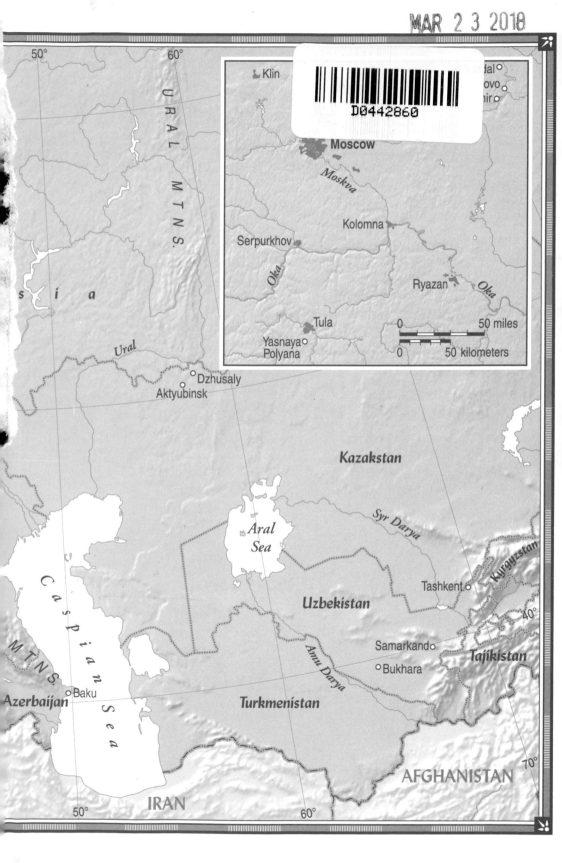

50°   60°

U R A L   M T N S.

s i a

Ural

Klin

Moscow

Moskva

Kolomna

Serpurkhov

Oka

Ryazan   Oka

50 miles

0

Tula

Yasnaya
Polyana

0   50 kilometers

Dzhusaly

Aktyubinsk

Kazakstan

Syr Darya

Aral
Sea

Kyrgyzstan

Tashkent

Uzbekistan

40°

Samarkand

Tajikistan

Bukhara

C a s p i a n   S e a

Amu Darya

M T N S.

Baku

Turkmenistan

Azerbaijan

70°

IRAN   AFGHANISTAN

50°   60°

THE YEAR I WAS
PETER THE GREAT

1956—KHRUSHCHEV, STALIN'S GHOST, AND A YOUNG AMERICAN IN RUSSIA

BROOKINGS INSTITUTION PRESS

Washington, D.C.

THE YEAR I WAS

PETER THE GREAT

MARVIN KALB

Overleaf: The author driving near St. Basil's Cathedral in Red Square.

Library of Congress Cataloging-in-Publication data
Names: Kalb, Marvin L., author.
Title: The year I was Peter the Great : 1956, Khrushchev, Stalin's ghost, and a young American in Russia / Marvin Kalb.
Description: Washington, D.C. : The Brookings Institution, 2017. | Includes index.
Identifiers: LCCN 2017020201 (print) | LCCN 2017044019 (ebook) | ISBN 9780815731627 (ebook) | ISBN 9780815731610 (cloth : alk. paper)
Subjects: LCSH: Kalb, Marvin L. | Television journalists—United States—Biography. | Kalb, Marvin L.—Travels—Soviet Union. | Soviet Union—Description and travel.
Classification: LCC PN4874.K26 (ebook) | LCC PN4874.K26 A3 2017 (print) | DDC 070.92 [B]—dc23
LC record available at https://lccn.loc.gov/2017020201

9 8 7 6 5 4 3

Typeset in Albertina MT

Composition by Westchester Publishing Services

To the young journalist on a first assignment,
whether to Moscow or City Hall:
just tell us what's happening, without fear or favor.

Contents

Contents

Preface

"Write a memoir, Marvin!"

The advice would come from family and friends, at first gently but then, after a while, with growing insistence. "You've broadcast from everywhere. You've written books about Russia, China, Egypt and Israel, the Vietnam War, and Ukraine. You've lectured on presidents from Truman to Trump. And at dinners and classrooms, you've told fascinating personal stories about your coverage of the Cold War." And, then, with a knowing nod, they'd add, "It's time for a memoir."

Until recently I had resisted. Journalists, I would argue, do not write memoirs; they write "the first draft of history," the stories they cover. At their best, they are observers of history. They cover major events, such as presidential campaigns, wars, summits, legislative battles on Capitol Hill. They interview presidents, senators, secretaries of state. But they are not actors in a story, or shouldn't be; they stand on the sidelines, or should, always attempting with an air of detachment to be fair and objective. Only then do they add their analysis, opinion, and perspective. They are the scribes of our time.

But over the years, when the advice to write a memoir began to come from my twelve-year-old grandson, Aaron, and my nine-year-old granddaughter, Eloise, who, separately or together, knew instinctively how to get to their eighty-seven-year-old "Grampa," I felt myself folding under their gentle pressure. But I did attach a caveat. I would not write a purely personal memoir, reminiscences of the ups and downs of family and friends. My private life was, after all, private. I would write a more professional memoir, focusing on my coverage of the major moments of the Cold War, of the leaders I met and the decisions they made.

For example, in 1956 I met the Soviet leader Nikita Khrushchev, who in jocular exchanges would often refer to me as Peter the Great. But he was also the Russian autocrat who brought the world to the brink of a nuclear war during the Cuban Missile Crisis. I had serious differences with Presidents Johnson and Nixon. The issue was almost always Vietnam. They objected strenuously to my coverage of the war. Nixon wiretapped my home phone and put me on his "enemies list." I enjoyed memorable conversations with three Israeli prime ministers—Golda Meir, Yitzhak Rabin, and Menachem Begin. I learned a lot about the Arab world during Henry Kissinger's groundbreaking shuttle diplomacy in the early 1970s, when I often met Jordan's King Hussein and Egypt's courageous Anwar Sadat. I reported on the Kremlin's suspected involvement in the assassination attempt on Pope John Paul II. And in the early 1990s I wrote about the sudden, but not totally surprising, collapse of the Soviet Union, which effectively ended the Cold War.

This, then, is my fifteenth book, but it is the first written as a professional memoir. It focuses on the uncertainties, fears, and challenges of the early years of the Cold War, at least as I saw them. Joseph Stalin had imposed Soviet control over Eastern Europe with the persuasive power of a Red Army bayonet, and Harry Truman had countered with the Berlin Airlift and the establishment of the North Atlantic Treaty Organization (NATO). During World War II the Soviet Union had been an

American ally against Nazi Germany; after the war, it quickly became an adversary—some even warned, an enemy. The phrase "Know Your Enemy" was widespread.

I had first developed an interest in Russia during World War II, when my bedroom walls were covered with maps of the Nazi blitzkrieg into the Soviet Union. By my junior year in college I was already toying with the idea of becoming what was called a "Russia expert," a journalist who would specialize in Soviet affairs, often at the time the subject of front-page news stories. When opportunity knocked and I got the chance in 1956 to go to Moscow as a diplomatic attaché at the U.S. embassy, a fancy moniker for an everyday job as a translator-interpreter and, when the need arose, also as a very, very junior press officer, I seized it. Apparently the embassy needed someone who spoke Russian and already had a high security clearance. I fit the bill. While serving in army intelligence during the Korean War I had a top-secret clearance, and of course I needed and knew Russian in order to do my work.

So in late January I left Cambridge, Massachusetts, where I was pursuing a Ph.D. in Russian history at Harvard, and a few days later arrived in Moscow, the frigid, snow-covered capital of the Soviet Union. Overnight, it seemed, I was transformed from a casually dressed graduate student into a buttoned-down diplomat with a special passport. I learned a great deal during my assignment: reading and translating the Soviet press every morning, enjoying my chance encounters with Khrushchev and other senior Soviet officials at national day receptions, talking to Russians whenever and wherever I got the chance, attending concerts, going to the theater and the Bolshoi Ballet, and traveling widely, from Tashkent to Kiev, from Leningrad to Sochi. In addition, there were always the mysteries, surprises, and wonders of Moscow. I loved nearly every minute of this invaluable experience.

I spent all of 1956 in the Soviet Union, a year the Russians dubbed "the thaw" for a very good reason. In early February, Khrushchev delivered a historic address to the 20th Congress of the Communist Party of the Soviet Union in which he stunned the world by attacking the once-omnipotent Stalin as a "criminal" who had violated communist doctrine and, by his idiosyncratic, personalized style of Oriental autocracy, endangered the Soviet state. To attack Stalin at that time was to attack a secular god, and many Russians shivered in fear and anxiety. A number of communist leaders, listening to Khrushchev, were said to have died on the spot of heart attacks; others pretended later that they had never heard of Stalin. Very quickly, by way of the often-reliable Soviet grapevine, Russian workers, artists, and students learned about the dismantling of Stalin's legacy and they felt as though a heavy overcoat of fear had been lifted from their shoulders.

A new day was dawning for a weary people. Professors could speak and travel more freely. Foreign artists were invited to perform in Moscow and Leningrad, and they did so before packed houses. I heard students at the Lenin Library in Moscow and the Saltykov-Shchedrin Library in Leningrad openly defy the party line and question the legitimacy of communism as their governing philosophy. These were amazing, unforgettable scenes. I soon realized that I was witnessing the early stages of the unraveling of a dictatorship.

Then, in the summer of 1956, the thaw spilled from Russia into Eastern Europe. Suddenly the Soviet empire itself was endangered. Anticommunist uprisings broke out in Poland, East Germany, Czechoslovakia, and, finally, in Hungary, where the entire country rose and boldly challenged communism and Russia. Khrushchev faced a crucial decision: to crush the Hungarian Revolution or risk the withering away of Russia's empire. He decided to crush the threat, believing he had no other option. Suddenly the streets of Budapest were awash in blood. Russia lost its claim to be Eastern Europe's comrade-in-arms. It was now unmasked as its brutal oppressor, a dictatorship that would stop at nothing to retain control over the whole region.

With Hungary, the thaw lost its magical appeal, the old chill returned, and Khrushchev, pressured by hard-line Kremlin critics, readjusted his anti-Stalinist melody. By year's end he was back to singing an old refrain. "God grant," he pronounced at a diplomatic reception, "that every communist be able to fight as Stalin fought." He put special emphasis on two words—"God" and "Stalin"—and then he said: "For all of us, Marxists-

Leninists who have devoted our lives to the revolutionary struggle for the interests of the working class and its militant vanguard, the Leninist party, the name of Stalin is inseparable from Marxism-Leninism."

In February Stalin had been demonized; by year's end he was again being eulogized as a Soviet saint.

At the time, many of us in Moscow speculated that Khrushchev had lost his struggle with the Kremlin hard-liners, led by the former Soviet foreign minister Vyacheslav Molotov. His thaw was over, we thought, and Stalin was now assured of a new life in the Marxist pantheon. But we were wrong. Stalin remained a disreputable figure, and, surprisingly, Khrushchev held on to power until October 1964, when a mediocre bureaucrat named Leonid Brezhnev replaced him. But enough of Khrushchev's de-Stalinization survived to ensure that this champion of "the thaw" would be awarded a retirement dacha and a limousine after his many years in power came to an abrupt and embarrassing end. If there had been no thaw, Khrushchev might well have been liquidated.

Much of this book is based on the only diary I ever kept, one that I wrote on a daily or nearly daily basis during my 1956 assignment in Moscow. If I had an interesting conversation with a Russian I met in Gorky Park, or bumped into at a concert, or shared a compartment with on a train in Azerbaijan, I would try that night to recollect the major themes, using the person's own words, on my portable Olivetti typewriter. Or if I met Khrushchev or another Soviet leader, I would write about the meeting and quote him—with accuracy, I hoped. Same for a visit to a famous site, such as Tolstoy's home at Yasnaya Polyana, or a trip to Kiev in Ukraine or Bukhara in central Asia. Kiev then was still Kiev, not Kyiv, as it came to be called after the 1991 proclamation of Ukrainian independence.

After a while the pages would pile up in my room at American House, a gloomy building along the Moscow River once owned in pre-revolutionary times by an aristocratic mortician. I had no place to hide my diary. I usually left it on my desk. It was personal, but it was not classified, and I always assumed that the Russians would read it as part of their normal snooping. That meant I had a special responsibility not to include anything that was official or secret, nor to use a Russian's real name if I thought what he or she had told me might get them into trouble. Therefore, the "Sasha" I described meeting in Leningrad was not really named Sasha. The diary helped me to remember people, places, and conversations. I also depended for insight and analysis on my university studies, on my memory, and on the stories my mother and father used to tell me about their early years in Eastern Europe.

My mother was born in Kiev, the capital of Ukraine, which was then part of the Russian empire. My father was born in Zyrardow, a small textile town west of Warsaw in Poland, also then part of the Russian empire. Their stories were not warm, nostalgic reminiscences of a happy time. They spoke of economic hardships, religious persecution, and fear of a war soon to erupt throughout Europe. When my mother reached New York and my father disembarked in Galveston, Texas, they were, like so many other refugees, thrilled to be in the United States of America. My father often referred to America in Yiddish as the *goldene medina*, roughly translated as the "blessed land."

My mother and father met and married in New York, where my father worked as a tailor. By the time I arrived in June 1930, a 10-pound, 2-ounce heavyweight—or, as the nurse informed my mother, "a two-ton Tony Galento," a famous boxer at the time—I already had a sister and a brother. Like many others, we had very little money during the Great Depression, but we had faith in ourselves and in our country. More important, I always felt honored to be the son and brother of such wonderful people. They set an example of honesty, decency, and loyalty unparalleled in my experience. I wish others could have been so lucky.

It could be said that my journey to Moscow began in the Bronx.

Roots

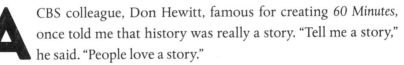 CBS colleague, Don Hewitt, famous for creating *60 Minutes*, once told me that history was really a story. "Tell me a story," he said. "People love a story."

So, here are three stories, each a brief glimpse into an immigrant family's determination to live the American dream. As best it could.

One story: During the Depression of the 1930s, a milk bottle, if returned, was worth a penny. Five pennies added up to the nickel my father needed to board a subway train in the Bronx for the ride to the garment center in midtown Manhattan, where, if he was lucky, he could find a day's or a week's work. But he needed the nickel, and there were days when he did not have even that. I remember several mornings when I got up at four or five in the morning to look through neighborhood garbage pails for discarded milk bottles. If I found five bottles, my father had his nickel, and the chance for a day's work. In the evening, when he got home, he would give his day's wages to my mother. She was magnificent at "stretching a dollar"; we never went hungry. It was only many years later when I wondered what would have happened if my father had gone downtown and had not found a job. How would he have gotten home? Even in the Depression, though, my father, a tailor born in the small textile town of Zyrardow, an hour by train west of the Polish capital, Warsaw, never lost his faith in America, his adopted home since 1914. If on occasion he did, he never showed it.

Another story: We lived in an apartment house on Southern Boulevard. During the summer my mother would often take me to nearby Crotona Park where I would play with friends, one of whom was named Benny. One day, when it was especially hot and humid, Benny's mother bought a Popsicle, unwrapped it, and gave it to her son. In those days, Popsicles could easily be split in two, each with its own stick. My mother had no money and could not buy one for me. She hoped and half expected that Benny's mother would break the Popsicle in two and give one half to me. That was what she would have done in a similar circumstance. But Benny's mother gave her son the whole Popsicle. I watched as he started to lick it. My mother, in a fury of frustration, took me by the hand, muttered something to Benny's mother, and we walked home. That evening I overheard my mother tell the story to my father. She was sobbing. "How could she?" she asked. "How could she do that? Marvin was standing right there."

And still another story about those times: Though a very hard-working tailor, my father always dreamed of becoming an entrepreneur. He was ambitious, the first in the extended family, years later, to own a car and a house. One day, shortly before the stock market collapsed in 1929, he came home with an exciting prospect. A friend who had done reasonably well in the hat business urged my father to buy a hat store (one was available at the intersection of Third Avenue and 105th Street in Manhattan), and my father was game. He knew nothing about hats and little about business, but he was thrilled by the vision, totally unrealistic, of becoming a successful businessman. As enthusiastic as my father was about this venture, my mother was doubly unenthusiastic, but she failed to abort the deal. My father became a hat merchant, assuming naively that the profits others enjoyed in those days, he would enjoy too. But then the market collapsed, and within a year he had to abandon his mercantile adventure and return to his more modest endeavors as a struggling tailor. But, remarkably undaunted, on the eve of the outbreak of World War II he bounced back and bought a dry cleaning and tailoring store on 188th Street in Washington Heights. My mother tended the store while my father continued working downtown in the garment district. After a while my family moved to Washington Heights. For me, this meant leaving P.S. 44, where I had many friends, and entering P.S. 189, where I had none. It was a challenge, but a manageable one.

George Washington High School would occasionally be referred to as a country club. It was no such thing, of course, though its location on a quiet corner of Washington Heights suggested a rather leisurely approach to schoolwork. The school sat, like a king at court, on a high bluff overlooking the Harlem River. It was a sprawling, four-story, red-brick bulldog of a building with a Roman tower and tall white columns looking down on a semicircular driveway at the corner of Audubon Avenue and 193rd Street. Its students were a middle-class mix of Italians and Jews, Greeks and Irish, most of them dreaming of college and careers, jobs and family. They entered GW during a hot war in 1944, and graduated in the early years of a cold war, in 1948.

I appreciated my years at GW. I was, most of the time, a serious student, though occasionally I would have "a real good time with plenty of noise and pushing around," as one of my teachers later recalled. In my graduating class, I was fourth in grade average—94.6, as I recall. Only Francis Randall, a slender, studious, bespectacled student whose father was a philosophy professor at Columbia; Alex Kessler, an incredibly brilliant, hard-working Jewish refugee from Germany; and Norma Leichter, the beautiful daughter of the neighborhood butcher, whom I adored, produced higher grades. If I sought an explanation for my fourth-place finish, which I did not (I was thrilled to be fourth), it was probably the many hours I spent running the prestigious Arista committee, composed of a dozen or so of the school's top students, who had banded together to help other students in need of academic assistance. For example, if a student was on the edge of flunking a course, and, knowing of Arista, sought our help, we would meet with the student once or twice a week or however many times it took to help him or her pass the course. And if, with our help, they did manage to pass, we would pat ourselves on the back—"a job well done," we'd proudly proclaim, and then go on to the next needy student.

Increasingly, by graduation time in 1948, more Puerto Rican students, freshly arrived in upper Manhattan and now enrolled at GW, found themselves in urgent need of help. Their English was poor, their study habits almost nonexistent. They had much to learn, and though we at Arista wanted to help, we came up short. We had too few "teachers" to meet the rising challenge of another generation of immigrant students. We tried, but failed.

In the spring of 1946, the editor of the *New York Herald Tribune*, a Republican newspaper that would survive in a heavily Democratic city for another twenty years, invited high school students to answer a deceptively simple question: What kind of world would you like to see? For many of us, even those aged fifteen, World War II was still a fresh memory: two atomic bombs had been dropped on Japan, Nazi Germany had surrendered unconditionally, tens of millions of people had been killed in Europe, including millions of Jews, and everyone wondered, what now?

I could not resist the editor's invitation. I had recently been chosen to represent George Washington High School in a mock United Nations debate. For a few memorable days, I enjoyed the thrill of being the "U.S. ambassador" in a "Security Council" exchange about European security. Fresh from this experience, I bubbled with the youthful notion that I had something of importance to contribute to the paper. I wrote my letter, and it appeared on the editorial page on May 26, 1946, under the headline: "The World We Want—Forum of High School Opinion."

"To the *New York Herald Tribune*," it began innocently enough. "The world I want? I want a world where all men are really and truly equal, not just an empty phrase. I want it stated in black and white that all the peoples are independent and have the same opportunities.

"I want all the peoples in the devastated countries of Europe and the South Pacific to feel they can rely on us for aid. I want to see them all get an even break until they are able to take care of themselves. We are indebted to them: let's show it.

"I want all the Negroes in our country to be recognized as a race equal to any other. They should be able to vote without a poll tax.

"Finally, we must start on the organization of a world government.

"That's the kind of world I want. I believe that it is about time that sovereignty bowed out and made room for international cooperation."

Reading and rereading the letter now, I am proud of the world I wanted in 1946, a world, I wrote, where "all men" were "truly equal," where the United States of America provided foreign aid and "all [got] an equal break," where "Negroes" (the parlance of that time) were "recognized as a race equal to any other," able to vote "without a poll tax," and where "sovereignty" yielded to the creation of a "world government." In fact, over the years, the United States did bestow hefty amounts of foreign aid on developing nations, African Americans did acquire full voting rights, and although "sovereignty" remained as sovereign an international force as ever, the UN did provide an international forum for the discussion and sometimes the solution of dangerous problems.

My letter might have forecast a career for me in politics or diplomacy, and although it appeared in a newspaper, it did not, on its own, point me in the direction of journalism. All that was to come later.

Late one winter afternoon, after an especially long Arista session, I bundled up and left GW through one of its large front doors. I was alone. The snow was falling, and a fierce wind was blowing. Across the street I could see a gaggle of GW students. I recognized them and waved. One student, named O'Reilly, waved back and, almost in the same motion, threw an icy snowball in my direction. He missed. His friends then joined him and, crossing Audubon Avenue, threw many more snowballs at me. One of them hit my head and drew blood. Frightened, I ran away from them. "Jew boy!" they hollered. "Running home to Mommy?" I could hear them laughing, but they did not run after me.

A few weeks later, I again left GW late one snowy afternoon, but this time the O'Reilly lesson having been burned into my consciousness. I arranged to be accompanied by a dozen of my Puerto Rican students. They were, in effect, my bodyguards. I had warned Pedro, a strong, self-confident student, that we might be met by a hostile Irish gang armed with icy snowballs. I had learned that O'Reilly's snowballs were actually pieces of rock or coal covered with snow and frozen in icy water. Pedro seemed unimpressed. "Don't worry," he said with a smile. "We know what to do." Indeed, he did. No sooner had we exited GW, Pedro and his friends forming a protective shield around me, than the Irish began their icy offensive, hurling snowballs in our direction from across Audubon Avenue. Many struck their targets. Pedro then screamed something in Spanish and, followed by his friends, raced across the avenue. To this day I do not know whether they had knives, but I suspect they did. What I do know is that within a few minutes the Irish were in full retreat, and the Puerto Ricans were slapping one another in satisfaction. The Great Snowball Battle was over. The Puerto Ricans won decisively, the Irish lost, and my youthful flirtation with pacifism died. Every now and then, I learned, overwhelming force, applied judiciously, could accomplish miracles. I never again had to face another Irish attack.

I had two memorable English teachers, neither of whom wore a wedding ring. One was named Miss Draddy. She was tall, spider thin, and chronically cranky. She opened her first class by telling her students, "There are two kinds of people in the world: the Irish and those who would like to be Irish." Otherwise, she was a good teacher, one whose command of American novels was unmistakably impressive. She introduced me to *Look Homeward, Angel* and its author, Thomas Wolfe, who quickly became one of my favorite writers. For that and much more, I would always be indebted to Miss Draddy.

The other English teacher in my hall of fame was Miss Bachner, a short, soft-spoken woman who had fallen in love with English poetry while still at Barnard and managed to retain her passion and convey it to her students many years later. We got on very well. Miss Bachner became my number one adviser. If several of my friends thought I had become her "pet," they were right. After a while, she decided on her own that I should become a lawyer, and while I was still a junior she arranged for me to meet her brother, Lester Bachner, a successful Wall Street attorney. He had a sparkling reputation; other lawyers described him as "the lawyer with the razor-sharp mind." He spoke crisply, smiled rarely, and dressed immaculately. In our first talk he offered me an extraordinary opportunity, starting with a part-time job, which I accepted on the spot. I held it for four years, until I was a junior in college. There was an unspoken understanding between us that once I earned my law degree, I would continue working with and for him. I would become one of his partners. Fantastic! And yet, despite the temptations he spread before me, I was not quite certain I wanted to be a lawyer. There was always the lure of journalism.

In late January 1948 I graduated from GW and promptly enrolled at City College. I never considered attending any other college, though I might have been able to get a scholarship to Columbia or Harvard. City was where my brother had gone, and so too would I.

War, College, and Basketball

Like a sudden storm, the Cold War came to City College on June 25, 1950, when the North Koreans invaded South Korea, puncturing a tender springtime bubble of March Madness basketball on St. Nicholas Terrace. The unpredictable Beavers had just accomplished a miracle, winning unprecedented victories in both the National Invitational Tournament (NIT) and the National Collegiate Athletic Association (NCAA). No other basketball team in college history had ever won both tournaments in the same season. Sportswriters called it the grand slam.

For the next ten months City College lived in a fairyland world of basketball championships won in tinseled gardens. Then, in the early-morning hours of February 18, 1951, everything on campus changed. Three of the team's top stars were arrested at Penn Station for shaving points in an illegal betting scheme run by Mafia gangsters. "Impossible," was my first reaction—someone's idea of a sick joke, surely. But it was true. The players, treated until that morning like secular gods, had betrayed their college, besmirching their truly memorable accomplishment—their grand slam.

As sports editor of the college newspaper, the *Campus*, during the 1949–50 academic year, I had covered nearly every game. It was an assignment made in heaven. In their improbable march to the championship, the Beavers had beaten many powerhouse teams, but no victory was more satisfying to me than their 89–50 demolition of haughty, hugely favored Kentucky, whose coach, the legendary Adolph Rupp, known as "the Blue Grass Baron," had boasted on his arrival in New York that his team did not have to practice to whip City College.

But now, with the news from Korea dominating the morning headlines, like so many other students I began to worry about the United States getting involved in another war so soon after World War II and, on a more personal level, about whether I would be drafted. Would I be allowed to finish my senior year? Would I be able to go on to graduate school?

The Cold War was not an unknown to us. In the alcoves ringing the ground-floor cafeteria there had been many heated debates about the origins of the Cold War: Who was responsible, the United States or the Soviet Union? Were the Red Army's moves into Eastern Europe a defensive operation, or was Stalin positioning the Soviet Union for a dramatic drive into Western Europe? Was communism really an existential threat to the United States, or just an economic and diplomatic challenge? These questions preoccupied statesmen and commentators—and they preoccupied us as well.

City College, especially in the 1930s but also when I was there, was a hotbed of political warfare: Truman Democrats opposing Wendell Willkie Republicans, Stalinists battling Trotskyists, Social Democrats fighting Norman Thomas Socialists, Newman Society Catholics struggling to be heard, and Orthodox Jews engaging in ecclesiastical battles with Zionist Jews. Each point of view had its own alcove, everyone sounding off as if there were no tomorrow.

Irving Kristol, who had graduated from City College in 1940, eight years before I got there, a socialist while a student, a conservative in his later years, wrote nostalgically about his alcove, occupied by the Young

People's Socialist League, otherwise playfully known as the Fourth International. "It was there one ate lunch," Kristol reminisced, "played Ping-Pong (sometimes with a net, sometimes without), passed the time of day between and after classes, argued incessantly, and generally devoted oneself to solving the ultimate problems of the human race." And it was all taken so seriously. Joining Kristol were such academic luminaries as Irving Howe, Daniel Bell, and Nathan Glazer, all later to be recognized as among the nation's premier scholars.

I used to drop in on an alcove debate, but I was never a member. If I had joined an alcove, it probably would have been with the Truman Democrats, tough on foreign policy, liberal on domestic issues. I especially remember one organization, the Young Progressives of America. It had muscled its way into one of the alcoves, earning a measure of notoriety by always blasting Washington for any problem besetting the world. The United States was on a heartless crusade, the Young Progressives argued: instead of helping anti-imperialist forces rise up against their colonial masters, the United States was either looking the other way or, for example, helping France reconstitute her colonial rule over Indochina.

Into this hot and often intemperate climate entered a new college newspaper, called the *Observation Post*, which challenged the editorial line of my paper, the *Campus*, and espoused an essentially anti-establishment position on nearly every subject—from the college's finances, which it found to be corrupt, to the many problems of the Cold War. It was critical of the United States, rarely so of the Soviet Union. Often, when discussing foreign policy, the *OP*, as it was soon called, seemed blind to Stalinist aggression, an editorial position I could not accept. During World War II, when the United States and the Soviet Union were allies, the *Campus* had had its own flirtation with the left, but after the war the paper adopted a moderate line on most issues. A number of good reporters, including a few of my friends, wanted to do more than just practice journalism; they wanted to make a political statement. They joined the *OP*.

The former British prime minister, Winston Churchill, struck a depressing but realistic chord when he described the immediate postwar challenge. On March 5, 1946, during a speech at Westminster College in Fulton, Missouri, he scanned the European horizon and reluctantly concluded that an "Iron Curtain has descended over the continent," creating a "Soviet sphere" of influence. Less than a year after the war had ended in Europe, he thought that a war with the Soviet Union, busy pushing into Eastern Europe, was becoming a distinct possibility. President Harry S. Truman, who shared Churchill's gloomy assessment, saw a world split in two: half free, and the other half "bent on the subjugation of others." Truman felt that the West, especially the United States, had no choice but to block further communist expansion in Europe and Asia. He did not want war, but he did not trust Stalin. In the face of unprovoked expansion, Truman felt he had to act. Opening the spigots of American generosity, he gave economic and military aid to Greece and Turkey. He started the Marshall Plan for the economic reconstruction of Western Europe and the North Atlantic Treaty Organization for its military defense, and he launched the remarkable Berlin Airlift in 1948, ferrying food and supplies to a divided and desperate German capital. On leaving office on January 20, 1953, Truman looked back on his Cold War tenure and said, "I have hardly had a day in office that has not been dominated by this all-embracing struggle."

A Washington-based columnist, Walter Lippmann, gave a name to this struggle. In a short 1947 book called *Cold War* he wrote that the United States and the USSR were already involved in a fierce global competition, jockeying for strategic advantage, using proxies in local wars, and building up their military strength—but stopping short of actually engaging in direct combat, or hot war. In this dangerous environment, he asked, what was the best strategy for the United States? George Kennan, an old Moscow hand, offered a possible answer in an article for *Foreign Affairs*, "The Sources of Soviet Conduct," which was a slightly sanitized version of his famous "long telegram," written while he was still a diplomat based in Moscow. He proposed the containment of expanding Soviet power—not, he later stressed, by depending on American military power but by gradually advancing a "smarter" policy of bilateral cooperation. Known as the containment policy, it was adopted by a succession of administrations, starting with Truman's.

The rise of the Cold War led me to a number of important decisions about courses and faculty. When I first enrolled at City College in February 1948, I found myself flitting, like a restless butterfly, from one major to another, never quite sure if I wanted to be a pre-med student, which would have satisfied my mother, or pre-law, which would have delighted my father, who was always convinced that I was put on this planet to be the best lawyer in America. Besides, I was already working for a lawyer and enjoying the experience. Lester Bachner used me for more than sharpening pencils or running out for coffee. He had me do research for his cases, and occasionally he even invited me to court to watch him argue a case. "How did I do?" he would ask after a trial, and I would praise him to the skies. Still, after a while at City College I was drawn toward a concentration in Russian language, literature, and history, prompted in part, I think, by my World War II obsession with huge maps on my bedroom walls. Using red-white-and-black-topped pins, I tracked the island-hopping American war against Japan in the Pacific and the ultimately unsuccessful Nazi invasion of the Soviet Union.

I was also inspired by the teaching and example of Hans Kohn, a Prague-born professor of European intellectual history who had recently come to teach at the college. He was all a professor was supposed to be: kind, encouraging, and stimulating. He made history exciting, basing many of his lectures on the adventures of real leaders. If not for Kohn's emphasis on the role of individuals in history, how else would I remember Charles Maurras and Maurice Barrès, two influential French nationalists, whom my roommate, Mark Maged, and I would affectionately refer to as "more ass and bare ass"? Also, with the rise of the Cold War, he took public positions that put him at odds with American foreign policy. Although he supported "vehemently [resisting] aggression anywhere in the world," he disagreed with General Douglas MacArthur's decision to cross the 38th parallel in Korea and advance toward the Yalu River, and he disagreed with the American decision to rearm Germany. For him and for others born in central Europe, Germany was often at the center of their strategic concerns.

The biggest issue for Kohn was always personal freedom. He feared that in our Cold War obsession with Soviet communism, we would lose sight of the one principle fundamental to our democracy, and that was our personal freedom. Even when I disagreed with Kohn (he was less concerned about the threats posed by the Soviet Union than I was), I admired him enormously. He was a decent, honorable man and a superb scholar. He had a major influence on my own thinking about U.S.-Soviet relations in a Cold War environment.

There was a very practical reason, too, for my growing fascination with Russian language and history. We were then in the early days of the Cold War, and knowing something about the Soviet Union—"Know Your Enemy" was the popular, often overused, cliché of the time—could open the door to a job. That certainly proved to be my experience. My older brother, Bernard—always Bernie to me—a reporter for the *New York Times,* had advised me on more than one occasion that if I wanted to go into journalism, which was always in a corner of my mind, I ought to have more than a degree in English literature. I ought to know something special, perhaps cultivate an area of expertise—something that would catch the eye of an editor or producer at a newspaper or a network. Harry Schwartz was a scholar and an expert on the Soviet Union and he worked for the *Times.* He set an example for others, like me, who specialized in Soviet affairs but who might not want to be a college professor. Every time I saw one of Schwartz's analyses in the *Times,* I realized that my brother's advice was golden. Maybe one day I could be the Harry Schwartz of CBS News. My father always believed, as did I, that in America, if you worked hard and obeyed the rules, anything was possible.

It was not surprising, then, that in my freshman year journalism beckoned, and I saluted. A shameful story, involving racial and religious discrimination, was brewing at the college. In October 1948 about 2,000 students, expressing their outrage, organized a sit-in. They demanded that two professors be fired. Six months later, on April 11, 1949, the college was shut down by similar mass protests, no different really from those that later rocked college campuses during the Vietnam War. City College was just ahead of its time. Many hundreds of students, carrying placards denouncing the professors and shouting "Jim Crow Must Go," blocked traffic on Convent Avenue. Police on horseback, wielding batons, rode directly into the demonstrators, as if they were trying to contain stampeding cattle. Many students were bloodied. Sixteen were arrested. A *Times* headline the next morning read, "City College Students Clash with Police in 'Bias' Strike."

The professors were William E. Knickerbocker, chairman of the Romance Languages Department, accused of blatant anti-Semitism in a college where roughly 80 percent of the student body was Jewish, and William C. Davis, an economist, charged with discriminating against Negroes, as African Americans were then called.

I always believed that Knickerbocker was a bigot. The evidence seemed overwhelming. I was never sure about Davis. In fact, at times I thought he got a bum rap. In any case, in the history of City College, Knickerbocker and Davis were forever twinned in infamy. They were unavoidable distractions from my studies, but they were essential lessons in journalism. I was one of a number of *Campus* reporters covering the protests. I did well enough, apparently, for my editor, Sandy Socolow, who was later to be a colleague at CBS News, to name me sports editor for the 1949–50 academic year. Soon I would be covering an unforgettable story—the grand slam of college basketball.

At City College basketball had been the most celebrated sport on campus ever since 1920, when Nat Holman began to coach the Beavers. There were sixteen varsity teams, but at the *Campus* we covered one more than any other, and the legendary Holman was the reason. Immodestly he referred to himself as "the master," and he looked like a British aristocrat.

Even in warm-up garb and sneakers Holman conveyed an air of elegance, like a character out of *Downton Abbey*, his dark hair speckled with gray and his soft hands looking like those of a surgeon. After practice Holman would emerge from the gym looking like a Wall Street banker—his dark, double-breasted jacket fitting perfectly, with a handkerchief folded neatly in its pocket and a tie always of the latest fashion. His accent was more London than New York, Rooseveltian with broad *a*'s and a roll of *r*'s. Only occasionally, during a close, intense game, did his original accent break through, betraying his humble New York roots. Before he shortened his name it had been Nathan Helmanovich. He was always fascinated by the spoken word. "Speech," he once said, "deserves the respect of using it as well as you can."

Basketball, I was soon to learn, was like a gem of many facets, sparkling with a hundred moves, reflecting a subtle beauty only a player or coach like Holman could appreciate. The City College style of basketball was urban ballet—*Guys and Dolls* with Nathan Detroit as the leading scorer. It was also a game of unexpected changes in speed and style: a team could be ahead by twenty points at halftime only to blow its composure in the second half and lose by as many as fifteen. How? Why? Not even a Holman could explain such swift, mercurial changes.

The 1949–50 basketball season began with an easy Beaver win over Queens College. One win followed another, many of them at Madison Square Garden in midtown Manhattan—a "medieval fortress," wrote reporter Stanley Cohen. It was a fortress for fans, sportswriters, and also bookies, though at the time I knew little about them and, in truth, cared even less. Of course, I did see them at the Garden. They were impossible to miss: Runyonesque characters, many of whom were Mafia mobsters wearing wide-brim hats, smoking fat cigars, and making money on their point spread betting. I once heard a gambler at courtside shout at a player who had just missed an easy shot, "What are you doing, you jackass? You are already four points under the spread." I heard what he said, but paid no attention to it. In the old days bookies bet on a team to win; now they were betting on a team to win by a certain number of points. Though the bookies were everywhere at the Garden, they were, as Elie Wiesel said in a totally different context, not my people. I had nothing to do with them, and at the time I thought they had nothing to do with Beaver basketball.

City College finished the 1949–50 season with impressive wins over metropolitan rivals such as Fordham, Manhattan, and New York University. Its win-loss record for the season was 17–5. Was that good enough for a tournament bid? I thought not, but late one afternoon Holman got a call from the NIT: Would City College agree to be the twelfth and last team to be invited to compete in the 1950 tournament? In those years, a bid to the NIT was more treasured than one to the NCAA. Holman, relieved, took no more than a second to say "Of course."

City College's first game was against San Francisco, the NIT's defending champion. Most of us thought San Francisco would win, but surprisingly the Beavers won, blowout style, in an easy 65–46 victory. Next came Kentucky, so accomplished a team that even the most optimistic fan could not imagine victory. In fact, we were certain this would be City College's last game of the year. Some of us thought of it as a culture war, a collision of fundamental values, attitudes, backgrounds. As sports editor I heard a strange mix of fanciful speculation, ranging from crazy predictions of victory to painful reminders of the Holocaust. When some of us thought about Kentucky, we imagined not a team but a disciplined strike force of Aryan giants, all blond and blue-eyed, advancing on the Beavers like a Nazi strike force during World War II. Wasn't their coach's first name Adolph, after all?

Was it a flight of exaggerated fear on my part to link the Adolph of Kentucky with the Adolf of Berlin? Not really, not for me, not then. Only a few years earlier, the Knickerbocker-Davis scandal had rocked City College and sensitized students to any whiff of anti-Semitism; and during World War II Adolf Hitler had killed millions of Jews. We did not know exact numbers. Was there not something magical about the recuperative powers of the Jewish people that, five short years later, three of them had been chosen for the starting lineup of the City College basketball team? Three of them, joined by two blacks, had the awesome task on March 14, 1950, of taking on Adolph Rupp's aristocrats of basketball.

On the big night, Madison Square Garden was noisy, sweaty, and packed, every one of its 18,000 seats taken. Because there were no elevators, ramps, or escalators in the old Garden, ticket holders would have to trudge up steep banks of stairs until they found their seats in the upper balcony. It was like climbing the Alps without skis. Then, squeezed in on all sides, they would catch sight of a large American flag hanging vertically from the roof above center court. "The game of basketball was a native ritual in New York," wrote Stanley Cohen, "and Madison Square Garden was its Mecca."

Rupp proudly led his Kentucky team onto the Garden floor, greeted by boos and catcalls from the predominantly New York crowd. He did not mind—indeed, he seemed to enjoy his notoriety. "This young team of mine," Rupp smugly told reporters, "is better than the group that won the Invitation Tournament as sophomores" a few years before.

From the press box I saw the City College players huddled around their coach. "Don't you think we ought to show these boys from Kentucky how polite we New Yorkers can be?" Holman asked. Something wickedly wise was on his mind. "Let's shake hands with each of them. That's right—just reach out and shake hands with each one of them. I think that would be the right thing to do." If the players thought their coach had suddenly lost his mind, they disguised their feelings behind nods of approval. "Sure, coach, sure," they grunted.

The 18,000 spectators were already standing and cheering. Holman inserted his tallest player, LeRoy Watkins, a rarely used six-foot seven-inch African American player, to jump-ball against Kentucky center Bill Spivey, who was five inches taller. What was the point? Holman's regular center, Ed Roman, was only an inch shorter than Watkins, and obviously the better player. But Holman wanted an African American center to confront Spivey, at least for the tip-off.

When the house lights dimmed, players and coaches on both teams stood quietly and listened to Gladys Gooding play the national anthem on her fabled organ, just as she had done at hundreds of other games. The moment she finished, pandemonium replaced decorum. The ten players took center court. Five of the players were tall, white, and Christian, three were Jews, and two were African Americans. Interracial basketball was common in New York, but not throughout the country, where most games were white-on-white encounters. As the referee juggled the basketball, bouncing it from one hand to the other in pregame pageantry moments before tossing it into the air and formally beginning the game, the three Jews and the two African Americans, as their coach had suggested, extended their hands to the Kentucky players. No Kentucky player returned the gesture. They refused to shake hands. Worse, they turned their backs on the City College players in full view of 18,000 astonished spectators. I was watching guard Floyd Layne in particular. He looked grim. Slowly he shook his head from side to side and hissed at the Kentucky player he was soon to guard: "You gonna be pickin' cotton in the morning, man."

The game started, and a miracle took place on the Garden floor, one that no City College student of that era will ever forget. The Beavers opened with a blistering running game. It was "motion offense," Holman's philosophy of the game, and it never stopped. Before the Wildcats of Kentucky had a chance to break a sweat, City opened a 13–1 lead. Ten minutes into the game the score was 28–9; at halftime it was 45–20.

In the second half, I waited for Kentucky to push back, but no matter what switch or tactic Rupp tried, what strategy he employed, nothing worked. With every Beaver basket, Kentucky seemed only to wilt further. With ten minutes left in the game, City was leading by thirty points. The final score was an unbelievable 89–50! It was the worst defeat in Kentucky's forty-six-year history of college basketball, the most embarrassing in Rupp's otherwise distinguished career.

I was so excited I had trouble coming up with a lead for my story. Many flashed through my mind until, finally, one seemed right: "Murder

Took Place Last Night before 18,000 Witnesses at Madison Square Garden." It was not the one that ultimately worked its way through the editing process, but it captured the spirit of the game. Under a banner headline, "'Five' Plows under Kentucky, 89–50," my edited story began: "The anticipated battle between two of the greatest basketball strategists in the country took place last night at the Garden. Nat Holman won, and his sensational Beavers murdered 2nd seeded Kentucky by the incredible score of 89–50 in full view of 18,000 astonished fans."

"We were sky-high for Kentucky," said a grinning Layne. "We were above the rim all night."

Holman, searching for a special way of saying thanks, took the entire team to Broadway, where they saw the Rodgers and Hammerstein musical *South Pacific*. Rupp led his moping marauders back to Kentucky, where the state legislature ordered the flag to be flown at half-mast.

On Saturday night, for the NIT championship game, it was City College vs. Bradley, considered by many sportswriters to be the best college basketball team in the country. Students stood on their seats, convinced that City would win, somehow, even though the bookies were betting heavily on Bradley. What did the bookies know? God was smiling down on the Beavers, and City College beat Bradley and then went on to beat Bradley again in the upcoming NCAA tournament. The next morning, the *Times* led its story with "Hats off to a real champion." Forward Irwin Dambrot was quoted as saying, "The team went crazy, the school went crazy and New York City went crazy. It was an unbelievable experience." The Beavers proved that Jews trying to make it in America, and blacks trying to make it in America, could make it in America—that we were as worthy as anyone else, even Rupp's favored Wildcats.

Immigrant parents might not have appreciated the full scope of City's basketball accomplishment until they watched the *Ed Sullivan Show* on CBS, their weekly exposure to American culture. When they saw, first, that Coach Nat Holman had been invited on the program, second, that the ovation for him from the studio audience was so loud Sullivan had to repeat his introduction of him three times, and, third, that Holman was there to discuss City's basketball triumph with Ed Sullivan, no less, then they understood that something truly momentous had happened at their children's college. From one end of the country to the other, City College was now recognized as the college of national champions. Even kids in San Francisco were chanting the college's famous "allagaroo" cheer.

For the next ten months or so, City College students lived in two worlds: one of sugared memories of basketball championships, and the other of grim news from Korea, an almost daily reminder that Lippmann's warning of a Cold War was real, that a new and dangerous chapter in global relations was unfolding before their eyes. China, torn by civil war, was now in communist hands, and the Soviet Union had broken the American monopoly in nuclear weapons. At home, Republican senator Joseph McCarthy railed against the State Department, Hollywood, and the northeastern intellectual elite. McCarthyism, for a few years, intimidated our national political discourse—perhaps everywhere except in the City College cafeteria, where all shades of communism, fascism, socialism, and democracy were debated with youthful vigor. We were hardly indifferent to the challenges of the Cold War, but we tried, when the draft did not intrude, to tend to our own gardens—to graduate school, to marriage, to careers.

And so, when, in the early-morning hours of February 18, 1951, WQXR, the classical music station in New York, broadcast the news that three City College basketball players had been arrested, I did not believe it. "No," I groaned, "there must be some mistake." I was then in my senior year, no longer sports editor, concentrating instead on Russian language, literature, and history. But my life still rotated around the *Campus*, and I felt I had to get there. My brother Bernie gave me a lift to the college. As we sped up the West Side Highway, he asked me questions about "point spreads" and "shaving points": What was that all about? My answers were skimpy on detail. I realized that I should have explored this corner of college basketball when I was still covering the team, but it had never occurred to me. I was certain that our team would never have had anything to do with point spreads or Mafia mobsters. Maybe other teams, but not City College.

At the time, reporters had not yet been infected by the skepticism of later years, the distrust of government and large corporations. The Vietnam War was far over the horizon, Watergate a political nightmare yet to happen. We still lived in a post–World War II optimism about ourselves and our country. We felt that our government protected us, and our team played for the glory of the game. We were still innocents at home and abroad.

I found the *Campus* newsroom strangely quiet, as if everyone were attending a requiem for a lost dream. Reporters knew they had to cover the story, but they seemed frightened by what they might find out. After a while I started making a few calls and learned that the New York district attorney, Frank Hogan, had sent two detectives to Philadelphia for the CCNY–Temple game the night before. They were Abraham Belsky and George Jaeger. After the game, which City won easily, the detectives joined Holman and his players on the train ride back to New York. Quietly, they informed Holman that they intended to arrest three of his players as soon as they entered New York's jurisdiction. Holman was stunned but offered no objections. "I have no sympathy for them if they are guilty," he said.

When the train passed through Newark and entered the tunnel to Penn Station, the detectives also told the three players that they were going to be booked on a charge of illegal point-spread manipulation in three Garden games, against Missouri, Arizona, and Boston College. The players had been cooperating with a once-jailed mobster named Salvatore Sollazzo and a former Long Island University basketball player named Eddie Gard. The players, in a state of shock, said nothing.

Moments after their arrival in New York, standing together on a damp, dreary platform, a devastated Holman told his players that if they had nothing to do with the gambling charges, he would support them "fully, to the best of my ability," but if they did have something to do with gambling, then he would let "the chips fall where they may." As the detectives hustled the players toward a police van for the short ride to the Elizabeth Street Station in downtown Manhattan, Holman walked off by himself, his coat collar pulled high around his neck, his head filled no doubt with denials and questions.

He walked into the misty darkness at the end of the railroad platform. It seemed like a scene from *Anna Karenina*.

The players were questioned by police detectives for several hours and then whisked to the Criminal Courts Building on Center Street. They looked frightened, their heads down, their hands in their pockets, as they were hustled from one place to another. News reporters and photographers snapped pictures of these "fallen idols," the title of a column I wrote that night for Monday's edition of the *Campus*. (I would occasionally contribute a column to the paper, even though I was no longer spending a lot of time there.) I was deeply disappointed in the players. The arrests were a heartbreaking introduction to the complex frailties of human nature, one I was never to forget.

A few days after the initial arrests, Hogan widened his net. He arrested three players from Long Island University—Sherman White, LeRoy Smith, and Adolph Bigos. They were charged with throwing games, not just spreading points. Eventually, Hogan was to arrest thirty-two players from seven colleges across the country, including Bradley and Kentucky. Coach Rupp, who had boasted, "They couldn't reach my boys with a ten-foot pole," watched in humiliation as his All-America center, Bill Spivey, among others, was arrested and led off by police.

My sense of gloom came with many questions. How could I have missed this story? More important, how could Holman have missed it? How could a great coach not have wondered why shots that should have been made were missed, why usually smooth players could become so sloppy? Almost every day I asked Holman for an interview. He waved me off. For a time he seemed to go into a shell.

The good old days were never to return. Holman knew it, but rarely second-guessed himself—he was, after all, "the master." I assume he must have indulged in what the Soviets used to call self-criticism, admittedly for Holman a tough thing to do. If he had simply alerted his players to the many dangers of gambling at the Garden, if he had urged them to report any approaches by mobsters, if he had had a closer personal relationship with the players and discussed their problems, he might then have been in a position to preempt the obvious temptations laid before the players by the likes of Sollazzo and Gard. But Holman was not that kind of coach. He believed his news clippings and he kept his distance. After the 1959–60 season, Holman retired, the questions "Did he know?" and "What did he know?" still hanging over his head and his legacy.

Did you ever hear of the "alveolar ridge"? I suppose I should have heard of it years before I was a senior at City College. I was a devoted listener of two CBS Radio newscasts: one was the World News Roundup at 8:00 a.m., and the other was Edward R. Murrow's 7:45 p.m. report. On both newscasts I heard superb reports delivered in a variety of accents. Howard K. Smith had a slight southern accent, Peter Kalischer had a New York accent, and Murrow had what was called "great American speech." Mine was closer to Kalischer's, but I would have preferred that it be closer to Murrow's, especially if I was ever to be a CBS reporter.

One day, while reviewing course opportunities for my senior year, I discovered that I needed to take and pass seven courses to get my degree, four in the fall semester and three in the spring, meaning I had room for an additional elective. Encouraged by a friend (I didn't really need much encouragement), I decided to take a course called "English Speech." I wanted to speak better. I wanted, if possible, to sound more like Murrow than Kalischer. In this effort, I learned about the mysterious alveolar ridge, which, from birth to death, affected the speech pattern of almost every New Yorker.

My professor, whose name I have forgotten, was a young Englishman who superciliously looked down on the speech patterns of all Americans, including Murrow. He would have us read Shakespeare as if we were all Globe actors, hitting every word with the right inflection, and of course we regularly failed to meet the impossible standards he set. One day, listening closely to my Hamlet, he asked, "When you say the word 'tight,' or 'nasty,' does your tongue tip your alveolar ridge?" In truth, I thought my professor had just gone mad.

"Alvila ridge?" I asked, thoroughly bewildered.

"Alveolar ridge," he snapped, correcting me. "Did your tongue tip the alveolar ridge when you were saying a word with a *t* or *d* in it?" I could not answer his question, and I was one of his better students.

Our frustrated professor pinned a large, side-view image of the human head on the blackboard and he pointed to two ridges, one on the roof of the mouth, just behind the front teeth, the other on the bottom of the mouth behind the lower teeth. With a pointer, he tried to explain the problem and offer a solution. It was not easy. "New Yorkers," he said, "have a special problem. When they use dental consonants, like a *t* or a *d*, they let their tongues hit the back of their teeth rather than the alveolar ridge in front. That more than anything else produces the so-called New York accent. But if they allowed their tongue to tip off the alveolar ridge, not the back of their teeth, they would be taking a big step toward 'great American speech.'" It was not that simple or automatic, but he had a point.

For the rest of the semester, leading to my graduation from City College, I practiced hitting my *t*'s and *d*'s off my upper alveolar ridge, and it worked. I began to move away from my New York accent toward "great American speech." Though my reading of *Hamlet* improved, I was still nowhere near Murrow. But I was improving my speech in English at the same time as I began speaking Russian, where, I learned, I did not have to worry about *t*'s, *d*'s, and the alveolar ridge. Russian had its own peculiarities and posed its own challenges.

Teddy, Joyce, and Journalism

O f all of my professors at City College, Theodore (Teddy) Goodman, the irascible one, stands on a dubious pedestal of his
own. In one scene, remarkable and for me unforgettable, he
opened my eyes to a career in journalism, but not in the way he, or I,
might have imagined.

Short, on the pudgy side though not heavy, bespectacled, balding, he
was always in motion, not just physically but also intellectually. He wore
jackets that seemed never to have been pressed, and his ties, always
loosely knotted, were spotted with leftovers. His round face was a study
in unpredictability, one expression shifting to another without warning:
a grimace suddenly collapsing into a smile, a frown into a silly cackle. His
hands, rarely content to rest in his pockets, drew odd patterns in the air
while he lectured. He would, most of the time, lecture behind a rickety
podium in the front of the room, but just as often he could be lecturing
from the back of the room, or the side—always, it seemed, with the

window wide open, winter or summer. He was a chain-smoker, one Camel cigarette after another. Ignoring every fire code, he would crush lit butts on the already filthy floor or flick them with a mindless abandon through the open window, striving, even at his age, to look bohemian. For Teddy Goodman, he seemed to be telling his students, there were no rules of etiquette.

His scholarship, such as it was, was not impressive. Over a long teaching career spanning thirty years, from 1922 to 1952, he wrote only two books: *Narrative Structure and Style*, a textbook of no distinction, and *Maria Edgeworth: Novelist of Reason*, a study of an early nineteenth-century Irish writer, which was quickly forgotten if remembered at all. Goodman was not a scholar; he was a teacher. His classroom was his pulpit; his students were his joy and frustration. His literary Bible was *Dubliners*, a collection of short stories by James Joyce, which Goodman discovered when he was a Phi Beta Kappa student at City College. His legacy was English 12, a creative writing course he started in 1926.

A charitable judgment of his pedagogical approach would be that he frightened as many students as he inspired. He could be brutal in his criticism of a student's paper; certainly he seemed indifferent to a student's feelings. One day my brother, Bernard, a 1942 graduate of City College, bumped into his friend Paddy Chayefsky, a student who had survived Goodman's English 12 course and become a successful playwright. They were discussing a homework assignment. "It's one word. That's the key," Chayefsky hinted, breaking one of Goodman's sacred sanctions. "Never share information about homework!"

In this way, armed, my brother attended class. The assignment was *Dubliners*, of course, which Goodman insisted that his students study with the ferocious dedication of Talmudic scholars. "You've all read 'A Little Cloud'?" he asked, referring to one of the short stories in Joyce's collection. "What is the key word in this story?" Goodman's question hung over his students. He glanced mischievously from one student to another. "The key word," Goodman repeated. The silence was church-like. Then, from the back of the room, came "the word," uttered by my brother. "Little," Bernie volunteered. It was an educated guess, but it was also the right answer. Goodman, rather than praising his student, felt the need to belittle him. "Someone must have told you," he snapped. "You could never have figured it out yourself."

Like so many other students who looked in the mirror and thought they saw a budding writer, I had heard about Goodman and English 12 from Bernie and others, and I summoned up the courage to enroll in his course. I had good grades, and I was accepted. I could not allow myself to miss this challenge, even though, in truth, I had premonitions of unhappy days.

If Goodman had a dream, unrealized after many years of teaching, it was that one day he would be able to create another James Joyce, another writer who would astonish the literary world. He had had modest success. Alfred Kazin, Bernard Malamud, and Chayefsky were graduates of English 12, but he could not escape the larger truth, noted in a eulogy at his funeral—he had produced far more journalists than "writers," and he died a disappointed man.

In my time with Goodman, we focused on "A Little Cloud." It was the story of two old friends, Thomas Chandler and Ignatius Gallaher. Chandler, wrote Joyce, is "slightly under the average stature." Not surprisingly, he is often referred to as "little Chandler." Gallaher, on the other hand, "had got on." Goodman loved this phrase, analyzing each word for hidden meaning, as though, taken together, they conveyed the power and majesty of the First Commandment. Eight years before Gallaher had left Dublin, like so many other young Irishmen, including Joyce, to become a journalist in London. Now he is back for a brief visit.

The two friends meet for a drink at a downtown bar. Gallaher is, in Joyce's hands, a sophisticated man of the world. Little Chandler, by comparison, lives a cramped life in a small apartment with his wife and infant son, all the while dreaming of the poet he might have become if he were not in fact a humble law clerk living on a tight budget. Gallaher dazzles Chandler with tales of cosmopolitan life in the big cities of Europe.

"Is it true," Chandler asks, "that Paris is so . . . immoral, as they say?" Gallaher, a cigar cocked out of a corner of his mouth, smiles. "How dull you must find Dublin," he replies. Soon thereafter he departs, leaving Chandler to go, not to Paris or London, but back to his "little" apartment, dazzled by his friend's descriptions of "rich Jewesses" with "dark Oriental eyes."

I read "A Little Cloud" a dozen times at least, praying I could extract a few nuggets of wisdom from Joyce's rhythmic linking of words into sentences and sentences into paragraphs—wisdom that I could then apply to my storytelling. Was it possible, I wondered, that Goodman thought I could become a "writer"?

Our responsibility as students in English 12 was to summon inspiration from Joyce's writing and guidance from Goodman's teaching, and then demonstrate both qualities in three short stories that we wrote for the course. Our final grades were based totally on Goodman's judgment of our stories.

I spent more time thinking, planning, worrying, and writing these stories than anything else I did in college. Well, almost anything else in college. I wanted my stories to appeal to this "teacher of teachers." I wanted to become a writer who would be admired by Goodman, a "living legend," as he was often described at alumni gatherings.

What was Joyce's secret? Clearly he wrote about what he knew intimately. He unmasked the souls of Dubliners. He used short sentences. He favored artful verbs. He seemed like a Hemingway in style, a Dostoevsky in his brooding insight. I thought that I was not indulging in a wild fantasy when I imagined that I could write a story that the other students would like and Goodman would at least accept as a stepping-stone toward a career as a writer.

But what was my story?

At the time I was among the relatively few City College students who lived on campus. There was only one dormitory building. It was called Army Hall, and it stood on the corner of Amsterdam Avenue and 137th Street like an unwanted child from a Charles Dickens novel. Immediately after World War II, Army Hall became home for hundreds of veterans who returned to school as the grateful beneficiaries of the GI Bill of Rights. It was a gloomy place. My roommate, Mark Maged, a happy warrior from Brooklyn, described it as "an overwhelmingly depressing Victorian orphan asylum."

For me, Army Hall was depressing for a reason having nothing to do with its architecture: it was a breeding ground for mice. Rarely was there a day when I did not see a mouse or even a rat racing through its dark corridors; and if there was a mouse, there was almost certain to be a cat trying to catch it. Often I found reason not to return to Army Hall for meals until late at night, preferring to work in the library or in the offices of the college newspaper.

Eureka! Was there not the beginning of a tale here? I began thinking about "A Little Cloud." How would Joyce have handled such ingredients: a student living in a dormitory that seemed more like a World War II battleground for mice and cats, wanting to study but afraid to stay in his room, painfully conscious of his guilt seeing his parents sacrifice so he could remain in college. Like any budding writer, I paced the floor, certain in my extreme naiveté that if I paced enough, I'd come up with a plot. It had happened with other writers, and it would happen with me.

And suddenly it happened. A plot popped into my mind. I needed two main characters—me, a shy student with an inordinate fear of mice, and my friend, a psychology student, a basketball star, an Army Hall resident. Over occasionally edible hamburgers, which sold for twelve cents each, the two friends delved into the dark corners of my guilt, my conflicted feelings about home and Army Hall, my parents. I put together a story of fear and emotion, of guilt and conflict, and of an underlying honesty that I felt even Goodman could appreciate. I considered calling it "A Little Obsession"; but then, anticipating criticism that I might have been excessively influenced by Joyce or fearful of Goodman, I decided on a clever alternative—"A Small Obsession." This was good stuff, I concluded with unjustified confidence. I even imagined that the *New Yorker* would make a bid for it.

I was dreaming, of course. When my turn came to read my story to the class, I rose with no small measure of trepidation, caused by Goodman's questioning the worthiness of my title. ("Were you trying to pass yourself off as another Joyce? Come on," he muttered disparagingly.)

I proceeded to read "A Small Obsession." Goodman had retreated to the rear of the classroom, mumbling to himself. Every now and then he would interrupt and ask a provocative question, but most of the time he just paced. My fellow students listened with what seemed like genuine interest; and when I finished, they applauded. Their questions reflected a genuine curiosity. One asked whether I had deliberately fashioned my story after "A Little Cloud." Another wanted to know whether my main character's obsession with mice was really my obsession with mice. A third student rose to say he thought it was the best story he had heard all semester.

I felt a rush of pride. Goodman walked slowly from the rear of the room to the front. For a few moments that seemed like an eternity, he looked at me and then asked for my paper, which of course I handed to him. Goodman examined the front page, still not saying a word. There was a strange look in his eyes. Was he going to echo the student compliments, or was he going to cut loose with one of his characteristic condemnations? The silence lingered for a few more moments. Then, with dramatic flourish, he held the paper aloft and proclaimed, "Kalb, this is a great story." He paused. I smiled, foolishly. "A great story," he continued, "for the wastepaper basket!" And, in one swift motion, he hurled the paper toward the basket, most of it going in, some pages ending up on the floor.

Goodman stared up at me, a weird grin on his face. A gasp of incredulity rose from the students. I stood before him and the students for only a second, then burst into tears and fled from the room, pausing only to pick up my briefcase. From the hallway, I heard Goodman shouting after me. "Kalb," he screamed, "all you will ever be in life is a journalist."

From Cambridge to Moscow

Poor Teddy Goodman. He wanted so much for his students to blossom into models of James Joyce, to become, as he put it, "real writers." In Goodman's judgment, Shakespeare showed definite promise, but he was no Joyce. So if Goodman ever, for a fleeting moment, imagined that I could become a "real writer," not just another journalist, he was to be profoundly disappointed with my first postgraduate decision. The question was the same one that had haunted me in my junior and senior years: Would I volunteer for the army, or would I first go to graduate school? Graduate school won the toss.

I could have applied to Columbia's Russian Institute, but at this point in my life Columbia seemed too much like City College, another stop on the IRT subway. I was drawn instead to Harvard's Russian Research Center, which specialized in offering a two-year master's program in Soviet studies considered by many to be the best in the country. It was, I thought, good preparation for a career in journalism, or teaching or diplomacy, whichever I would ultimately choose. I always had Bernie's advice in mind: know something! Russia and Russian seemed the right mix for me.

I loved Cambridge almost from my first day there. I shared early impressions with my parents. "I'm thrilled," I wrote in one letter. "Harvard is magnificent." I had a comfortable room in Richards Hall. I actually considered the meals in the nearby Harvard Law School cafeteria to be "wonderful, seconds too if you wish." I met students from all over the country and the world, many friendly and very bright. I enjoyed walks along the Charles River as much as crisscrossing the Yard in search of a classroom.

Most impressive was the faculty. I met within days of my arrival with Professor Robert Wolff, an accomplished historian and student adviser. A large, bespectacled man, always it seemed in a dark three-piece suit serving as backdrop for a bright, striped tie, he was avuncular in manner and precise in organizing my academic program—this course in the first semester, that one in the second—always stressing the importance of language as the essential tool for understanding Russian society. Russian became my constant companion. Because I had a special interest in communism as the ideological backbone of the strategic threat to the United States, Wolff recommended that I also start studying Chinese, an undertaking that, together with my study of Russian, proved to be too formidable a task. I dropped Chinese after six weeks of headaches and frustration, but stayed with Russian. I was again open to the excitement and wonders of Russian and Chinese history, politics, sociology, and economics.

Like Wolff, Professor Michael Karpovich, who expressed enormous admiration for Hans Kohn, welcomed me into his crowded office shortly after my arrival. Karpovich had left Russia after the 1917 revolution. He was a small man, blessed with a ready smile. Amid small mountains of manuscripts, magazines, and books, he talked to me for more than an hour about his fascination with Russian history, especially Russian intellectual history. He recommended that I read Sir Bernard Pares's 1926 classic, *A History of Russia*, which he considered a door opener to understanding his homeland. "Read Pares, then Vernadsky, and then

Klyuchevsky," he said smiling, bubbling with pleasure, "and then you'll understand why I am so happy to be here at Harvard, to be able to teach Russian history." I took his course and loved it, and, much to my surprise, he asked me to be one of his teaching assistants. He even asked me, on more than one occasion, to teach his class when he was away or ill. It was, for me, an extraordinary experience—rich, responsible, and rewarding. After a full semester as a teaching assistant, I began to think more positively about a Ph.D. and a career as a teacher of Russian history.

All of my professors were experts in pre- and postrevolutionary Russia. Each in his own way helped me develop an appreciation of Soviet society so close to the reality that very little surprised me when I first arrived in Moscow in late January 1956 on a State Department assignment. I had already read about the icy Russian winter that had stymied Napoleon and ultimately defeated Hitler's vaunted Wehrmacht. Now, in Moscow, by visiting the peasant market in Moscow or the GUM department store in Red Square, I could see vivid examples of the unevenness of the Soviet economy, clothing of rough fabric with no discernible style and surpluses of cabbage but shortages of such basics as flour and salt. Professor Alexander Gerschenkron had provided precious insights into the strange ups and downs of the socialist economy, its ability to build massive weapons but its inability to build simple homes. Professor Adam Ulam introduced me to Kremlin intrigues, and the sociologist Alex Inkeles described the many ways Soviet citizens survived in a whacky, unfriendly society. The great writer Vladimir Nabokov was a visiting professor, an unforgettable character, and many of my friends and I rushed to enroll in his class on nineteenth-century Russian literature. He almost always arrived ten to fifteen minutes late, trailed by his pale, ascetic wife, Vera. He went through a routine before ascending to his teaching podium. He would plop down in a student's chair, any student's chair, as though weary from a day in the mines, while on her knees in front of him Vera would remove his galoshes. Then, as though mysteriously infused with energy, he would lecture with humor and eye-opening brilliance about such Russian writers as Alexander Pushkin,

Nikolai Gogol, and Anton Chekhov. Sometimes he would stop and say to his wife, "Sweetheart, dear, write Dostoevsky's name on the blackboard—you know, the way I like it spelled, with an *iy* and not the plain *y* others use incorrectly." I wondered, why couldn't he write Dostoevsky's name on the blackboard himself? Although, to my way of thinking, he treated Vera as an aristocratic landowner might a peasant in prerevolutionary Russia, she never said a word, never fussed—at least, not in class.

I was also attracted to two young professors, Richard Pipes and Alfred G. Meyer, who helped solve my problem of choosing between teaching and journalism (add a modest flirtation with diplomacy) as a career choice. Both professors came up with variations on the same theme, in the process producing an approach to graduate teaching and learning that was innovative and highly practical, at least for me.

A teacher of remarkable instinct and academic accomplishment, Pipes produced a proposal for a one-on-one course (one professor, one student) that would be devoted to a subject undiscoverable in the Harvard syllabus—undiscoverable because we were constructing our own course, never seen or taught before. Pipes suggested that I research and write monthly *New York Times Magazine*–type pieces about current developments in Eastern Europe. It was a serious game of make-believe: I'd be the reporter, he'd be my editor. I'd suggest a theme, he'd approve or disapprove. Then I would be essentially on my own, meeting with Pipes once a week to discuss my progress. My deadline was the end of each month. Four months per semester, four articles. My final grade would be determined by his judgment of my magazine pieces. His judgment was an A.

Meyer, a brilliant refugee from Nazi Germany, taught a course in communist ideology. He knew about my interest in journalism when I enrolled in his course. Because he, too, was a daily reader of the *Times*, he knew about Harry Schwartz's analyses of Soviet policy. He thought Schwartz was making an important contribution to educating the American people about the Soviet Union. He wanted to help me. Like Pipes, he produced an original formula that satisfied both Harvard and me. Every two weeks Meyer would arrange the following scenario: an imaginary secretary of state had a sudden and serious problem, and of course he would turn to his chief analyst of Soviet affairs (that was me) for advice. I would write a four-page recommendation and then, orally, present it to Meyer and the class. I did eight such papers, enjoying the challenge of each one and learning a great deal about different aspects of the Soviet strategic challenge and possible American responses.

Both Pipes and Meyer had adjusted Harvard's normally procrustean rules to satisfy my interests and needs, and I was indebted to them for these absorbing, valuable exercises in journalism and scholarship.

Over this two-year period, in all of my course work, my Russian-language skills improved considerably and my appreciation of Soviet politics, economics, and foreign policy deepened in meaningful ways. Throughout I was aware that I would soon face a critical crossroad: to go on for a doctorate, allowing me to avoid the draft (that issue hung over all of us, an almost constant reminder of the war in Korea), or to pre-empt the draft by joining the army now, not waiting for an official draft notice, serve the required two years, and then make up my mind about next steps. I chose the army, in large part because I felt it was the right thing to do. I wanted to "give something back" to the country that had opened its doors to my father and mother and provided all of us with a chance for a better life. In those days, a sense of old-fashioned patriotism was felt with pride; it was not something mentioned with a trace of embarrassment, as happened during the Watergate scandal and the Vietnam War. My father understood my decision and supported it. Not my mother.

In July 1953 I visited the neighborhood selective service office, explained my thinking, volunteered for immediate service, and in early September 1953 began my two years in the army (actually twenty-one months) at Fort Dix, New Jersey. I was offered the option of attending officers training school, which would have meant three years of active duty and seven years of reserve duty, and I declined. A two-year tour was enough, especially since the war in Korea was winding down to an unhappy truce. Had the war continued, I might have made a different decision and gone to OTS. As it happened, I spent only four weeks at

Fort Dix. Basic training was tough but, in an odd way for me, satisfying. I met people I would not otherwise have met—southerners who had never exchanged a word with a black or a Jew, westerners who had trouble adjusting to eastern ways, and Californians who seemed to live in their own world. I enjoyed singing rhythmic songs during endless marches, and I found kitchen patrol—KP—usually considered so onerous soldiers would feign illness to avoid it, to be an entirely natural chore. I had often done the dishes at home.

My commanding officer during this rigorous four-week program was a tough, wiry Floridian who had only recently returned from Korea. His full name was James Todd Warner, but he was always to be addressed as "sir" or "Sergeant Warner." He was always lighting up a cigarette, or so it seemed, inhaling slowly and then exhaling even more slowly, while quite deliberately flicking cigarette ash on floors that had just been washed. He cursed in ways I had never heard, while demanding absolute propriety from all of us. "You're in the army now, you assholes," he'd say. "You're representing the United States of America. No cursing allowed. Show respect, you fucking recruits." He wore his uniform with enormous pride, as though he were parading before the company commander, and he demanded the same of us. He was, in every imaginable respect, an impossible person—always angry, impolite, rigid, rarely bowing to even the smallest measure of humanity, and yet if I ever had to go to war, I wanted an SOB like Warner to lead my platoon into battle. He exuded a sense of total self-confidence, and I'd have followed him anywhere.

I was, though, quickly detached from Warner and Fort Dix and dispatched to the Army Security Center at Fort Meade, Maryland, where I found myself in an elite unit of Russian-speaking soldiers who had studied Soviet communism. They knew the enemy. Several were teachers, others lawyers, and some were hoping to become diplomats, Foreign Service officers. For the better part of the next two years I worked as an intelligence analyst focusing on the Korean War, in particular the cruel, inhumane treatment of American POWs. If I had not been an anti-communist before my time in the army, I would have become one as a result of my training as a POW analyst in the Korean War.

One way the North Koreans got intelligence information from an American POW was to put him in a box, doubled-up, knees to his chin, in absolute blackness, and then raise the box off the ground, no more than a few inches, tilting it slightly so the POW would slide into a corner—and then leave him there for twelve hours, or twenty-four hours, or even longer if he was still unwilling to disclose more than his name, rank, and serial number. Then, in bright light, they would suddenly pull a cord and the bottom of the box would snap open, and the POW would drop to the ground, startled by the light, frightened, embarrassed, covered in his own excrement. Most of the boxed POWs told the North Koreans whatever they wanted; several did not and they were returned to the box for thirty-six hours or longer. Almost everyone talked.

Another one of my responsibilities was lecturing to senior officers about communism. I did a four-lecture course at the Pentagon. My own commanding officer, a tall, resolute, Virginia-born colonel named Lively, admitted to me that I was not his choice for this assignment—I had been selected by more senior officers who had reviewed my résumé and had made the call. I was a PFC, a private first class, meaning among other things that I had a single stripe on my uniform, and apparently Lively did not want someone from his unit, a PFC no less, lecturing to field-grade officers, many of whom were his friends. He recommended that I lecture in civilian clothes. It was not an order. In fact, my orders noted my rank. Something inside me went into revolt, and I mischievously responded that I was "very proud of my uniform" and would prefer lecturing in uniform. By implication, I was saying that he was not proud of my uniform, nor of me. For a moment I thought he was going to punch me in the jaw, but he controlled his temper and signed my orders.

My first lecture started one Monday at exactly 8:00 a.m. I arrived at 7:45 a.m., more than a few butterflies dancing in my stomach, checked that my handouts had been distributed, went to the men's room when I didn't have to, watched as the auditorium gradually filled up with majors and colonels, and, with only a minute to go, I walked briskly to the podium. The officers, obviously not expecting their lecturer to be a PFC, saw me but kept right on talking. I said nothing but stood my ground behind the podium. Slowly the thought must have dawned on them that I was the lecturer. I started as the minute hand hit eight. According to unofficial army protocol, lectures begin with two jokes, everyone relaxes, and then the serious stuff begins. In defiance of protocol, I started with substance.

"Good morning," I said, "this is a course on Soviet communism," and off I went, the large auditorium descending into silence as I launched into a lecture about Marx and Engels and, later, Lenin and Stalin.

After a few minutes I violated one other element of protocol. I asked a question of a colonel in the third row. That was a no-no, for if the colonel did not know the answer, he would be embarrassed. I asked a simple question: Who was more important, Marx or Engels? He gave me the right answer, and we continued. Why?, I wanted to know. The course proved to be a success. I got a round of applause after the fourth session. A crazy thought ran through my mind: maybe I'll now make corporal.

One night, back at Fort Meade, when I was on guard duty, Major Ernest Netzloff, executive officer of the Army Security Center, entered command headquarters, where I was monitoring two phones resting mute on a clean desk. He was a handsome, graying-crew-cut native of Oklahoma, who had fought in both World War II and Korea. His khaki shirt was covered with medals. His manner was always correct and friendly. I leaped to attention, but he quickly dispensed with formality. It was two o'clock in the morning.

"I've wanted to talk to you for a long time, Private," he said, taking the seat behind the desk.

"Yes, sir?" What was on his mind?

"Have you ever wondered why you haven't made corporal?" he asked, to my astonishment. Actually, I had wondered why a number of my colleagues had been promoted, and I had not. PFC was my apparent ceiling. I did not answer him. I just stood there.

"You've never made corporal," he continued, "because Colonel Lively doesn't like Jews." Colonel Lively was Major Netzloff's commanding officer, too. "You've done your work admirably. Your lecture course was well received. You deserve a promotion, but he will never give it to you." Clearly, Major Netzloff was violating every rule in the army manual. He was accusing his commanding officer of anti-Semitism. He could get into bad trouble. I was suddenly tongue-tied, not my usual condition. What was he doing?

"I just wanted you to know," he said, pushing back on his chair. Then, more softly, "Just wanted you to know." He stood up, snapped to attention, turned smartly toward the door, and left. Years later, when I had already become a network correspondent, I got a letter from Major Netzloff, saying he had retired from the service shortly after our time at Fort Meade. I lost his letter, but I remember he wrote that no form of discrimination was acceptable to him in the U.S. Army and that so long as Livelys remained in the service, he had to leave. He did not fight against fascism in World War II, he continued, to be a silent witness to anti-Semitism in the U.S. Army. He offered an apology, saying he hoped that one day Colonel Lively would do the same.

A footnote: My army service ended in June 1955 and I immediately returned to Harvard, where I enrolled in summer school, preparatory to pursuing work on my Ph.D. I met a lovely student from Virginia. Her name was Ginny, and her father was an army general. One day I shared the Netzloff story with her. She was shocked. She asked if she could tell the story to her father. Why not?, I thought. Months later I got a letter from Ginny, telling me that Colonel Lively had been officially reprimanded and told that he would never make general and that perhaps he should resign. He did, shortly thereafter. In a way, his resignation was my promotion to corporal. Thanks, Ginny.

Govorit Moskva —*"Moscow Calling"*

ecember 1955 was Cambridge, cold and intellectually stimulating. January 1956 was Moscow, colder still and even more intellectually stimulating. What a difference a month could make—from one month to the next my location and life had changed. I went from being a Ph.D. student at Harvard to being a translator for the American embassy in the Soviet capital. On occasion, I also served as a press attaché. It all seemed to happen overnight.

One day in late December, Marshall Shulman, once Dean Acheson's speechwriter at the State Department and now associate director of the Russian Research Center, asked a question that took me totally by surprise: Would I accept a Moscow assignment as a State Department translator, and would I be prepared to leave in a week or two? It was helpful, he said, that I had recently held a top-secret clearance at the Army Security Center. And, by the way, he added, he needed an answer by tomorrow. I gulped.

"Could I have another day or two?" I asked.

"No," he answered, a smile spreading across his face.

Shulman was my friend, a man of exceptional decency and good humor. If he could have given me more time, he would have, but only that morning he had received an urgent call from friends at the State Department.

"Know anyone who speaks Russian, has a clearance, and can leave for Moscow in the next week or so?" they wanted to know.

"Yes," Shulman replied, guessing correctly that I would jump at this opportunity.

I checked with a few of my colleagues, who all responded with the Monopoly equivalent of "Go! And don't stop to collect two hundred dollars." My father shared their enthusiasm but my mother, characteristically, was more cautious and proved to be more prescient. She wondered whether it would be wise for me to accept a Moscow assignment when I was only a month or two into my Ph.D. program. Might the allures of Moscow not preempt serious scholarship?

There was another reason, too. My brother, a reporter for the *New York Times*, was then covering another of Admiral Richard Byrd's missions to the South Pole, and she did not want her other son to be in Moscow at the same time her first son was in the Antarctic. Too dangerous, she thought. Besides, who would believe that one son would be at the South Pole and the other in Moscow?

Still, Moscow beckoned. I had been studying Soviet policy and communist ideology for more than five years and I was intensely eager to see whether a deep immersion in Soviet studies could ever properly prepare someone for the real thing.

When I told Shulman the next morning that I would be honored to accept the State Department job in Moscow (and, for me, "honored" was the right word—it was not just a matter of protocol), I thought I might even find a way of combining my official job with some unofficial scholarship for my dissertation. Shulman was pleased. We then talked about the Cold War. He was worried that we might be misreading Soviet intentions and they misreading ours, producing a deeper spiral of distortion and distrust in superpower relations. Ever since 1949, when the Russians exploded their first atomic bomb and Mao Zedong seized control of the Chinese mainland, two events of global consequence, the Cold War had turned frigid and Shulman saw troubling signs of habit, not reason, governing policymaking in Washington and Moscow.

"Observe and write," he urged as we said good-bye. "Observe as much as you can, and write to us as often as you can." Then, whispering, he added, "Wish I were going with you. There's so much we have yet to learn." Shulman, patting me on the back, gave me the name and number of a State Department official. "Call him when you get a chance," Shulman added. "Like now."

The official's name was Robert, and he had a soft, cultivated voice suggestive of an upbringing in New England. He was all business. "When can you get to Washington?" he asked. "Monday," I replied, and we arranged an 8:00 a.m. meeting at the State Department. I would be briefed in Washington for a week. I went to my room, packed, and headed for the train station. I had a job. I was going to Moscow, and I could not have been happier.

My week in Washington was intense, interesting, and even, in its way, amusing. I went from one briefing to another, most of them devoted to my new job as a translator, not literally for the American embassy in Moscow, as it turned out, but for an international organization called the Joint Press Reading Service (JPRS), which lived in Moscow under a separate diplomatic umbrella funded by the United States, Great Britain, Australia, and Canada. The JPRS, I was told, was run by Anna Holdcroft, a remarkable Englishwoman of exceptional charm and wisdom who knew more about Russia than an army of "Russia experts." Staffed by a dozen or so translators and typists from the four sponsoring nations, it serviced many foreign embassies in Moscow—too strapped for cash to employ their own translators—by providing them every afternoon with translated articles or editorials from the Soviet press at the modest cost of roughly $140 a year. (A few years later the Russians took a page out of a lesson book on capitalism; they set up a similar operation but charged only $100 a year. They eventually put us out of business.) The United States, by supporting the JPRS, was not engaging in an exercise of mindless generosity; the JPRS was a small corner of the Cold War. Reading the Soviet press was a political necessity in those days. It was as close as many of us got to the reality of Soviet life.

At the time we met very few Russians. They were not our friends. They lived in their world, we in ours. When we, who were associated with the American embassy, did talk with a Russian, it was generally in the context of an arranged meeting, a chance encounter in a marketplace, or an innocent exchange on a train or trolley. Rarely would we meet the same Russian twice, and if we did, we knew from experience that the encounter had to have official clearance. The few Russians we met with regularity at embassy parties or national day receptions, such as the July Fourth holiday party, were likely to be KGB officials in the guise of diplomats or journalists. They would shoulder up to foreigners, create artificial friendships, and pick up any fragments of information or intelligence that were considered interesting, possibly valuable. CIA officials did the same thing with Russians.

Buried in a long, tedious article about communist ideology might be the early signs of a power struggle, or in a difficult-to-digest discussion of Soviet agriculture the first indications of a new approach to solving the old problem of food shortages. Which articles, therefore, should be translated? Which editorials? Clearly these were political judgments, and Holdcroft, whose experience as a Russian-language translator for the British Foreign Office went all the way back to 1921, made these judgments every morning. Our job was to translate. I was told that the JPRS served America's national interest by spotting, translating, and distributing the selected articles to as many foreign embassies as possible. In this way we were giving them our assessment of what was important in judging Soviet reality. It was not exactly casting a light on all of Soviet society—it wasn't a form of translated transparency. But in a society where, in those days, weather forecasts were regarded as military secrets and telephone books were classified, the insights the JPRS provided on a daily basis were invaluable.

The last briefing of my Washington week concerned what was called "personal security." It was my favorite. "Please don't be late for this one," my advisers stressed. "It's really important."

I was intrigued. I had not been late for any of my briefings. Why the warning? My imagination ran wildly from one possibility to another, from wiretaps to Mata Haris. At the scheduled time, not a minute too early or late, I entered a gloomy room on the second floor of the State Department. An official sat behind a cluttered desk. "Sit down, please," he said, not lifting his head from a file he was reading. "You're Kalb, right?" he asked, still not lifting his head.

"Yes, sir," I answered.

"Good," he said. "Let's get on with this then, okay?"

"Yes, sir."

"You're single, aren't you?" he asked, flipping through my file.

"Yes, sir."

"Do you date?" Bob asked, still not looking up.

"Date?" I was puzzled.

"Yes. Do you date? Do you go out with girls?"

"Of course I go out with girls." What was he getting at?

The official looked up at me. "This is important," he said, a note of urgency in his voice. "In other words"—here each word left his mouth as if, strung together, they composed a phrase as meaningful as a declaration of war—"you are straight?" he asked, with a knowing nod. "You like girls?" he added.

I understood, finally. "Yes, of course," I said, summoning every ounce of masculine self-confidence to ease his concern, "I like girls. I go out with girls. I am not a . . ." I paused.

"Okay," he said, raising his hand. "I understand." He took a deep breath. "This is always a difficult interview, but I have to ask these questions, you know."

"Of course." I tried to be reassuring.

"So, let's see," he continued. "You are single. Handsome, in a way, and you like girls." He again looked down at my file, as though to avoid looking at me. "You can see where I'm going, can't you? The Russians will spot you immediately. You're a target, a potential target, someone they can compromise, get secrets from."

"No, no," I replied. "I'm no target. You don't have to worry about me. I'm—"

"You're wrong," he said, trying to hide a trace of irritation in his voice. "Quite the contrary, you are the perfect target." I shuffled from foot to foot.

"Do you like the ballet?" he asked.

"I love the ballet," I answered, hoping we were going on to another subject. "Love it. I hope I can get to the Bolshoi as often as possible."

Wrong answer. I could see a wrinkle of concern cross his face. "That's what I was afraid of," he said with a sigh. "They often use ballet dancers."

"Use ballet dancers?"

"Yes, it's happened before. They send ballet dancers to do the job."

"The job?"

"Yes, the job. You know, seduction."

My knees wobbled. Was he saying that the mighty, nuclear-armed Soviet Union might be concerned enough about me—totally unimportant know-nothing twenty-five-year-old me—to send a Bolshoi ballerina to seduce me? Crazy, I thought. Silliest thing I ever heard!

"One day," he went on, looking out a State Department window that hadn't been cleaned in months, "a Russian ballerina will knock on your door, and—who knows?—try to seduce you." My throat felt very dry.

"You know the way it works. They get photos of the two of you in bed, and they use them to embarrass you and your country. Your family, too." He was looking straight at me now. "They get state secrets. You get . . ."

I must admit, listening to him, that two thoughts from two different planets passed through my mind at the same time: One, I wouldn't want to embarrass my country and certainly not my family—that was abso-

That's Kalb, statue-like, on Red Square. What's not visible are the 22-below-zero temperature and the 20-mile-an-hour winds.

lutely true. But two, a Russian ballerina sent on a secret diplomatic mission to seduce me? Oh, my God! Visions of a Bolshoi seduction danced before my eyes, visions I attempted immediately to block from anyone else's view, especially Bob's.

I reassured him that I would fend off any advances by a Soviet ballerina. "I completely understand your concerns," I said, hopefully with conviction, "and please understand that I will never allow anything like that to happen to me. Never."

The official rose from behind his desk. Shaking my hand, he said in conclusion. "Marvin, I trust you completely. It's the Russians I'm worried about. Please be careful."

"Yes, sir," I replied, and left with a joyful bounce of anticipation in my step.

Bob was not being excessively cautious. The Russians did engage in seduction. One example—of many, no doubt—involved the columnist Joseph Alsop, who was photographed in early 1957 in a Moscow hotel room with a male KGB agent. Using these photos the Russians hoped to be able to embarrass Alsop and convert him into becoming a spy. He refused, and the Russians did not press the issue.

Dear reader, you are entitled at this point to hear my confession: Not once, over the next thirteen months of my first Moscow assignment, during which time I traveled through central Asia, the Caucasus, Ukraine, and large parts of Russia, attended scores of plays and ballets, studied at the Lenin Library and frolicked in Gorky Park, not once did a Russian girl, ballerina or not, approach me and suggest we spend a glorious night together reading Pushkin's poetry, looking up at the Moscow stars, and promising to love each other forever. Not once.

And so, with Bob's warning about Cold War sex and seduction framing my excitement about my Moscow assignment, I left Washington and hurried to New York for a farewell dinner with my parents. They were both very proud, even my mother. The next morning my father, sporting a new fedora, escorted me to the airport and I was off to Moscow on a giant Pan Am Stratocruiser, a 5,400-mile journey by way of Prestwick, Bremen, Copenhagen, Stockholm, and Helsinki, and then the rest of the way by train from Helsinki to the Finland Station in Leningrad (as St. Petersburg was then called) and finally on to Moscow. Because I had a diplomatic passport, the U.S. embassy put me in charge of a large food shipment. It was my first official responsibility. As we were clearing customs at the Finnish-Soviet border—why was it that the grass was green on the Finnish side and scraggly and unkempt on the Soviet?—a Russian customs officer asked to see my passport. Was I the officer in charge of the shipment? he asked. Yes, sir, I replied. He examined my passport, saluted, and returned it. I felt relieved. My modest mission, accomplished!

When we arrived in Moscow on the morning of January 28, 1956, it was 42 degrees below zero. As I stepped from the train onto the platform I felt the cold in a way utterly new to me, like a physical force so overpowering that for a moment I could not breathe. It was as if the cold had frozen my nostrils, throat, and lungs. I doubled back into the comparative warmth of the train. "You'll get used to it," shouted the embassy officer who had come to the station to greet me. He grabbed the back of my heavy coat, stopping my Napoleonic retreat.

"Welcome," said Nat Davis, who quickly became my embassy savior and friend. "Welcome to Moscow."

I have always believed that a person who loves ice cream has to be a good person, even if, by chance, he or she works for the KGB, the Soviet secret police. So it was with a special pleasure that the day after my arrival in Moscow, where everyone was luxuriating in a comparative heat wave (the temperature had climbed to 15 below zero), I came upon indisputable evidence of the healing properties of "ice cream diplomacy," years before "ping-pong diplomacy" had a positive effect on U.S.-China relations.

Because I was a bachelor and the embassy was short of housing space, I was not given an apartment in the embassy building but rather a large single room at American House, a three-story, red-brick building on Kropotkinskaya Naberezhnaya, an embankment road running alongside the Moscow River. Before the Russian Revolution it had been a mortician's home and also his place of business. It was still a gloomy place, I felt, and I wanted to get out of it as quickly as possible. On my first full day in Moscow I decided I would visit Red Square. Where else, after all? I dressed warmly, left American House, and headed toward the neighborhood stop of the Moscow Metro. Remembering my Washington guidance about personal security, I glanced from side to side, checking everyone and everything. Across the street I spotted a young man in a heavy black overcoat. My first reaction was, in truth, ambivalence: "He couldn't be following me, and yet maybe he is," I thought. I entered the Metro, bought a ticket, and waited for the next train. Within minutes one arrived, and I boarded it for the quick ride to Red Square. The train was crowded, but—no doubt about it—there was the same young man in the black overcoat. He stood not more than three or four steps from me. He looked at me and twitched his mustache.

Three stops later I got off the train, ascended an escalator to the street, and found myself looking at the beautiful Bolshoi Theater. But not for long—it was too cold. I pirouetted and—whoops—bumped into the man in the black overcoat. "Excuse me," I said. He did not reply. I walked toward Red Square. Around a busy corner I saw two stunningly beautiful throwbacks to Czarist Russia: the Kremlin and St. Basil's Cathedral. Like many other visitors I stopped for a moment to admire this famous scene, but unlike the others I was being followed by a young man in a black overcoat, and I decided to enter GUM, a giant department store fronting Red Square. The young man—undoubtedly my tail, I figured—followed me. I turned and smiled at him, but he did not smile back.

There, in a crowded corner of GUM, I saw an ice cream vendor. Even on icy days in a Moscow winter, Russians love their ice cream. I approached the stand and on a whim purchased two ice cream cones. I started to eat mine and, without looking back, extended the other to the young man, who I assumed was standing directly behind me. He took the cone, never said "Thank you," and started to lick it with the same delight I derived from licking mine. I turned and smiled at him. He did not smile back. But I felt I had made my first Russian conquest—a KGB tail who liked ice cream.

The JPRS was my job. Sergei Semyonovich Uvarov, the minister of education under Czar Nicholas I, who came up with the popular conservative slogan of "Nationalism, Autocracy, and Orthodoxy," was the subject of my Harvard research. In my mind, but considering, too, my mother's concern, I felt I could link the two. Somehow.

The JPRS was located on Kropotkinsky Pereulok 26, a narrow street in what must have been a fashionable neighborhood in prerevolutionary

Moscow. At one end was the Arbat, a busy avenue where one could still find bookstores and modest art galleries, and where in czarist Russia one could imagine Russian noblemen and -women showing off their best imported finery, sprinkling their speech with French colloquialisms, strutting about, or being whisked in horse-drawn carriages to a Kremlin reception or a Chekhov performance at the famed Moscow Art Academic Theater, or the MKhAT, as it was popularly called. At the other end were side streets with decaying mansions, most still walled off by tall iron fences that had kept the aristocracy safely protected from the workers—ostentatious wealth and privilege separated from the people. The JPRS was housed in one of those old mansions, one that a hundred years earlier had belonged to the Kropotkin family.

On my first morning, as snowflakes fell from a charcoal-gray sky, I got a lift to the JPRS in an embassy car, which stopped at the entrance to Kropotkin's home. A uniformed militia man, the sort seen in front of all buildings where foreigners worked or lived, asked for my personal *propusk*, my crisp new identification card. He looked at it, then slowly looked at me, and then again at the card, until he finally turned and entered a small, cone-shaped sentry box, where he picked up the telephone. Obviously he had never seen me before and he wanted a higher-up's permission to allow this stranger into the courtyard. After a minute or two he returned to the car, again looked at me and my card, and only then, after a pregnant pause, did he stand tall, salute, and wave me in.

On the front of this two-story mansion, which had clearly seen better days—paint was peeling from old classical columns—I noticed a plaque from which jumped the proud, bearded face of one of its prerevolutionary owners and just below it the words "P. A. Kropotkin was born in this house in 1842." I was delighted. I was going to be working in the home of one of Russia's greatest anarchists, an aristocrat who devoted his life to the destruction of the centralized state his family had helped build 700 years earlier. Peter Kropotkin's *Memoirs of a Revolutionary*, required reading in a course I had taken on Russian intellectual history, eloquently told the story of an idealistic aristocrat who hated the unquestioned powers of the czar, though he enjoyed all of their benefits, and concluded that societal bliss could come only from the destruction of such state power. For many years he had lived in Western Europe, banished from his homeland by the czar. After the Russian Revolution of 1917 he returned to Moscow, believing he now had a chance to infuse communism with his fiery brand of anarchism. But an intolerant Lenin had other ideas, and Kropotkin was unceremoniously exiled to a small town near Moscow, where he died a slow, unhappy death of disillusionment in 1921, never to see his ancestral home on Kropotkinsky Pereulok ever again.

That night I wrote in my diary: "The Russians are their own greatest admirers, and they love even the 'bad boys' of Russian intellectual life, like Prince Kropotkin. Therefore, they read and worship not only the Lenins, but also the Turgenevs, the Herzens, the Belinskys, and the Kropotkins.... In the Russian political tradition, there have been at least two powerful currents. One is communism, or the extremist sentiment that led to it.... The other is the humanitarian liberalism [of those] who placed the cause of individual freedom above all others."

This contest between liberal democracy and communist totalitarianism continued through the intellectual upheavals of the nineteenth century and into the twentieth century—indeed, for a time, even after the Russian Revolution. The communists operated on the assumption that they would be the ultimate winners, and for a time they were. They believed history was on their side. But in 1956, the "year of the thaw," as it came to be called, I stumbled upon a Russia in kaleidoscopic change. Russians knew where they had been—the wars, the purges, the fear, the collectivization of agriculture, the communization of their lives—but they did not know where they were going. Most Russians waited for their leader, their *vozhd*—a person of awesome, frightening power—to point the way.

Among the elite, even among the communist elite, one sensed impending change, as if the ground under the Soviet regime was beginning to rumble with uncertainty, doubt, and questions: Was communism, as the governing philosophy of the Soviet Union, losing its way? Was the Soviet regime itself so ragged, corrupt, and inefficient that it was demanding reform, and were Soviet leaders not listening? A question seemed to surface in random conversation: Was it now possible that communism was heading toward a historic collapse, or might it stumble along for another few decades, meeting increasingly meaningless industrial quotas, swearing loyalty to a political faith fewer found relevant to their everyday lives, flexing Cold War muscles while at the same time swearing allegiance to "peaceful coexistence"? No one knew the answers.

This was a problem of enormous importance for Russia and for the rest of the world. With my pursuit of the nineteenth-century minister of education and with my job at the JPRS, I was able to observe "the year of the thaw," or, as I later realized, the beginning of the end of Soviet communist rule as it had been practiced for decades. Armed with nothing more than a burning curiosity about what made Russia tick, I read the usually dull Soviet press, occasionally coming upon a small gem of insight into the functioning of a closed dictatorship. I traveled from one end of this vast country to the other; whenever possible I listened to what the Russian people were saying in parks, libraries, trains, or busy marketplaces. And because I worked under the auspices of the U.S. embassy, I had occasion to meet a number of Soviet leaders, including the ebullient, unforgettable first secretary of the Communist Party of the Soviet Union, Nikita Khrushchev.

De-Stalinization = Destabilization

It was the sort of clue Anna Holdcroft could spot before her morning tea.

The dictator Joseph Stalin had died on March 5, 1953. Nine months later, on the seventy-fourth anniversary of his birth (and on the seventy-fifth, the following year), the official Soviet press was predictably stuffed with tributes to his genius, his brilliant leadership during World War II, his awesome contributions to the worldwide communist movement. But then, suddenly, on the seventy-sixth anniversary of his birth, in December 1955, just a few months before the 20th Congress of the Soviet Communist Party, *Pravda*, the official party newspaper and mouthpiece, barely mentioned his name or birthday.

Mistake? Hardly, concluded Holdcroft.

Pravda would not have decided on its own to ignore the great man's birthday. She knew, from instinct and experience, that the missed opportunity for another round of Stalin-soaked adulation was deliberate. A major political upheaval of some sort was on the near horizon.

When I arrived for work at the JPRS in early February 1956, the place was aflutter with excitement. What was going to happen? The phrase "collective leadership" had begun to appear more frequently in authoritative editorials. Why stress "collective," Holdcroft asked, if it was not to suggest that the Party had become obsessed with something at the other end of the political spectrum—a "cult of personality," or a "cult of the individual," a phrase that was soon to become shorthand for Stalin's maniacal rule.

It was, I thought, revealing that everyone at the JPRS, using nothing more lethal than the tools of Kremlinology, in this case simply reading and analyzing the Soviet press, could spot the missing adulation of Stalin and then the two politically charged phrases and conclude, ipso facto, that the unimaginable in Soviet life and politics—an attack on the almighty Stalin himself—was in fact imaginable. There it was, emerging for all to see, in the pages of *Pravda*.

Reading *Pravda* in Soviet times was an adventure into the unknown. Let's say that four paragraphs into an unenlightening editorial about Soviet agriculture you came upon the word *odnako*, Russian for "however" or "but." The word was a signal that some sort of criticism of established policy was about to follow; and indeed most of the time *odnako* did lead to criticism. Words were considered literary weapons, used in a class or proletarian struggle against "the last vestiges of capitalism."

What a time to be in Moscow, what a sobering moment in the Cold War, at least for me and others absorbed with the shifting mysteries of Soviet politics!

At the JPRS, our tea breaks in Kropotkin's home often sounded like university seminars, Holdcroft holding forth as the judicious mentor and we translators as graduate students bursting with questions.

Is Russia plunging into another power struggle?

Will heads roll?

Could Khrushchev be building his own personality cult while criticizing Stalin's?

Most important, was Stalinism dying, and, if so, what would re-place it?

Yet while we at the JPRS were absorbed with Kremlin politics, ordi-nary Russians, it seemed, were generally indifferent to politics. One day soon after my arrival I met a forty-year-old Russian, a television engi-neer by profession. He told me he earned the equivalent of $650 per month, meaning he was a member of the new, rising middle class, no different in his outlook than millions of others who were beginning to enjoy the fruits of modern industrialization. His wife, he said proudly, "loves just being a housewife." I tried to get him to talk about politics. "No, no," he said, waving me off. "Politics is for them." He pointed toward the Kremlin.

The next evening, after a diplomatic dinner at which the dismissal of a top Soviet official was topic number one, I flagged a taxi for the ride back to American House. The driver told me that he worked in a cement factory during the day and drove a taxi at night to supplement his in-come. I wondered if he had even heard of the dismissal. "Not my busi-ness," he said, with a firm wave of his hand. "That's the government's business, not mine." In Russia, it was safer to be ignorant or to feign ignorance.

I could not escape the impression, even after so brief a time in Mos-cow, that the city seemed to be divided into two worlds, as I noted in my diary. One was the party, which dominated everything; the other was the people, who felt little connection to the party. "There appears to be political apathy, bred either of fear or indifference, or both," I wrote.

███

Change could be found even on a battered bulletin board. You had only to look.

Late one snowy afternoon in early February, while wandering through an annex of Moscow University located near Red Square, I spotted a handwritten notice on a second-floor bulletin board announcing a spe-cial course. The subject was not what made it special—that was "The

Role of the People in the Soviet Novel." What made it special was its lecturer, S. I. Stalina, identified only as a "Candidate of Philological Sciences." I was not the only one who did a quick double take.

Stalina? The lecturer had to be Stalin's daughter, Svetlana, who had not been seen or heard from in a very long time. One student wondered, "Is it Svetlana, do you think? Really?" Another, trying to be helpful, suggested they check with the main office on the third floor. I followed them.

Above the door to the main office was a large photo of Stalin himself, as though the faculty had not yet got the word that Stalin was in a period of transition—from god to scoundrel. An announcement was tacked to the right of the door: "In the second semester starts the special course of Candidate of Philological Sciences, Stalina, S. I. on the theme: 'Role of the People in the Soviet Novel.' Registration for this course held in Literary Office."

I rushed to the Literary Office but I was told that foreign graduate students would not be permitted to enroll in her course. Technically I was considered a graduate student. Many Russian students did enroll. Svetlana was a draw. At a time when her father was being unceremoniously stripped of his glory, she, ironically, was being given the chance to emerge from the dark shadows of forced anonymity and teach a course at Moscow University. For those skeptics still wondering whether the signals of change in Kremlin politics were real, here was yet another sign that indeed they were.

If you stood at one of the three main gateways into the Kremlin at 10:00 a.m. on February 14, 1956, you would have seen a procession of black limousines carrying communist dignitaries from all over the country and the world pass into the citadel of global communism. The snow-covered scene was one for the history books—the formal opening of the 20th Congress of the Communist Party of the Soviet Union in the Great

Kremlin Palace, the first party congress since Stalin's death three years before. TASS, the official Soviet news agency, reported the next morning that some 1,355 voting and 81 nonvoting delegates, representing 6.8 million full members and 620,000 candidate members of the Communist Party, had joined the leaders of 55 "fraternal" Communist Parties, all except rebellious Yugoslavia's, for this historic conclave. Of all these delegates, only a handful knew in advance that the 20th Party Congress would soon rewrite the history of Soviet communism and the legacy of Stalin.

As the delegates entered the mammoth meeting room, they noticed that for the first time in decades the huge photo of Stalin, which had always stared down on them, was missing. Lenin's statue was still in its customary place of honor, but Stalin's photo was gone. No delegate had the courage to pause in front of the missing photo. No one asked any questions. Perhaps a furtive glance up, followed by a quickened stride to a preassigned seat, but no more. Explanations, if there were to be any, would come later.

Like earlier congresses, this one opened with the first secretary of the Communist Party, in this case Nikita Khrushchev, delivering a lengthy report on the domestic and foreign policies of the Soviet Union. He was followed by the prime minister, Nikolai Bulganin, outlining the new five-year plan. Everything seemed normal, except it wasn't. Every delegate at the 20th Party Congress knew, or sensed, that something big was stirring, but how big? Who would win, and who would lose? And, most important, what would happen to Stalin—to his status? This was not an academic question. Most delegates knew that their futures were linked to Stalin's. If he was being downsized, which was likely, then they would be, too. Suddenly their futures were decidedly uncertain.

With Stalin's death in 1953 everything had become uncertain. His death, described years later by the Russian dissident Vladimir Bukovsky, "shook our life to its foundations. Classes virtually came to a halt, the teachers wept openly.... Enormous unorganized crowds streamed through the streets to the Hall of Columns, where Stalin lay in state. There was something awe-inspiring about these immense, silent, gloomy masses of people.... The vast procession continued on for several days, and thousands of people perished in the crush." Stalin was, wrote the scholar Walter Reich, "the only father they had known. Through all the terror, through the mass death and privations of World War II, he was the symbol of authority, the ultimate protector, the source of all sustenance, because all power was in his hands. He had been their supreme leader." And now there was this frightening hint in the air that their supreme leader stood on the edge of official criticism.

Of course, the Stalin legacy was so deeply carved into the Soviet mentality that many delegates simply refused to accept his downsizing. For example, when the French communist leader Maurice Thorez rose at one point to praise Stalin, many cheered. They thought that the jarring uncertainties surrounding the 20th Party Congress could probably be explained in more familiar terms—perhaps that Stalin's successors were engaged in another of their power struggles. And if they were so engaged, what did that have to do with Stalin? He stood above petty politics. He was the untouchable one, wasn't he? But if Stalin was untouchable, who had removed his photo? Eyes turned to Khrushchev. What would he say to explain the meaning behind the missing photo?

No fan of short speeches, Khrushchev opened the congress with a seven-hour report on the state of Soviet communism. He started in the late morning and finished in the early evening. He seemed never to tire. He spoke in a style that could only be described as bombastic, pounding the lectern for emphasis and attention. At the same time he spoke with an air of supreme self-confidence, looking for all the world, wrote the *New York Times*'s Harry Schwartz, like "the successful corporate lawyer reporting to a stockholders' meeting." Except for the mention of Stalin's death, Khrushchev did not allow the name Stalin to cross his lips. He spoke instead of the "cult of the individual." He stressed that this cult must be "resolutely condemned" because it was "alien to the spirit of Marxism-Leninism." It led, he added, to "an atmosphere of lawlessness and arbitrariness." In this opening speech Khrushchev did not detail the "lawlessness"; it was enough that he linked Stalin to "lawlessness." His message was clear.

In for a penny, Khrushchev decided to go in for a pound. He had already begun to criticize the leader he had once worshipped. Now Khrushchev would go where no sensible communist leader would have dared to go—into Stalin's once-sacred interpretations of communist ideology. Everyone knew that for many years it had been Stalin's belief, firmly etched into dogma, truth as taught in Soviet classrooms, that war between the communist and capitalist systems was inevitable. It was only a matter of time. To his credit, Khrushchev tossed the "inevitability of war" into a Kremlin graveyard. Indeed, he planted the flag of "peaceful coexistence." In a world teetering on the edge of a nuclear war, in which, he said, "the living would envy the dead," Khrushchev decided that although the triumph of communism was still inevitable, it would no longer have to be achieved by way of war, let alone nuclear war. In Khrushchev's 1956 tinkering with communist dogma, different countries could now take different roads to communism. Even a peaceful, nonrevolutionary road to communism would be possible. Of course, Khrushchev insisted, competition between the communist and capitalist systems would still continue, perhaps even intensify, but now the ground rules would be changed—the Stalinist doctrine of "inevitable war" would now be replaced by the Khrushchev doctrine of "peaceful coexistence."

In his veiled but still powerful critique of Stalin and his legacy, Khrushchev was joined publicly by two recent allies: Anastas Mikoyan, an old Bolshevik bureaucrat and statesman who had himself stood on the brink of liquidation a few weeks before Stalin's death but now stood just one step behind Khrushchev as top man in the Kremlin; and Georgy Malenkov, another old Bolshevik who had gained Stalin's favor only to lose it and who, on the dictator's death, joined Khrushchev in forming an ideological crusade against the cult of the individual. As Mikoyan recalled years later, "For about twenty years we actually had no collective leadership; instead the cult of the individual flourished." Malenkov was

*Changing of the Red Army guards near the Lenin-Stalin Mausoleum
on Red Square in the spring of 1956.*

even bolder in his criticism of Stalin's one-man rule, charging that his
"personal leadership" led to "crimes" that could never be explained nor
justified.

How different for Mikoyan and Malenkov must the 20th Congress
have been from the 19th! At the 19th Congress, chaired by Stalin, Mikoyan
referred to him nineteen times. His praise of Stalin was embarrassing
though expected: "the genius work of Comrade Stalin . . . the bright flame
of Stalinist genius . . . Comrade Stalin enriches our life, gives us a program
of action and directs our victorious advance toward communism." But at
the 20th Party Congress Mikoyan referred to him only once—and that

was to sneer at him. As for Malenkov, at the 19th Party Congress he mentioned Stalin fifty-one times; at the 20th, not even once.

The 20th Party Congress ended officially on February 24, a remarkable ten-day journey that included praise for the Soviet system but also unmistakable criticism of Stalin's crimes. This criticism had the unintended effect of delegitimizing the whole Soviet system. Every day *Pravda* ran long reports on the 20th Congress. The newspaper was actually read by some while being used to wrap fish by many others.

At the JPRS these were heady days. Early every morning, with anticipation and excitement, we showed up at Kropotkin's home. I for one wondered what the idealistic anarchist would have thought about the 20th Party Congress. I was totally absorbed with it—I could imagine nothing in the world that could possibly be more interesting and important. We translated Khrushchev's opening speech and, a few days later, on February 18, we translated Mikoyan's and Malenkov's speeches. At tea time we discussed and debated the speeches—their importance, their underlying message. I suspected that Russia's political and literary elite were engaged in similar analysis, carefully reading *Pravda*, checking impressions with trusted friends or colleagues, and asking what was then the unanswerable question—what's next?

In my diary I made note of two issues especially. I could not help but notice that there were many more editorials than usual, and in all of them Khrushchev was being hailed as a first secretary who believed in the collective leadership of the party. His name began to appear with such extraordinary regularity in the state-controlled media that I assumed editors must have gotten the word—build up Khrushchev! "On the coattails of a vigorous propaganda campaign against a personality cult," I wrote, "rides the small but growing and powerful personality cult of Khrushchev and his Central Committee."

It was almost as if the Russian people required a personality cult, a leader of unquestioned authority and power, to help them survive the day-to-day hardships of a lousy, unproductive system. As one cult of the individual was being dismantled, another was already being constructed. One delegate after another lavishly praised Khrushchev's opening day speech, using the same hyperbole they had heaped upon Stalin only a brief time before.

I also felt that the speeches and the speculation about the 20th Party Congress were only a curtain raiser on developments far more significant looming on the near horizon. "There is something in the air in Moscow," I noted on February 18, "and it would not be surprising for a big story to break soon. Big, sensational, explosive, and terribly significant. The groundwork is being laid." At the time I knew nothing about Khrushchev's final speech to the congress given on February 25; nor did anyone else at the embassy. I simply felt the ground trembling.

It is rare indeed that one speech can change history, but the one Khrushchev delivered unexpectedly on the morning of February 25 did just that. Technically, the 20th Party Congress had ended the night before. Foreign delegates were packing their bags, preparing to leave for the airport and flights home, when they noticed Soviet delegates rushing back to the Kremlin. Khrushchev had summoned them to an emergency meeting. The ax, they feared, was about to fall.

When everyone was seated, Khrushchev, looking "red-faced and excited," according to one observer, launched into a devastating, four-hour attack on Stalin. It was, wrote Khrushchev's biographer William Taubman, "the bravest and most reckless thing he ever did. The Soviet regime never fully recovered, and neither did he."

Stalin was guilty of "a grave abuse of power," Khrushchev charged. He reminded the delegates that during Stalin's one-man rule there had been "mass arrests" and the "deportation" of thousands and thousands of people. There had also been "executions without trial" that created "insecurity, fear, and even desperation." Delegates listened in stunned silence.

Khrushchev then reminded delegates of the phrase "counterrevolutionary crimes"—these were "absurd, wild, and contrary to common sense." Communists, "innocent communists," had been accused of such crimes, and they had confessed to these crimes "because of physical methods of pressure, torture, reducing them to unconsciousness, depriving them of judgment, taking away their human dignity."

And Stalin's role in all this? Khrushchev fingered his former idol: Stalin "personally called in the interrogator, gave him instructions, and told him what methods to use—methods that were simple—to beat, beat, and, once again, to beat." Stalin governed by "suspicion, fear, and terror."

One observer later recalled that Khrushchev was speaking with "agitation and emotion." Another marveled that he "could have brought himself to say such things before such an audience."

Khrushchev then assailed Stalin's "mania for greatness." "I'll shake my little finger, and there will be no more Tito," Khrushchev quoted Stalin as saying of the Yugoslav renegade. Praise of Stalin was "nauseatingly false," said Khrushchev. Worse, Stalin "never went anywhere," Khrushchev charged, "never met with workers and collective farmers." What he knew about the countryside came "only from films that dressed up and prettified the situation." Russia was for Stalin a Potemkin village.

But nothing seemed to upset Khrushchev more than Stalin's astounding misreading of Hitler's intentions in 1941. The Soviet leader had struck a deal with the Nazi dictator in 1939. The two had cold-bloodedly rearranged the map of Eastern Europe, and Stalin naively believed that Hitler would stick to its terms. When Hitler invaded the Soviet Union in 1941, Stalin at first refused to believe the news. He fell into a deep depression, for a time leaving Russia without a leader. The effect on the Soviet military was cataclysmic, the effect on public morale even worse. German troops and tanks cut effortlessly through porous Russian lines. They decimated the Ukrainian capital of Kiev, and then Kharkov, and still Stalin did nothing.

Khrushchev was devastated. In the early months of the war he was the Kremlin's man in Ukraine, and although he was a Russian ruling with a tough hand, he still had a soft spot in his heart for the region. One reason was that Khrushchev had been based in Ukraine during his early rise to power; another reason was that his wife was Ukrainian.

When Khrushchev described Stalin's unbelievable ineptness, he left one delegate with the impression that he truly "hated" Stalin. "He was a coward. He panicked," Khrushchev had shouted. "Not once during the whole war did he dare go to the front."

If Stalin's failures were so obvious, then why didn't Khrushchev and other communist leaders challenge him? Khrushchev himself asked the same question—it was on everyone's mind. "Where were the members of the Politburo? Why didn't they come out against the cult of personality in time? Why are they acting only now?"

The silence, so "deathly" quiet "you could hear a bug fly by," according to one Kremlin leader, slowly turned into an anxious hum. Delegates still did not have the courage to look one another in the eye. What was the answer to Khrushchev's question, they wanted to know. It was a moment of fear and anticipation. Dmitril Goryunov, chief editor of *Komsomolskaya Pravda*, the newspaper of the Young Communist League, was seen taking five nitroglycerin pills for his weak heart. A few delegates reportedly suffered heart attacks on the spot; some later committed suicide. Almost all of the delegates saw Stalin as an awesome god, powerful and omnipotent, who knew everything, bestowed goodness on his people, yet was feared by everyone. Children sang songs about him. "Stalin outshines the sun," they sang. "He flies higher than all. He defeats all enemies. He is our very best friend."

Many weeks later, after the news of the Khrushchev attack on Stalin had begun to circulate in the markets of Moscow, I heard stories about the 20th Party Congress. One told of how Khrushchev described Stalin's humiliation of other Kremlin bigwigs.

"Once he turned to me," Khrushchev explained, "and said, 'You, *khokhol*, dance the *gopak*.' So I danced." *Khokhol* is a derogatory Russian description of a Ukrainian, and the *gopak* is a quick, snappy Ukrainian peasant dance, difficult for someone short and stocky, like Khrushchev, to perform. He must have looked and felt like a fool, but he danced the *gopak* because he felt he had to—Stalin had told him to dance the *gopak*! In those days, he had no choice.

Another story heard in the Moscow market had one troubled delegate jumping to his feet and shouting, "Well then, why didn't you all get rid of him?"

Khrushchev, interrupted by the question, looked slowly around the chamber. "Who said that?" he asked.

No one answered.

"Who said that?" he repeated more forcefully.

But again there was no answer, only a sudden chill and silence.

Khrushchev grinned. "Now you understand why we didn't do anything," he said drily before continuing his speech.

In his memoir, years later, Khrushchev admitted that "doubts had crept into my mind . . . but we couldn't free ourselves from his pressure even after he died. . . . We were told not to stick our noses into things. . . . We did everything to shield Stalin, although we were shielding a criminal, a murderer."

Khrushchev told the delegates of a time when he and Nikolai Bulganin, then one of his key aides, were driving home from a meeting in Stalin's dacha. "Sometimes when you go to Stalin's," Bulganin related, "he invites you as a friend. But while you're sitting with him, you don't know where they'll take you afterward: home or to prison." A constant drum of anxiety and fear ran through Khrushchev's thinking about Stalin. He thought Stalin, shortly before his death, was on the edge of arresting and killing the old guard in the party Politburo, including himself, Mikoyan, Molotov, and Malenkov. Stalin wanted to "destroy them," Khrushchev said, "so as to hide the shameful acts about which we are now reporting."

Khrushchev ended his emotional tirade against Stalin with an odd plea for silence. "This subject must not go beyond the borders of the party, let alone into the press. That's why we are talking about this at a closed session of the Congress. . . . We must not provide ammunition for our enemies. We mustn't bare our injuries to them. I assume Congress delegates will understand this correctly and evaluate it accordingly." And yet by his own order, Khrushchev's speech was quickly distributed to communist officials throughout the country and, shortly thereafter, to communist officials in his East European empire. His son, Sergei, who left Moscow to teach at Brown University and rarely returned, said, "I very much doubt that Father wanted to keep it secret. On the contrary! His own words provide confirmation of the opposite—that he wanted to bring his report to the people. Otherwise all of his efforts would have been meaningless."

Of course, at the time the fact and drama of the "secret speech" were hidden from public view. A few days earlier I had written in my diary that I expected a "big, sensational, explosive, terribly significant" event. Though there was such an event, the Khrushchev speech, I did not know anything about it, as it happened. Nor did 99.9 percent of the Russian people. Nor did the diplomatic corps, with all of its connections. Nor did the CIA.

Not until March 10, two weeks later, did Ambassador Charles Bohlen, one of the wisest, most superbly connected diplomats in town, get a wisp of a rumor of a Khrushchev tirade against Stalin, at a reception at the French embassy.

CHAPTER SEVEN

The Thaw

t was as if the Kremlin had not been dusted for decades. From February 1956 to 1957, a year later dubbed "the thaw," Nikita Khrushchev opened the windows and a fierce gale of change blew through the old fortress on Red Square. Suddenly Stalin was no longer a god and Russia was no longer a frightened police state. It was still a communist state, to be sure, was still the governing patron of an Eastern European empire, still the self-proclaimed head of a worldwide Marxist movement, but for those of us who worked in Moscow during the thaw, it was clear that Russia was turning a corner in its turbulent history.

Cautiously, Russians began to appreciate the change. They slowly shed the heavy overcoat of fear they had been wearing through decades of Stalinist terror. A few even spoke to foreigners, which had been unusual. One man asked me with wonder in his eyes whether I had ever been to Detroit—and driven a Chevrolet? Many were just then being released from Siberian prisons, eager to reacquaint themselves with their families, careers, and lives. I heard defiant university students openly raise questions in the Lenin Library about the Soviet political leadership, even about the continued viability of communism. American artists such as the violinist Isaac Stern and the tenor Jan Peerce, participating in a new East-West exchange program, performed at the Moscow Conservatory before rapturous audiences. Long lines of Muscovites eager to buy tickets blocked traffic on the busy Arbat. Hope, often in such short supply, was again in the air. Nirvana had not yet arrived; many questions remained about tomorrow and the day after tomorrow, but Stalinism as a way of life and government was clearly on the way out.

Sergei Khrushchev had suspected that his father really wanted to publicize his "secret speech," and Sergei was right.

On the night of February 25–26, only hours after Khrushchev had delivered the speech, communist leaders of Soviet bloc countries, who had attended the just concluded 20th Party Congress but had not been invited to hear the secret speech, were summoned to a special midnight briefing at Central Committee headquarters. Trusted Russian officials were told to read the speech to them very slowly so they could take notes. They were not given copies. A few days later, on March 1, Khrushchev sent an edited copy of the speech to his closest colleagues. He wanted it checked and wanted to know "if there arise no objections to the text," distributed to party and Komsomol members all over the country, all 25 million of them (Komsomol was the Communist Party youth organization). The speech had been labeled "top secret"; now it was downgraded to "not for the press." Khrushchev wanted to "acquaint all Communists and Komsomol members, and also nonparty activists including workers, white-collar personnel, and collective farmers," with the essential message of the 20th Party Congress. He also wanted to stimulate broad public support for the new party line and leader.

All of this took place behind closed doors, but rumors quickly sprouted all over Moscow, like weeds in spring. Once a Komsomol leader in Kazan had been briefed on the secret speech, it was only a matter of time before a cabdriver in Leningrad would pick up the theme of Khrushchev's stunning denunciation of Stalin, once the saint, now a killer. The Polish communist leader Boleslav Beirut, who had just been briefed and who routinely would inform the editor of the Polish communist newspaper about all major developments, told the editor about the midnight briefing. Naturally, over drinks, the editor would then share the news with reporters from other Polish newspapers, and they in turn with their Western colleagues. In communist times secrets were sacred, and most were kept, but this was one that the Kremlin leadership clearly wanted leaked to the public. This was hot news, and hot news traveled through the Soviet empire by rumor, by whisper, by sensible deduction, and, on occasion, by official proclamation.

At the U.S. embassy we could feel the political ground trembling beneath us, and, in the embassy courtyard, where we thought we were safe from Soviet electronic eavesdropping, we would swap stories and impressions. Khrushchev was now the boss, clearly, towering over Stalin's corpse, but what next? In Moscow's rarefied social circles, at dinner parties and receptions, we would share gossip, rumor, and occasionally facts. At the theater we might by chance bump into a Soviet official we had met elsewhere, and in a brief conversation pick up a phrase, a look, a reference to a *Pravda* article. At the JPRS, where I spent most of my time, I had the added benefit of being able to listen to Anna Holdcroft, a genuine expert on reading Soviet tea leaves and, it seemed to me, Khrushchev's mind. She was a remarkable resource, and on more than a number of occasions her insights would end up in my Moscow diary, but never with her name attached to them. I decided, shortly after starting my diary, that I would not include names, conversations, or incidents that might be harmful to American interests or to innocent Russians. I kept my diary, which was not classified, in my room at American House, where I imagine anyone could have read it.

By March 19, a day after stories appeared for the first time in Western newspapers about a secret speech, I noted in my diary that the Central Committee of the Communist Party of the Soviet Union, led by

Khrushchev, had "launched dramatic charges against the memory and legacy of Joseph Stalin." I cited no specific source, but mentioned four of the charges.

"Stalin is said to have 'murdered' three-quarters of the membership of the 1934 Congress of the Communist Party."

"He is said to have brutally slaughtered nine-tenths of the Red Army officer corps in the great purges of the 1930's and thereby seriously affected the morale of the military just prior to the outbreak of World War II."

"He is accused of ignoring intelligence reports from Germany and warnings from Churchill that Hitler was going to attack Russia in 1941."

"He is accused of having concocted the 'doctors' plot' as a perverted excuse for initiating a new bloodbath of the Communist Party leadership."

Then, in summation, I used the phrase "it is believed," suggesting I had gotten the information on "deep background" from a senior diplomatic source, more than likely Ambassador Bohlen, who by this time had learned definitively, from Israelis based in Warsaw, that Khrushchev had indeed delivered the rumored secret speech. "Deep background" meant I could use the information without attribution to any named source. I adhered rather rigidly to the rules of deep background while I worked as a translator at the JPRS and later, for many years, as a journalist. But now, more than sixty years later, I'm breaking the rules and taking the liberty of citing Bohlen. "It is believed that at some time during the 20th Party Congress," I wrote, citing no source, "Khrushchev launched a vicious attack against Stalin as a man. He is believed to have called Stalin a madman, driven by a persecution mania. Further reports indicate that throughout the Soviet Union, these charges are now being discussed."

Nine days later, on March 28, using a kind of coded language, *Pravda* went public with Khrushchev's dethroning of Stalin. Deep background was no longer needed to protect a source. In a long article, spread across the bottom halves of the second and third pages of the four-page newspaper, Khrushchev buried the Stalin era, even though photos, paintings, and busts of the disgraced Soviet leader were still in evidence throughout the city. Not enough time had passed to remove them. *Pravda* drew an interesting distinction between Stalin in his early years of power and in his later years. In his early years Stalin actually made "creative" contributions to Marxism-Leninism, the newspaper noted, but "with the passage of time, this personality cult assumed more and more ugly forms and seriously damaged the cause." My impression was that now that *Pravda* had spoken, Stalin's image would soon follow Stalin's crimes into the dustbin of Soviet history.

Everywhere, as it happened, except in the Soviet Republic of Georgia, Stalin's birthplace. We were hearing from different sources in the diplomatic community that there, pro-Stalin demonstrations erupted throughout the country when word of Khrushchev's speech reached Tbilisi. Not only were photos and paintings of Stalin not being removed; new ones were being plastered on trolleys and buses or hung in museums. As many as 60,000 Georgians carried flowers to the Stalin monument in Tbilisi. They shouted "Down with Khrushchev" and "Glory to the Great Stalin." When they marched on government buildings, tanks and troops interceded. Clashes followed. More than twenty demonstrators were killed, sixty wounded, and many others arrested and imprisoned. I noted in my diary, "The Georgians are not interested in seeing Stalin, one of theirs, blasphemed, perhaps because in his downfall they see a new attack upon Georgians in general."

I stopped one afternoon at the impressive Tretyakov Gallery, where a famous painting of Stalin and Kliment Voroshilov standing together on the Lenin Hills overlooking Moscow had been hanging for many years. Now it was gone. Muscovites ambled past the empty wall space as if the painting had never been there.

Snow was falling and the traffic was heavy, but I rushed over to the nearby Lenin Museum to check on whether paintings of Stalin were still hanging there. Until recently this architectural monstrosity had featured paintings of the young Stalin being tutored by an older, wiser Lenin—the ardent and ambitious revolutionary joined at the hip to the brilliant, visionary, inspiring leader of global communism. Many of the paintings were still there but the talkative docent, while discussing the paintings, never mentioned Stalin's name, not once. It was as if you were still able to look at Stalin and yet not see him. I assumed that the paintings showing Stalin would soon be replaced by less offensive paintings showing only Lenin. As I started to leave the Lenin Museum I happened to pass a sign that read "*Zal 21*," "Room 21," hanging at an odd angle on the door. Just at that moment a heavyset man carrying a tool kit opened the door. I glanced in and saw two huge paintings of Stalin being removed from a wall. "Black magic, Soviet style," I thought— Khrushchev's way of rewriting Soviet history.

For the next few wintry months, a time in Moscow of short days and long nights, snow and ice, and only occasionally a teasing flash of sunlight, I met many young Russians who were feeling the first flush of freedom caused by the thaw. They were experimenting with a new notion of free speech, sort of—what to say, how much to say, and when to say it. At the same time I was also fighting a nonstop war with the stuffy bureaucrats guarding access to Uvarov's papers at libraries and archives. On reflection, I think I had better luck with the young Russians than I had with the library bureaucrats.

Early one evening I met Volodya, a twenty-nine-year-old graduate student at the History Institute. He was tall, bespectacled, sleight of build, and he spoke excellent English. After only a few minutes it was obvious that Volodya was probably a member of the Communist Party. Using the stilted language generally found in *Pravda*, he defended the Soviet position on every issue. He debunked the United Nations and expressed deep reservations about NATO and American policy in Europe. Over dinner at the Grand Hotel we discussed our dueling definitions of history.

"How would you define history?" I asked.

"History is the examination of the objective facts of a given period," he replied, as if by rote, "in order to understand the vast forces at play."

I raised a hypothetical question: let's suppose, I said, a Russian student wanted to do an "objective" study of the 1905 revolution. He would have to have access to all relevant documents. "Could he do such a study?" I asked. "With all relevant documents?"

"Of course," Volodya answered.

"You know," I went on, "Trotsky was a very important figure in the Petersburg Soviet. In fact, for a while, he was chairman of the Soviet. Could this student read Trotsky's speeches?"

Volodya took a long time searching for an answer. The band was playing a Russian version of "Love and Marriage," a very popular American song. "Volodya," I said, breaking into his reverie, "could an average student study Trotsky's influence on the revolution, and, if not, can you still claim that Soviet scholarship is 'objective scholarship'?"

When Volodya looked at me, he seemed not just troubled but trapped. His eyes, usually dark and piercing, looked vacant, searching for comfort suddenly by examining his shoes. "You hit the nail on the head," he said, exhaling, lowering his voice to a whisper. "It's that kind of question my friends and I have also begun to ask of late." I chose not to press the issue. Probably for the first time in their lives, graduate students like Volodya felt they could discuss the role of Trotsky, an ideological enemy at the top of Stalin's hit list, even with foreigners. One totally unintended consequence of the secret speech was that even the evil Trotsky was being liberated from Stalin's hell.

A JPRS colleague and I went to dinner one evening at an Uzbek restaurant. We met a young Russian who told us he was, by the weird standards of Soviet education, a "master of basketball." He was very tall, accessible, stylishly attired, and he loved his vodka. After only a few minutes of conversation he offered his unorthodox definition of communism. He spoke in a loud voice and seemed totally oblivious to the fact that he was sounding off in a crowded, popular restaurant in downtown Moscow.

"A communist," he pronounced, "is a person who has a car, a family, a dacha, and earns lots of money every month."

"That's all?" I said. "What about communism as an ideology, as a revolutionary doctrine, as a way of changing society?"

"No," he replied, with a mischievous grin. "A great communist has a car, maybe two, a dacha, maybe two, and a lot of money."

"Who are the greatest living communists?" I asked, enjoying the exchange.

"Khrushchev and Bulganin," he replied, "because they have cars, families, dachas, and lots of money." He equated communism only with material benefits. There was no idealism in his definition, and there was no fear in his manner.

By the time we got to dessert, he had already had a few more vodkas. "War is inevitable," he announced, echoing Stalin's now discarded dogma. "Two years," he said with absolute certainty. "It will come in two years." I challenged him, arguing that Khrushchev had replaced the doctrine of "inevitable war" with one of "peaceful coexistence." Besides, I insisted, there was no need for war between the United States and the Soviet Union. It made no strategic sense. But our Russian friend stuck to his gloomy timetable.

"No," he insisted, "two years."

But why? I wanted to know.

"Because the capitalists want to come here and dominate us. The Russian Ivan may not like the Khrushchev communists, but he loves Mother Russia, and he will crush the invader, as he has done many times before in her name." Though I met many young Russians who, like our "master of basketball," were skeptical about communism, some even sharply critical of communism, there were others who felt, as one told me, that "the communists have brought incalculable advantages to our country. They industrialized the country. They made peasants literate. For this," he concluded with pride, "we Russians have Stalin and the party to credit. Now you in the West must look up to us. We, too, are a great power."

On any given day I would ask myself what was more exciting: talking with Russians or hunting for Uvarov? And then I would answer myself: I can do both, or at least try. My only problem during the thaw was that the day had only twenty-four hours.

A most unusual source, a waitress at American House who was an employee of the UPDK, a security and domestic service that looked after foreigners, was baffled one evening at dinnertime when I told her of my search for Uvarov. Why in God's name would I want to write about a nineteenth-century reactionary, she wanted to know. It made no sense to her—and, every now and then, not to me either. I told her about Harvard's Ph.D. requirements and about my reasons for selecting Uvarov. She looked at me with puzzled impatience, shook her head, muttered "That is insane," and then advised me that a good place to start my quest would be the Historical Library. If I thought I could not crack the state's central archives, I would probably get nowhere.

So off to the Historical Library I went after work the next day. It was a very old building on an even older prerevolutionary street, Starosadsky Pereulok, which translated roughly as "the little street with the ancient garden." I didn't get there until 7:30 p.m. I joined a long line of students waiting to register for admission. After a few minutes I found myself looking down at a librarian so old and frail she must have had the job since czarist times. She did not look up but asked for my name. When I answered "Kalb" and then added "Marvin" but without my patronymic (with my patronymic I would have had to say "Marvin Maksimovich," "Marvin, the son of Maksim"), she did look up. "Where are you from?" she asked, obviously picking up from my accent that I was not a native Russian. "From the United States," I answered. Her attitude turned frigidly professional. She pushed hard against the back of her seat, as if she wanted to get as far away from me as possible.

"What are you doing here in Moscow?" she asked cautiously. I told her I worked at the JPRS, but I was also a Ph.D. student.

"What university?

"Harvard," I replied.

"Do you have your documents?"

I showed her my diplomatic *propusk*, my identification card. She looked at it, then at me. A group of students congregated around us, asking if there was a problem. The old lady rose slowly, ignoring the students. *"Tovarishch,"* she said, pointing at me, "you come this way, please," which I did, following her into a small adjacent room. "Wait here." She nodded toward a wooden chair. I waited for more than fifteen minutes. Finally she and four others returned. One was apparently the chief librarian. Everyone deferred to her.

"Why are you here?" she asked brusquely.

"To do research," I replied.

"What kind of research?"

"I am doing work on Uvarov, Sergei Semyonovich Uvarov."

The chief librarian smiled skeptically. "Why would anyone want to do research on Uvarov? He was a reactionary." I agreed, yes, he was a "conservative" but an interesting subject nonetheless, and no one else was writing about him.

"Why don't you write about Lenin?" she asked. "He's much more interesting. He's a progressive."

I answered, "Everybody is writing about Lenin, but no one is writing about Uvarov." I smiled, trying to be both serious and charming. The chief librarian shook her head in bewilderment, conferred briefly with her colleagues, and then, much to my surprise and delight, said simply *"Khorosho,"* "Okay," and led me into a large reading room, where she pointed to a desk and a card catalog. "Look through it, and tell me what you want."

I was astonished. One hour after arriving at the Historical Library, I was given a pass and access to several interesting studies of Uvarov. All were secondary sources, but I was actually doing research in Moscow—I had broken the ice. I was to learn in time that not every Soviet library, and certainly not the Central State Archives, would similarly open its doors to a non-Russian student of Uvarov, but I had taken one big step toward my twin goals of doing research on Uvarov while working at the JPRS—and for the moment that was good enough. My mother would be pleased.

One foreign correspondent who had worked in Moscow for many years told me the next day that I was the first foreigner allowed to do research in the Historical Library. Ever. True or not, I was positive I had one person to thank: that person who had delivered the secret speech and launched the year of the thaw.

A day or two later, encouraged by my victory at the Historical Library, I decided to take my next step and go to the official office that registered all deaths in Moscow. I knew that Uvarov had died in Moscow in 1855. Where was he buried? Was there a plaque? What did it say? This was basic information; naively, I expected no problem in obtaining it. An old woman sitting near the entrance to the gloomy building, apparently a docent of the bureau, said she knew nothing about a burial site in Moscow but did know of a monument to his memory in Leningrad. Indeed, she added, even where he lived in Leningrad—that is, "if the house is still standing." The docent seemed unable or unwilling to go further.

Undeterred, I decided on the spot to go directly to the State Museum, a large, oddly shaped red-brick building at the opposite end of Red Square from St. Basil's Cathedral, looking for all the world as if it had been mistakenly plopped there by a distracted architect. It contained, I was told, the prerevolutionary archives of Russian aristocrats, among many other things. Maybe I'd have better luck there. And for a brief time I thought I had.

Another very old woman was in charge of the "historical division." How interesting, that—in Moscow, so many museums, staffed by so many old women! Unlike many of the other female staff, though, this one was gentle, neatly dressed, and, to a degree, cooperative. When I told her about Uvarov, she directed me with no apparent hesitation to Hall 30. Hurriedly I went to Hall 30 and there it was, a document with Uvarov's famous formula, "Nationalism, Autocracy, and Orthodoxy," on a table under glass and surrounded by a small gaggle of giggling students.

"Uvarov?" one asked. "Who's he?"

The others shrugged with obvious indifference. It was clear they had never heard of Uvarov, though he was a leader of the nineteenth-century conservative movement. Nevertheless, I was delighted. For the first time I was getting close to my subject. Here was his famous formula, and I was able to read it and take notes. Guards stood near the doors but did nothing.

I walked back to the old woman near the entryway. "That was really wonderful," I said with excitement. "But would it now be possible to see all of Uvarov's papers, his letters, everything?" She shook her head and explained that although she would like to help me, she had no authority to do so. Only the *uchenyi sekretar* (learned or academic assistant) could help. I went directly to her office. She too was surprisingly friendly, saying she had a great deal of material on Uvarov's son, an outstanding Russian archeologist, but little on Uvarov himself. I expressed my disappointment, but we got on so well she promised she would do "everything in my power" to get me admitted to the state archives. There, she was certain, I'd find Uvarov's papers.

Two days later I was back at the State Museum, hoping her "power" had been pervasive enough to produce miracles in the Soviet bureaucracy. The *uchenyi sekretar* was again friendly but her message was decidedly discouraging. She had tried, she said, but had failed. She could do nothing more on her own, and she recommended I try . . . the Historical Library.

"I've been to the Historical Library," I said. "Indeed I have a pass and a desk there."

Her eyes widened in surprise. "You have a desk at the Historical Library? Well then"—she smiled—"why come here?"

I explained that I needed primary source material, that the Historical Library had provided me with books and articles but nothing original— and that for a Ph.D. I needed primary sources. "I want to see his letters, his papers, his home," I pleaded. "I want to see Uvarov firsthand." The *uchenyi sekretar* had a good heart. She wanted to help, but since I had already been to the Historical Library, she suggested with apparent reluctance that I visit the Central State Archives, which were then under the control of the the dreaded Ministry of Internal Affairs (MVD), the secret police. As she led me to the exit she offered her best wishes, adding with a smile, "Maybe your friend Khrushchev can get you in."

It was not too wild an idea. The respected journal *Party Life* had only recently run an editorial calling for "unveiling the dusty shelves of the state archives to the clean light of scholarship." Could the editorial have meant that even a renegade communist such as Leon Trotsky could now get a fair hearing? Moreover, at the 20th Party Congress the education minister, Anna Pankratova, echoing a line from Khrushchev's opening speech, had appealed for a rewriting of Soviet history based on fact. What a splendid idea, I thought. Could even Uvarov be far behind?

One day after work I set out for the Central State Archives on Bolshaya Pirogovskaya Ulitsa. No building in Moscow could have looked more Soviet, more a reflection of Stalin's tasteless feel for modern-day architecture. It was huge, gray, and intimidating. As I wrote in my diary that night, "I [might] have appeared brave and self-confident as I opened the heavy metal door and strode quickly to the main desk, but my stomach was doing strange somersaults. I was plain frightened."

The guard at the desk wanted to know the purpose of my visit. I told him about my desire to do research on Uvarov. He grinned, wickedly, I thought, before telling me that I was standing in the main lobby of the MVD. The Central State Archives were just around the corner. With pleasure I fled the MVD and headed for the archives, which were in the same building but approached through another entry.

A stern-looking guard wearing what appeared to be an MVD uniform asked the purpose of my visit. I explained, once again, that I wanted to do research for an Uvarov biography. My Russian was quite good by this time, but I did have an accent. The guard must have heard it but he said and did nothing about it. "You need a *propusk*," he advised, an ID card, "and you can get one over there." He pointed to a large door about half a football field away. Up to this point, I felt, everything was proceeding smoothly, maybe too smoothly. I approached the *propusk* office. Another MVD guard asked the purpose of my visit, and, with patience and politeness, I informed him of my interest in Uvarov. He suggested I wait

*Standing patiently in Red Square, notebook in hand, the author is ready
for interviews with ordinary Russians.*

in a small dark room to his right. Ten minutes later a heavyset woman
wearing thick glasses entered the room. She identified herself as an archivist. Like everyone else she wanted to know "the purpose of my visit."
I told her about Uvarov.

"Uvarov!" she exclaimed. (At least she had heard of Uvarov.) "Why
write about him? He was a reactionary. You should write about Lenin." I
came up with a new response. I told her I was interested in prerevolutionary Russia. Since Uvarov was minister of education under Nicholas
I, and since I wanted to be a professor, I wanted to know more about his
approach to education and teaching, an explanation she found hard to
reject. She said she would give me a *propusk*. For a minute I thought I had
cracked my way into the Central State Archives. I was exultant. The
archivist was about to tell the guard to grant me a *propusk* when, out of
curiosity, I imagine, she asked where I was from. The United States, I

answered. The poor woman's jaw dropped. She looked at me once and then twice and said, "Please wait here." She nodded to the guard to watch me. I thought about racing to the front door but instead sat down and waited.

Ten minutes later the archivist returned with a tall man, who looked like a muscular World War II statue of a heroic Soviet soldier. He was wearing a shiny dark gray suit. His shirt was clean but not pressed, and his tie had seen better days. But he exuded authority. He asked the same question I had already been asked by the archivist and a number of guards: "What is the purpose of your visit?" I repeated, as though for the first time, that I wanted to do research on Uvarov. He told me about a regulation, in effect since 1948, that obliged non-Russians wishing to do research at the Central State Archives to have their embassy send an official request to the Ministry of Foreign Affairs. If the Ministry of Foreign Affairs chose to look favorably upon the request, then it would inform the Ministry of Internal Affairs, which had administrative authority over the Central State Archives. If the MVD agreed with the judgment of the Ministry of Foreign Affairs, it could authorize the Central State Archives to cooperate with the non-Russian scholar, that is, if the Central State Archives considered the subject to be worthy of serious and safe study. I asked how long he thought this process would take. He paused before answering, and then, using almost the same words, repeated what he had just outlined. I was trapped in the Soviet bureaucracy. I thanked him and left.

That night, reflecting on the experience, I decided to ask the first secretary at the U.S. embassy to submit a letter on my behalf to the Ministry of Foreign Affairs. Why not? Maybe the thaw would open the door to the Central State Archives. If not, on this one occasion I would have experienced the powers of the tangled Soviet bureaucracy, something Russians experienced in different ways every day. The first secretary, in an example of embassy bureaucracy, nodded sympathetically and promised to discuss my request with the ambassador.

"When?" I asked.

"As soon as he has a moment," he answered.

Mikhail Gorbachev, the last of the Communist Party leaders, remarked years later that Khrushchev had taken a "huge political risk" in "beginning the process of unmasking Stalin's crimes." As a young Komsomol leader, Gorbachev had the responsibility of reporting on the speech to a meeting of rural officials near Stavropol in southern Russia. His party boss had warned him that "the people don't understand; they don't accept it." Actually, the people were divided in their reaction to the speech. Younger, better-educated Russians supported it. Others angrily rejected it. And still others asked, "What for? What is the point of washing one's dirty linen in public?"

It was my good fortune in those days, largely because I spent so much of my spare time in libraries and museums, to meet many students who were in their own post–20th Party Congress world of rebellion, confusion, and frustration. For much of their lives they had been moored to a rigid communist dogma, trained to worship Stalin's genius, dedicated to the Soviet system. Then, by nothing more powerful than a speech, their world was shattered. What they had been taught all of their lives was suddenly subjected to withering criticism, mostly directed at the legacy of the one man who was always accepted as a kind of secular god, unquestioned, inviolable, a brilliant *vozhd*. But now his legacy was beset by doubts, questions, accusations, and criticism of a sort unimaginable only a few weeks before. What in heaven's name was happening?

At the Lenin Library I was able, after much effort, to gain access to one file of Uvarov's official papers. I spent two, sometimes three, evenings a week reading the file, taking notes, and then listening to a rising rumble around me of student discontent and anger at communism. Normally the large reading room was quiet, students respectful of one another's reading and research. I think I was the only Westerner in the library, and I kept a very low profile. I did my work, and when I was finished, I left. But one evening, much to my surprise, the rumble became a roar as one student after another rose, spontaneously it seemed, to ask questions about the Khrushchev speech, specifically about his attack on Stalin. Library guards stood at the doors, listened, shook their heads in disbelief, but did nothing to stop the raucous crowd. Even after a few of the students leaped on top of the library tables, stomping on official papers, bellowing questions, tearing up copies of *Pravda*, the guards still did nothing to stop them. Could they have done anything? Were they waiting for an order from above?

I realized quickly that I was observing a memorable moment in Russia's thaw. Students seemed to be in rebellion. They were no longer listening; now they were in rhetorical revolt, many of them shouting epithets against the government and communism. I was an outsider listening in on a national upheaval. I tried my best to look innocuous. Occasionally I would raise my head, but only briefly, lest I attract attention. I just kept taking notes, describing the scene, listening carefully to the outbursts.

"How did Stalin develop a 'personality cult'?" one student shouted.

"Why didn't they stop him?" another asked.

I heard someone yell from a corner of the reading room, "Khrushchev is developing his own 'personality cult,'" and many others muttered, "Yes, yes" under their breaths.

"Down with communism!" "Down with Stalin!" "Down with Khrushchev!"—fearlessly students demanded dramatic change.

"Will there be a war?" I heard a student ask.

"No, no war," many shouted. A widespread hum developed, first in a low tone, then louder and louder, "No war, no war, no war."

So far as I could tell, there was no violence. For a long time, or so it seemed, this explosion of student unhappiness continued, and then slowly subsided. Students began to pack up their books and papers and leave. I stayed for a little while longer. I thought the students would continue their anti-government and anti-communist tirade outside the library, but I was wrong. The street was empty except for a straggler or two.

I had no intention of returning to American House. I felt I had to report this episode to someone, and who better than the American ambassador? I went directly to Spasso House, where the ambassador lived. Normally no one would disturb him, certainly not in his home after 10:00 p.m. If I were a professional diplomat, a true Foreign Service officer, I would never have bothered the ambassador unless there was a genuine catastrophe. But I was a translator for the JPRS. I had just seen and heard something of importance, and I wanted to share it with him.

Russian police guarded the old mansion. As I approached, I flashed my diplomatic ID card, which they examined and returned; then they stood back. I could proceed to the main door. I rang the bell and a U.S. Marine sergeant opened the door. He recognized me. We both lived at American House. I gave him a thumbnail sketch of my reason for wanting to talk to the ambassador. His eyes widened. "Wow!" was all he said. He escorted me to the waiting room.

Ambassador Bohlen, when he appeared a few minutes later, was, as always, gracious. He immediately eased my anxiety about whether I was "bothering" him, as I put it. "Just tell me what happened," he said. I described the scene at the Lenin Library. I read from my notes. The ambassador listened carefully, asked a few questions, and then called the sergeant and told him to get a car. We were going to the embassy, where Bohlen drafted an urgent cable to the State Department. "Thanks, Marvin. Good job," Bohlen said. "Can I give you a lift to American House?" He was not only a superb diplomat; he was also a gentleman. We were to go through this routine one more time during my tour in Moscow. A week or two later, I happened to be at the Historical Library when students there exploded in similar fashion.

At the time I was the embassy's only source for tracking student discontent with the communist status quo. The story was to appear for the first time in the Western press in early June, after the CIA leaked a copy of the Khrushchev speech to the *New York Times*. I was thrilled. Every time I read a story about the students, I remembered how I "bothered" the ambassador and earned a pat on the back for doing so.

The Khrushchev revelations about Stalin's crimes affected everyone in Russia, but especially two groups. One was the senior leadership of the military; the other was the chief ideologues of the party. Both groups had suffered grievously under Stalin's fanatical rule.

Ever since the late 1930s, when Stalin eliminated the top generals and marshals of the Soviet military, dramatically weakening its strength on the eve of the Nazi invasion, the Red Army had been sensitive to any party encroachment on its military responsibilities. The post–World War II leaders, such as Marshal Georgy Zhukov, the new minister of defense, wanted to build a big, thick wall between themselves and the party—but they failed in this effort. The party almost always prevailed. Until the Khrushchev speech! The military wasted no time, quickly seizing upon it as proof that the fault for Russia's lack of preparedness lay entirely with Stalin, not with them. One day at the JPRS I spotted a small article in the influential journal *Military Messenger* charging that Stalin, not Hitler, had been the greatest threat to state security in 1941. Military intelligence knew about Nazi plans to attack. Stalin was informed—but Stalin did nothing to repel the Germans. He was at fault for the early setbacks and heavy casualties, and the military demanded that its good name be restored.

The party ideologues had their own problems with Stalin, but until the Khrushchev speech they, too, kept these problems to themselves. Fear ruled the day. Among the ideologues, though, nothing upset them more than Stalin's suppression of the so-called Lenin Testament. Written by Lenin in late 1922, finished in early 1923—a few months after he suffered the first of a series of strokes that made it impossible for him to manage the fledgling Communist Party of Russia—it outlined his considered judgment (in effect, his last will and testament) about the party's internal struggles, then threatening to tear it apart. At the time, while Lenin lay dying, Stalin and Trotsky were in mortal combat about who would ultimately emerge as the party's leader. Lenin had surprisingly positive things to say about Trotsky and decidedly negative things to say about Stalin, describing him, among other things, as "coarse," "unfit," and "intolerable" for party leadership. Lenin then went one critical step further, recommending for these reasons that Stalin be removed from his current position as general secretary of the party's Central Committee.

Every single leader of the party knew about the Lenin Testament. It was political dynamite. How would Stalin handle this crisis? Lenin's widow, Nadezhda Krupskaya, who had reportedly been bullied by Stalin, had demanded that the party not only discuss her husband's testament but act on it—Stalin was to be dismissed. But at meeting after meeting, Stalin managed to manipulate the levers of power and retain his job until, finally, during the 1930s, he eliminated his party rivals and became the ultimate czar of the Soviet state. As a result, the Lenin Testament was never discussed or published in Russia until the 20th Party Congress in 1956, three years after Stalin's death.

On June 30, 1956, the highly influential party journal *Communist*, on Khrushchev's direct order, published the full text of the Lenin Testament. It became topic number one at party meetings, dinner tables, and university seminars.

In the meantime, while communist officials pondered the underlying significance of the Lenin Testament, diplomats yearned for a break from the daily demands of Kremlinology, and Queen Elizabeth II of Great Britain provided it.

The Queen celebrated her birthday twice a year—once on her actual birth date of April 21 and the other on a day of official celebration later in the spring or summer. In 1956 that day was May 31. All over the world, British embassies hosted elaborate parties honoring the Queen on her thirtieth birthday. In Moscow the British embassy occupied hallowed ground, across the Moscow River facing the Kremlin. During the worst days of the Cold War, Stalin had ordered the embassy to be moved because he did not want to look out of his office window and see the Union Jack defiantly waving in the Moscow breeze. The British, careful not to violate existing diplomatic protocols, promised to move as soon as they could find another appropriate place for their embassy. On May 31, 1956, they were still looking, and looking, and looking.

Meanwhile, on this day, the garden behind the embassy was dressed beautifully in spring flowers and crowded with hundreds of diplomats and journalists eager to partake of the delicious strawberries topped with fresh whipped cream flown from London to Moscow that morning. The sun was shining, as was appropriate on the Queen's birthday, and roses were in bloom.

All of the embassy's guests entered through the front door and mingled briefly in the huge lobby before spilling into the garden, where champagne was served and gossip shared. After a while the large iron doors to the garden slowly opened, which attracted immediate attention, and Nikita Khrushchev, of all people, accompanied by his prime minister, Nikolai Bulganin, entered, to be greeted by Sir William Hayter, the British ambassador.

Khrushchev wanted to pay his respects to the Queen, whom he had met the month before on a groundbreaking visit to Great Britain. He respected her, he later said. He admired her style. She wore a "plain white dress . . . and looked like the sort of young woman you'd be likely to meet walking along Gorky Street on a balmy Sunday afternoon." Before meeting Elizabeth, Khrushchev had been concerned about protocol: Would he dress the right way? Would he say the right things? The Queen made things easy. She was, he remembered, "completely unpretentious, completely without haughtiness."

For her birthday celebration the Soviet leader wore a wrinkled white suit and a flat white hat. I had seen Khrushchev on television, in photos and, most recently, at the May Day parade, when he stood atop the Lenin Mausoleum enjoying the cheers of the Red Square crowd, but I had never before seen him up close, and certainly had never before exchanged a word with him. My initial impression was mixed. As I noted in my diary, "Khrushchev looks like a short, fat, strong, peasant-type leader. He has practically no hair. He has bad teeth. His trousers were baggy. He laughs heartily, and seems to have a good sense of humor." He wandered into the embassy crowd like a New York politician hustling for votes, willing to talk to anyone about anything. Though raised in the suffocating atmosphere of Stalinist terror, he acted like a Bronx boss ready to fix a parking ticket. He projected the image of a tough communist leader, unafraid to scuttle Stalinism and welcome a new day.

Isaac Stern, a guest at the party who was preparing to leave Moscow after a very successful tour, asked Khrushchev why he was holding up the American tour of the famed Moiseyev Ballet. Khrushchev responded sharply. "No Russian will submit to fingerprinting," he said. "That is only for criminals." An American diplomat, overhearing the exchange, volunteered that the fingerprinting of foreigners coming into the United States was the law of the land, and just as he observed Soviet law while working in Moscow, the dancers would have to observe American law while working there. Khrushchev snapped, "Well then, change the law." Bulganin, standing nearby, parroted, "Yes, change the law," at which point Khrushchev burst into laughter, prompting all of the other Russians near or around him to burst into laughter.

Khrushchev, enjoying the moment, then told a story that reflected his disdain for Congress and, it seemed, all other legislative assemblies, even the prerevolutionary Russian parliament, the Duma. "A young Duma official," he began, "leaped from a government building into his *droshky* [a horse-drawn carriage] and suffered a terrible accident. His head hit the road, and his brains fell out of his head and spilled out on the road." Khrushchev looked around for approval, and from the Russians got it. They all laughed. Khrushchev continued, "The young official thought nothing of it, left his brains on the road, and marched off. An old woman, seeing the accident, ran after him, and said, 'Sir, you left your brains on the road.' 'That's all right,' he replied, 'I can still do my job. I'm a member of the Duma.'" Khrushchev could barely muffle the sneer in his voice, but he laughed and the other Russians laughed and even a few diplomats, who apparently wanted to be on good terms with the Soviet government, laughed, too—though his story was not funny.

At this moment CBS's Dan Schorr, who did tell funny stories and had a wonderful sense of humor, grabbed me by the arm as he approached the Soviet leader. "You're going to be my interpreter," he said.

"Chairman Khrushchev," Schorr began. "I have a serious problem, a personal problem, and I hope you can help me."

Khrushchev looked at Schorr, and smiled. "Of course, how can I help?"

Schorr was smiling, too. "You see, there is a rumor in Moscow. You've undoubtedly heard of it—that there is going to be a very important meeting of the Central Committee at the end of June. Probably big announcements, big changes. And I really wanted to go on vacation at that time."

"Yes?" Khrushchev said, still playing the game.

"Now this is not for a news story," Schorr insisted, as he tried to keep a straight face. "This concerns only my vacation. You see, my office in New York says if there is going to be a meeting of the Central Committee, I have to stay here to cover it. So, and please understand, this is not for a news story. But, sir, do you think I can go on vacation?"

Khrushchev nodded slowly and seriously. "I understand," he said. He waited a few pregnant seconds before adding, "Mr. Schorr, go on vacation." Schorr, thinking he had just got confirmation that there would be no meeting of the Central Committee, began backing away from Khrushchev, almost as one would royalty. "Thank you, sir," Schorr said. "Thank you very much. I'm so grateful for your help." At which point Khrushchev added, with a grin that spread from one ear to the other, "And Mr. Schorr, If we decide to have a meeting of the Central Committee, we'll have it . . . without you."

Khrushchev had the last laugh, but Schorr had a joke that he would tell again and again. He always got a laugh.

June 2. Bernie was visiting. He was on his way to a Southeast Asia assignment for the *Times*, and a stopover in Moscow was a twofer: time with his kid brother and a look at Russia at an interesting time.

The day started with a discussion of an announcement in *Pravda*: Vyacheslav Molotov, an old Bolshevik for more than thirty years, a close protégé of Stalin, the foreign minister who signed the historic Nazi-Soviet pact in 1939 and the Kremlin order in 1948 expelling Yugoslavia's Tito from the Soviet orbit for "revisionism," was "relieved" of his official duties. Molotov was out.

At the JPRS and later at the embassy lunch counter, the questions were obvious. Why? Why now? The answers were, as usual, complicated, involving important policy differences between Molotov and Khrushchev. They argued at a July 1955 Central Committee meeting about the "virgin lands" project, which Khrushchev considered crucial for expanding grain production and Molotov described as not only "premature" but "absurd." They also argued over housing construction, Molotov favoring more of Stalin's ugly "wedding cake" skyscrapers and Khrushchev wanting to help ordinary Muscovites who lived in what he called "overcrowded, vermin-infested, intolerable conditions, often two families to a room." But the disagreement that led ultimately to Molotov's downfall focused on Kremlin policy toward Marshal Tito of Yugoslavia. Molotov had pressed for Tito's expulsion from the Soviet orbit because he and Stalin believed that Yugoslavia, under Tito, was "no socialist country." Khrushchev believed, just as strongly, that Tito's expulsion was one of Stalin's gravest errors and that Tito should be brought back into the socialist fold. For one thing, Khrushchev felt, it would strengthen the communist world, and for another, a rapprochement with Tito would allow him finally to get Molotov out of his sight. Every time Khrushchev saw Molotov he saw Stalin, and he wanted desperately to turn the page.

Khrushchev's moment came after the 20th Party Congress. If he was to abolish Stalin and his policies, which he was in the process of doing, he could at the same time correct the late dictator's decision to expel Tito. He could also get rid of Molotov, who was a drag on his new post-Stalinist policy. Khrushchev arranged for Tito to visit Moscow in early June and for Molotov to be officially demoted on the same day—hardly a coincidence.

Tito arrived by train. Bernie and I rushed to the Kievsky Station, buttoned down by heavy security, to observe this special moment in communist reconciliation. We joined a bursting contingent of foreign diplomats and journalists. The railroad station, like Moscow, was dressed for the occasion, and Soviet and Yugoslav flags crisscrossed on the top of flagpoles. Senior Soviet officials, led by Khrushchev and, remarkably, including the just ousted Molotov, stood waiting on a red-bunting-decorated reviewing stand. Tito, looking vigorous and ramrod straight, alighted from his compartment as the railroad clock struck 5:00 p.m. Khrushchev greeted Tito with a warm handshake but no hugs. Both leaders watched the honor guard march by with brisk, almost Teutonic, precision and then listened respectfully to the playing by a military band of their national anthems. I suspected that everyone on the platform noticed that one large flag bore a face strongly resembling Stalin's. As it was carried past Tito, a brisk wind suddenly snapped it to show its full expanse, and the Yugoslav leader as well as Khrushchev must have seen it and realized that the late dictator's ghost was also present to observe this repudiation of one of his major policy moves. De-Stalinization was comparatively easy to proclaim, but much more difficult to implement.

From Zhukov to Poznan

Khrushchev always knew that his decision to dethrone Stalin was a huge risk—to himself, to his party, and to his country. Yet he took it. He was convinced that without meaningful change the communist system would slowly rot. Stalin's legacy had to be uprooted and destroyed: fear had to be replaced by hope, economic stagnation had to give way to genuine reform, and the pervasive paralysis of Kremlin politics had to yield to new ideas and new leaders. Unfortunately, the speech accomplished only half the job—it demolished the Stalinist legacy, triggering a tidal wave of popular confusion and relief. But it did not initiate a program of political and economic reform, without which nothing much could be changed. The system survived the speech.

By June 1956 Khrushchev faced a rising crescendo of doubts about his controversial policy. At JPRS we were beginning to find hints in the controlled press of Kremlin concern about "opportunistic vacillations" and "hostile propaganda," which in the context of the time suggested antiparty sentiment was on the rise, and the public had to be on alert.

On a trip to Sverdlovsk, Khrushchev warned that a "principled and disciplined struggle" must be waged against these "opportunists." He blasted the sudden upsurge of "slanderous fabrications" and attacked "anti-party slanderers," although he did not name them. Bulganin, on a trip to Warsaw, noted that "in connection with the struggle against 'the cult of the individual,' not only have hostile and opportunistic elements become more active, but unstable and vacillating people in our own ranks have also come out into the open. These people, misled by 'hostile propaganda,' at times incorrectly interpret individual propositions connected with 'the cult of the individual,' and this has found its reflection in some press organs of the socialist countries, Poland included." In other words, some communists in Russia and Eastern Europe had openly defied Khrushchev, even in the press, and argued against his anti-Stalin policy, and this had to be crushed.

That evening I noted in my diary that "it is no easy job running a totalitarian government in a half-totalitarian, half-free manner."

But on July 4 Khrushchev arrived at Spasso House, the Moscow home of the American ambassador, as if he did not have a care in the world. He had begun to make a habit of dropping in on national day receptions, his way of telling the world that a new day was dawning in the Soviet Union. Ambassador Bohlen had been informed the night before that Khrushchev and several other top government officials would be attending America's national day celebration, and Bohlen alerted the embassy's three other Russian speakers, me among them, that each of us would be responsible for a Soviet leader, meaning we had to make certain that he was enjoying himself. The ambassador, of course, would get Khrushchev, and I got . . . Marshal Zhukov! Why, I don't know, but there was something wildly incongruous about my new responsibility. Zhukov was a sixty-year-old marshal in the Soviet Army, a World War II hero who had led troops into battle at Kiev and Stalingrad, a minister of defense in charge of nuclear weapons. I was a twenty-six-year-old, ex-PFC (private first class) in the U.S. Army, a translator who happened to have learned enough Russian to get a job at the American embassy in Moscow.

Zhukov was as short as he was wide, his chest was adorned with a forest of medals, all richly deserved, and he loved his vodka. I was tall and thin and indulged in a glass of wine once every week or two, if that. I decided almost immediately that if I was to do no harm to U.S.-Russian relations, I had to find a way to drink with Zhukov without consuming any vodka. Early on July 4 I raced to Spasso House and conferred with Tang, the ambassador's Chinese-born butler-waiter-handyman, who I always thought was in the employ of at least six secret services. He was short, wiry, and imaginative. More important on this special July 4, he was a master of conspiracy. How, I wondered, could Tang serve vodka to Zhukov and water to me? That was the challenge, rivaling in importance, I imagined, the U.S.-Russian competition for influence in the oil-rich Middle East. Thinking for no more than a minute, Tang, with a broad smile on his face, exclaimed, "Got it!"

He ran to the kitchen, where he found the large round tray, on which he would serve drinks at the reception. He held it out in front of him. "When I come to you and the marshal," he said with a mischievous glint in his eyes, "I shall be holding the tray just like this." He nodded to the right side of the tray. "That's where the vodka will be. The water will be in the same type of glass, but always on the left side." Tang looked up at me. "Understand, sir?" he asked playfully.

"Indeed, I do," I replied, feeling as though I was party to a diplomatic conspiracy that only a Metternich could appreciate.

At exactly 3:00 p.m., Khrushchev and company arrived. The garden in back of Spasso House was magnificently aglow with colorful flowers, none more stunning than the red roses hanging from red-white-and-blue trellises. Tables groaning with food and drink were situated strategically so that none of the hundreds of guests had to move more than a few feet for replenishments. And of course Tang led a small army of waiters, each carrying a tray of goodies, including Russia's best caviar and America's best hot dogs. Everywhere, American flags fluttered in the breeze. Khrushchev, as usual during the summer, wore a suit that was off-white in color and in desperate need of pressing. He seemed to be in good spirits. Bohlen greeted him with a friendly handshake.

"Happy July Fourth, Mr. Chairman," he said in his fluent Russian. "I extend the best wishes of the president of the United States, Dwight Eisenhower, and all of my staff here at Spasso House." With the easy grace only the best ambassadors seemed to possess, Bohlen spoke a little about the weather, which was uncharacteristically hot for Moscow, and then joked a bit about the American presidential campaign, which attracted Khrushchev's full attention, before introducing his designated Russian speakers to their official guests.

When the ambassador introduced me to Marshal Zhukov, I of course shook his hand. "Welcome, Marshal Zhukov," I said. "It is a special honor for me to meet one of the great heroes of World War II, a time when the United States and the Soviet Union were allies against Nazi Germany." It was a well-rehearsed, well-planned greeting—it flattered him and recalled a time when both superpowers were reading from the same script, and I spoke his language.

"Very good, young man," Zhukov replied, then adding, "We must then raise a toast to 'peace and friendship.'" It was the popular Soviet greeting of the day. I beckoned to Tang, who was standing on alert only a few feet away. Drinks were served. (I remembered—vodka to the right, water to the left.) But in truth it was only when I felt the cool water sloshing down my throat that I was able to take a deep breath. Tang bowed ever so slightly. He could not conceal the grin forming around his mouth.

"Come, Marshal," I said. "Let me show you our beautiful roses," and off we went to a convenient trellis, where we quickly slipped into a conversation about his wartime exploits at Stalingrad. "What was the turning point?" I asked with excitement. Zhukov was happy to answer my questions. Tang seemed always to be available, his vodka tray conveniently at hand, as the marshal, one after another, downed his vodkas and I my waters.

After the better part of an hour, during which time I introduced Zhukov to a number of diplomats and journalists, we walked back to the patio, where Bohlen and Khrushchev were chatting. I thought the marshal was a bit tipsy. He must have drunk seven or eight vodkas by this time.

"Nikita Sergeyevich," Zhukov bellowed, as if he was preparing to announce a scientific breakthrough, "I have finally found a young American who can drink like a Russian. Meet Marvin Maksimovich!" I heard a few giggles, mostly from the Americans, but Khrushchev extended his hand, which I shook with unaccustomed vigor. I wanted to prove, if nothing else, that Zhukov had taken a proper measure of me as an American who could hold his vodka. Bohlen, who knew I didn't drink except for that occasional glass of wine, looked at me with questions in his eyes, but none were asked and the illusion of me as a tough, heavy-drinking American held.

"How tall are you?" Khrushchev asked, changing the subject.

"Very tall, but still six centimeters shorter than Peter the Great," I replied, reaching back into Russian history for an interesting but unimportant fact. Peter stood six feet, eight inches tall—204 centimeters. He was a giant of a czar who tried mightily to modernize his backward empire by importing Western engineers and craftsmen and exporting Russian noblemen to study at Western universities. Why show off my familiarity not only with Peter's height but also with Russian history? And why do this with Russia's supreme leader? To this day, I have no sensible answer. Maybe it was because Zhukov and I had spent part of our "happy hour" discussing Russian military victories, and on one occasion I had mentioned Peter the Great's victory at Poltava, when he defeated Charles XII of Sweden.

Khrushchev apparently liked my answer. "Peter the Great," he grinned. "Wonderful, absolutely wonderful." Then a cheerful thought entered his mind. "You must play basketball." Khrushchev was not a man of few words; it was clear he wanted to talk.

Interrogation in Red Square—a Moscow policeman asks for the author's identification, while a Russian friend explains he has a diplomatic passport.

"Yes, I play basketball," I said. "I love the game."

"Then," Khrushchev continued, "you must know that last night, our best team, from Lithuania, won the national championship." I had actually followed Soviet basketball while reading through my morning newspapers. I even saw a game, and I was left less than impressed by the quality of Soviet basketball. I often thought about City College's remarkable twin championships—how could I not? In my mind I compared the Beavers with the Soviet teams. No doubt they were better and could beat the Russians!

Khrushchev then struck a theme common those days in Soviet propaganda—that Russia (or the Soviet Union) was better than anything non-Russian. Not only better, but the best ever. "The Lithuanian team is the best team in the entire world," he boasted, emphasizing each word. "I'm sure there is no team in the United States that could possibly beat our national champion." In the oddest ways, I thought, Russians would disclose chronic feelings of inferiority, in this case by boasting wildly about basketball. They had made major contributions to literature, music, and science, and much else. There was no need for Russians to feel inferior, and yet they did.

It was clear that Khrushchev did not really understand the beauty of basketball, but in my answer I tried to be diplomatic. "Well, maybe one or two on an especially good night might be able to provide some competition. Just one or two."

"No." Khrushchev shook his head. "No team could beat our Lithuanian team. It is the best team in the world." Bulganin and the other Russians nodded in predictable agreement. For them it was the thing to do. As for me, I felt a strong urge welling within me to speak truth to power, even though it made no diplomatic sense and ran a risk of creating unnecessary trouble.

"With all due respect, Sir, I believe that any really good college team, like Kentucky or Bradley, could beat your Lithuanian team." I do not know what possessed me. Who was I to challenge Khrushchev on an issue that was truly of no significance? Maybe I had mistaken Tang's vodka for water.

For a very brief moment Khrushchev's peasant eyes flashed with anger—I cringed, expecting a storm, wondering how I could explain my comment to Bohlen; it was, I knew, totally uncalled for—but then, as quickly as the clouds had gathered, they vanished. Khrushchev again smiled, and his smile had the instantaneous effect of a sunburst of reassurance to anyone, American or Russian, listening to our exchange. "Let's start an international basketball competition," he proposed with both hands making strange motions of excitement. "You against us. I know we'll beat you." In Khrushchev I found in one man two Russians raised under communism: one a brutal party apparatchik, capable of both pride and shame in his work; the other a tough politician with a striking blend of humanity and humor.

The diplomat in Bohlen seized the moment. He leaped into the conversation and blessed Khrushchev's proposal. "Superb idea," he said with a smile. "I shall discuss it with the president immediately." Everyone laughed, and the crisis, such as it was, subsided into relieved chatter about how difficult it would be to get tickets.

In short order Khrushchev gathered his flock and proceeded to the door. Everyone followed him. The Americans quickly formed a line to wish him a proper farewell. As the Soviet leader passed me, he paused and tossed a comment to his buddies: "Here is Peter the Great," he said, "and Zhukov says he can drink." I never told Khrushchev the truth, but I did tell the whole story to Bohlen later in the evening.

"You had me worried there for a moment," he admitted. "I didn't know where you were going."

"Neither did I," I replied.

Bohlen continued, "Khrushchev is a remarkable politician, and he is learning to be a good diplomat."

The following morning, when I shared this story with Holdcroft and my other JPRS colleagues, we all agreed that Khrushchev was indeed a "remarkable politician." But we all wondered whether he would have delivered his secret speech, demolishing Stalin's legacy, if he had known in advance that it would eventually lead to destabilizing unrest throughout the communist empire. I didn't think so then, and I don't now.

Now, as I look back upon the year of the thaw, I can be detached, analytical, cool, but in 1956 events "left me breathless," as I unashamedly noted in my diary in late June. "Russia these days is like a hurricane of change. One change tumbles down upon another, and the spectator [I guess I meant myself] is left dazzled, bewildered, and dizzy." I was trying especially to understand the impact of the Lenin Testament on ordinary communists, and I was eager to get more information about the recent bloody riots in Poznan, Poland, and the deepening party upheavals in Budapest, Hungary, and other Eastern European capitals. "It is difficult to grasp the full significance of the change which has taken place in Russia and the satellites since the 20th Party Congress," I wrote. "We are too close to the source to draw back . . . and contemplate the events. They pile up day after day."

I did notice, though, that the Chinese reaction to the Khrushchev speech was exceptionally cautious, suggesting that the ideological split between the two communist giants, which became apparent four or five years later, was already opening. Whereas the rest of the communist world bubbled with change and uncertainty, China was officially mute for the better part of three months; and when it did react, it spoke only of Stalin's "mistakes," not his "crimes." The Chinese did not want to run the risk of encouraging any possible comparison with Mao Zedong's rigid rule, his own "cult of personality."

One day, while driving along the Moscow Embankment toward American House, I was talking to the cabdriver about the Lenin Testament, specifically about Lenin's recommendation that Stalin be removed from power. The driver, surprisingly well informed, preferred another topic, but I insisted on hearing his opinion about the many changes in Russia since Stalin's death in 1953. "It is surprising what is going on here," he answered finally. "It is amazing, even funny to us, because we were here three years ago. You weren't. It is like a peaceful revolution. A quiet major change is taking place."

That night I bounced the idea of a "peaceful revolution" off a young woman I had met at the Lenin Library. She offered her own refreshing definition. "Now we are not afraid to think or ask questions," she said, but there were "limits."

Troubles in Poznan, Poland, were big news in most parts of the world, but in the Soviet Union there was just a short item on the back page of *Pravda*. It was also symptomatic of Khrushchev's growing concern that the anti-party agitation spreading through Russia was now beginning to spread through Eastern Europe as well. The news, as portrayed by *Pravda*, was that "a broad and carefully prepared provocative, diversionary action" had disrupted an international fair in Poland, leading to its "destruction." The message, in *Pravda*-ese, was clear. Anti-communists were behind the destruction; they were on a reckless rampage against state authority, and they had to be crushed. Fortunately I did not have to depend on *Pravda*. In addition I had access to the Voice of America, the *International Herald Tribune*, embassy reports, and diplomatic chatter that I was able to pick up at JPRS.

What I learned at the time was that the trouble started early Thursday morning, June 28, when angry workers (no one was sure of exact numbers) converged on Poznan's City Square, demanding better living conditions. The demonstration began peacefully but soon turned violent. I noted in my diary, "Workers attacked Communist Party headquarters. The prison was torched. Trams were overturned. Soon, shooting was heard, and tanks were seen lumbering through the streets of Poznan. Armed soldiers appeared on the streets shortly thereafter. All communications to the town were cut, and aircraft diverted to other points."

What I learned at the U.S. embassy was that many thousands of workers had demonstrated, at first calmly but then, after a while, going on the attack. One foreign observer recalled, "As the sound of their steps intensified, so did the temperature of emotions. Such a mood is like dynamite. Any spark becomes dangerous." Soon the demonstrating workers, demanding "bread and freedom," began to shout anti-communist and anti-Soviet slogans.

"We want a Free Poland."

"Down with Bolshevism."

"Down with the Russians."

"We demand free elections under the UN."

"We want God."

"We demand religious classes in schools."

Hearing the slogans, seeing the chaos, fearful of the proletarian workers they claimed to represent, Polish communist leaders, encouraged by the Russians, ordered two infantry divisions and two armored divisions, totaling more than 360 tanks and 10,000 troops, into the City Square, where they smashed the uprising, killing more than 70 workers and residents and wounding hundreds of others.

Was it an "uprising," a "revolt," or a "rebellion"? Poles argued about a proper term for many years. Russians at the time preferred the word "provocation." A Russian professor, probably a member of the party but one deeply disturbed by the revelations flowing from Khrushchev's speech, told me that "there are really two histories. One is ours—what we read in our papers. The other is yours, the kind we cannot read. I think I like yours better. Our history gives us only our side, our course. But we know from the story of our own country that many things can happen in history, and usually do."

Here was a Russian in transition, caught between two definitions of history. He, like millions of other Russians, probably did believe, before Khrushchev's speech, that Stalin was a genius, that he alone transformed the Soviet Union into a modern nuclear power. But a day or two after the speech, told that Stalin was actually an evil coward who had killed millions, he changed his mind not only about Stalin but about communism itself. He has become a bewildered agnostic. Cut loose from Stalinism, he has begun to look for a more satisfying port. But he has not yet found one.

By summertime Khrushchev could see clear signs that his secret speech had unleashed not only hope for a better future but also strong currents of impatience and anger, not only in the Soviet Union but also throughout the communist world. Would he be able to contain the rising demands for change? My sense at the time was that Khrushchev would eventually lose power, but in the meantime, when challenged, he would crush his political opponents. The Russians had done so in East Germany in 1953 and they had just staged a repeat performance in Poznan in 1956. Because they believed they were in the catbird seat, riding the crest of history, they saw no reason to change their position: once in power, they had a right that bordered on an obligation to retain that power. The use of force, then, was only a minor consideration in the flow of communist history.

Into the Heartland

S it on a bus or a train, walk through Red Square on a sunny Sunday, watch passengers boarding a plane, mingle with young people in Gorky Park, check out their parents at the Bolshoi Theater—and you would again be reminded that the Soviet Union was a mix of many nationalities, as many as 179. The Russians, Orthodox Christian by faith, dominated this polyglot mix: their language was the official language of the state, and their faces—oval, with high cheekbones, a stubby nose, and dark eyes—reflected the map of this vast country. I made it a practice wherever I was to look at the passing parade of faces. It made me appreciate one central fact: although the Russians ran the show, they had to manage people of many different backgrounds, religions, and customs—and they did so with characteristic insensitivity, which made smooth governance impossible. This was true under the czars, also true under the commissars, and now true under Khrushchev.

I wanted to see as much of this fascinating country as I could squeeze into my year-long assignment at JPRS. But the rules governing the Cold War made travel an uncertain endeavor, mostly because of the deep distrust each superpower felt for the other. Soon after the outbreak of the Cold War, the Russians decided, as a matter of both protocol and security, to limit a foreign diplomat's travel to an area within a twenty-five-mile radius around Moscow. This meant we could travel to Zagorsk, site of the treasured Troitsky Monastery about twenty-five miles from Moscow, by simply informing the Foreign Ministry. But if we wanted to travel beyond the twenty-five-mile limit—to Leningrad, or Kiev, or Tashkent—we had to both inform the ministry and get its permission. We would send a letter detailing when we wished to leave and when we planned to return. Of course, since the Russians controlled the airlines, hotels, limos, translators—everything involved with domestic travel—they knew where we would be anyway. But we both played the game. In the United States we imposed the same restrictions on Russian diplomats based in Washington and at their UN mission in New York.

Here is an example of the official notification that the U.S. embassy would write to the Foreign Ministry:

EMBASSY OF THE UNITED STATES OF AMERICA
Moscow

Ministry of Foreign Affairs of the USSR   *July 25, 1956*

The Embassy of the United States of America presents its compliments to the Ministry of Foreign Affairs of the Union of Soviet Socialist Republics and has the honor to inform the Ministry that Marvin L. Kalb, Attaché of Embassy, plans to travel to Kiev on Friday, July 27, returning to Moscow on Sunday, July 29. The trip will be made by Aeroflot.

I made many short trips, several requiring this sort of official notification, in my first six months in the Soviet Union.

On February 19, an unusually bright Sunday, I joined a small group of diplomats and journalists for a forty-five-minute ride to the official American rest house, or dacha, in the Moscow suburbs. "Once you leave the immediate heart of the city, you enter Russia," I wrote in my diary. "For the heart of Moscow, big and blaring, is not Russia. Russia, it seems, is the small wooden cottages, or huts, which sit at different points of a wide expanse of white, snow-covered plains."

The Soviet Union was a superpower with thousands of nuclear weapons, but it was also a third world country. Hard to imagine, but true. Away from the glitz of the capital and a few of the other large cities, such as Leningrad and Odessa, Russians continued to live in Slavic squalor. Small towns in 1956 resembled small towns a hundred or so years before.

On April 2, I took a train on a 100-mile journey northeast of Moscow to a troika of towns that centuries earlier symbolized czarist power: Vladimir, Suzdal, and Bogolyubovo.

The town of Vladimir dates back to the early twelfth century, when it became the unofficial capital of Russia. A kremlin, or fortress, was built on a summit overlooking the town. From there, the Russians fought the invading Mongols in 1238. Now this kremlin served as headquarters for the local branch of the Ministry of State Security (MGB). The doors were shut—no one allowed in, a guard informed us. Not discouraged, we walked quickly to the astonishingly beautiful Dmitriyevsky Sobor, translated roughly as "monastery," built in 1194, where we marveled at the old frescoes painted by Andrei Rublev, one of Russia's greatest painters. Vladimir, though endowed with an impressive history, looked tired.

Then, instead of eating lunch in Vladimir, we rented a car and drove twenty-five miles to Bogolyubovo, once a center of religious learning, now a tiny, unwashed town known for the small, white square church with the single cupola sitting on a lonely hilltop in the near distance. Regarded justifiably as an architectural masterpiece, this magnificent church, now empty, called Pokrov Na Nerli, looks down on miles of snowy countryside, a reminder for me of the historian Sir Bernard Pares's observation that in Russia sky and earth seemed to meet and become one, giving rise to a mystical belief in many Russians that somehow they were closer to God than other people.

The following day we drove to Suzdal, thirty-five miles northeast of Vladimir. It had a courageous past, battling the Mongols, but its present-day life seemed sad and dull. Once it was home to thirty-six churches; now not one functioned as a church. It had three monasteries; now one served as an electric power station, another as a training center for KGB troops, and the third we were not allowed to see.

"Why?" I asked the guard.

"There is nothing inside," he replied.

"Well then," I said, "can we see the nothing inside." The guard did not appreciate my humor. He walked away in a huff.

Yet, as I noted on the train ride back to Moscow, our farewell from Suzdal was memorable. A small group of people gathered around our car, waiting for us. They wanted to talk. More than anything, they wanted to stress that they did not want war.

"The American people are a good people," one of them said. "We Russians are a good people." Nodding for emphasis, he added, "You don't want to fight. We don't want to fight. That's good."

One young man pleaded for greater understanding and proposed increasing exchanges between the two countries. I asked no one in particular what people thought about Stalin's now-discredited "personality cult." "Better late than never," someone said.

I continued on this theme, "Where were your current leaders when Stalin did all these terrible things?"

An uncomfortable silence descended on our conversation, broken only when a young man spoke of his faith in God. "I know that God will help us all," he said loudly, "all of us, no matter. He will wish us well. God can do such things, you know."

Throughout this friendly exchange, an old man held my hand. He did not let go. He kept repeating in a low mumble, "Please tell the American people we love them very much and do not want war." He started to cry, still refusing to let go of my hand. Like so many Russians, he feared war.

He wanted us to appreciate the depth of Russian suffering during World War II. It was for me a very moving experience.

The train stopped once on its way back to Moscow. I took advantage of the stop to breathe fresh air. I had not been feeling well since lunchtime. On the platform I asked a peasant woman running an improvised snack bar for a glass of tea. She did not have tea but she did have vodka. "No," I said, waving her off, "no vodka." She looked at me with sudden sympathy.

"Your stomach?" she asked.

I nodded.

"Where are you from?" she wanted to know.

"America," I replied, puzzled. What did my nationality have to do with my stomach problem?

The woman, reading my mind, explained. "I have met other Americans with stomach trouble. Always the same reason—Russian food is too greasy. Trust me," she said, "one hundred grams of vodka with each meal, and you won't have problems anymore." She was right, although sometimes I needed 200 grams.

On April 22 a few reporters and I drove to Zagorsk to see the famous Troitsky Monastery, a wondrous sight of high walls, priests in training, and parishioners in prayer, with church bells breaking into the musical liturgy every fifteen minutes. Zagorsk played a key role in the sixteen-month defense of Moscow against the attacking Poles during the Time of Troubles, a brief but intense period of political upheaval in the early years of the seventeenth century.

As I prepared to leave a young Russian approached me. "Are you an American?" he asked softly. No sooner had I replied, "Yes," than he urged me to follow him into the museum's men's room. I did so, reluctantly. There, from under his coat, he removed two files. "These are my father's. They will show you, prove to you, point by point, how awful things are in this country." I told him I could not take his father's papers. I was concerned that he might be KGB, setting me up for a classic sting. He appealed to me again and again, describing himself as an expert mechanic who had been out of work for three months.

"Take me with you," he pleaded.

I shook my head. "No, that is not possible." As I headed toward the door, I asked, "Aren't you afraid that people will see you with a foreigner?"

He laughed. "If they threw me into prison, what difference would it really make?"

I wondered on the drive back to Moscow how many young people were desperate enough to ask a foreigner for help.

On June 17 I drove three and a half hours to Yasnaya Polyana, the birthplace and home of Leo Tolstoy, Russia's greatest novelist. Millions have read his books *War and Peace* and *Anna Karenina*, and his life story has been studied for an understanding of his doctrine of nonresistance, which profoundly influenced Mahatma Gandhi and the Reverend Martin Luther King Jr. Tolstoy had served in the Russian army during the Crimean War and then in smaller wars against Muslim tribesmen in the northern Caucasus. Toward the end of his life he was regarded as a saint, and many Russians brought their children to Yasnaya Polyana, hoping they would be impressed and influenced by the wisdom and wonder of Tolstoy.

I overheard one docent telling her group that Tolstoy especially admired Russian writers. She raved about his love of Maxim Gorky. He considered Gorky a "great artist." Puzzled, I asked my guide whether that was true. He waited until we had left the main building before answering. "When peasants come to Yasnaya Polyana, that's the sort of thing we tell them. But that's propaganda," he said with no shame. "That's not for you or me."

On July 23, I drove sixty-five miles on the Leningrad road to Klin, a small town known now as the home of Peter Tchaikovsky, one of Russia's most prized composers. Actually, Tchaikovsky lived in Klin for only fifteen months, starting in May 1892, but for the first time in his vagabond life, he felt he had a home. It was there that he finished his Sixth Symphony. The house was large and yet modest, bright red in color and yet subdued. His desk was a wooden table, and his bed, in the same room, was like a cot. He loved his garden, where he regularly walked and rested.

Now the garden was open to visitors. My friend and I thought we would enjoy a picnic lunch there. We were not the only ones. We shared a table with an old man and woman. Soon we were in conversation, and when we told them we were Americans, they were wide-eyed with incredulity. "It doesn't seem possible," the man said. "A few years ago, we thought we'd never be able to meet Americans again." He explained that he had lost both of his legs during the war (in Russia the "war" was always World War II) and had lived in Klin ever since. I offered to share our lunch with him and, we assumed, his wife, but he declined. As I told them about America, Harvard, my parents (both of whom were born in Eastern Europe), and my family, I noticed that the old man's eyes welled up with tears, and as we talked, he began to cry openly. The woman explained that they were both Jews and had few friends. Their life in Klin was lonely. Occasionally, during outbursts of anti-Semitism, they lived in fear even of their neighbors. A postmidnight knock on the door could have meant their arrest. She asked if I was Jewish, and when I said yes, she smiled and, with sadness, told us that in 1904 her mother had expressed her wish to emigrate to the United States, but her father, who had the last word, decided that Russia would be a better place for his family. "So, you see," she said, "if it were not for him, I'd be an American." I could not help but think that if my father and mother had not decided to come to the United States before World War I, I might have shared their fate.

On July 27, after a terrifyingly rocky three-hour flight in an Ilyushin-14 from Moscow to Kiev, as the Ukrainian capital was then called, I vowed I would never again fly in a Russian plane. No seat belts. People smoking on takeoff and landing. Passengers standing in the aisle. Restroom unbelievably filthy. Yet it was a vow I was repeatedly to violate when I took many other trips through the Soviet Union.

Kiev, though, was worth the experience—for many reasons. It was, first of all, my mother's birthplace. It was, and remains, a beautiful city with a rich history. It was the capital of what historian Pares called "the first Russia," known too as Kievan Rus. At the time of my visit it was the capital of the Ukrainian Soviet Socialist Republic, one of fifteen republics in the Soviet Union. After 1991 it was to become the capital of an independent Ukraine. Although I reached the hotel at a time when most good boys were asleep (it was almost midnight), I decided to take a walk.

My first impression was that Kiev did not sleep. What I saw was a city of cobblestone streets, trolley cars and hills, and many parks. Couples walked arm in arm, hugging, kissing, teasing. In a city where housing was tight, park benches served as private places for lovemaking and mating. It was all so different from Moscow. Kiev was southern, Moscow northern, and if the Russian capital was never quite sure her seams were straight, Kiev walked with a distinct pride, knowing they were. At 1:30 a.m., the trolleys were still crowded, people were still standing on street corners, and Kiev refused to end the night.

Back at the hotel I met Patrick O'Regan, a British diplomat, and Leo Haimson, an American scholar. O'Regan told a story about Russia's rush to restore her old churches. It was a national obsession. During a visit to an old church, known for its fabulous Rublev frescoes, he saw an old worker energetically chipping away at a wall with still visible Rublevs. Piece after piece fell to the floor. O'Regan was as puzzled as he was angry.

"Why are you chipping away at the frescoes?" he asked. "They are invaluable."

The old worker looked at the diplomat with contempt. "I am not chipping away at the frescoes, you fool. I am restoring them."

Haimson had a better story. He had just been to Leningrad and had been given permission to visit the storehouse of the Russian Museum. He expected to find discarded works of Russian painters. Instead he found hundreds of paintings of Stalin.

Before going to sleep I ordered breakfast for the next morning. I asked the hotel manager, who took my order, whether he thought the hotel would have oranges. "We don't have oranges in Moscow," I explained.

"Of course," he answered. "We have everything. This is Kiev."

At 7:30 a.m., as requested, a waiter knocked at the door. He had my breakfast, but he had no orange. "Not today," he said. "Maybe tomorrow."

After breakfast, I left for the Khreshchatyk, Kiev's beautiful main street, a gathering place for leisurely strolls and angry demonstrations.

A young Ukrainian walked alongside me for a block and then asked, "Are you an American?" My reply was an affirmative nod. "I knew it," he said with the pride reserved for finishing a tough test. "I could tell by the way you walk."

"By the way I walk?" I was puzzled.

"Yes, you walk very freely, not the way we walk." He was obviously referring to my ducklike walk, the kind that used to infuriate my army sergeant.

The Khreshchatyk was a broad boulevard, now bustling with traffic, but during World War II it had been destroyed. Major "remont," or renovation, started in 1946 with tall, Soviet-style buildings on both sides. Trees and flowers happily obstructed much of the view, leaving behind a feeling of an old, lived-in Kiev, disturbed only by the occasional black limo racing down the center of the boulevard. Last week, I noted in my diary, these limos were called ZISs, short for Zavod Imena Stalina, meaning "factory in the name of Stalin." When one needed a limo, one ordered a ZIS. Now the ZIS has been renamed ZIL—"factory in the name of Lenin," infinitely safer after the Khrushchev speech.

The Khreshchatyk was a historic boulevard that screamed "Ukraine" to a visitor from any other part of the Soviet Union. "I'm different," it proclaimed. "I'm me." It conveyed not only a feeling of youthful energy but also a link to the past, a place where a Ukrainian poet such as Taras Shevchenko could stride while creating sentimental odes to Cossacks and damning condemnations of Russian leaders such as Peter the Great and Catherine the Great. I enjoyed the simple pleasure of buying an ice cream cone from one of the many vendors on the Khreshchatyk and then finding a park bench and watching people, young and old, strolling by, many of them seeking an adventure they may never find.

In the afternoon I visited the Kiev Pechersk Cathedral and Monastery, whose golden cupolas glistened in the bright sunshine. Located on an elevation on the right bank of the Dnieper, it was surrounded by a yellowish wall, which from a distance looked like a giant snake frozen into the green mountainside. The cathedral, called the Lavra, was built in the tenth century on orders of Yaroslav the Wise. It ushered in the golden age of Kievan Rus. For Russians the Lavra had special appeal. It was believed to be the first Orthodox church in Russia, and the famous Russian Chronicles, recording the early history of Russia, were written there by monks. Though the cathedral itself no longer served as a church, a number of smaller churches within its massive walls were open to the public. Each was overcrowded. On a pathway to one church were the ruins of another, leveled by the Germans in the early days of World War II. I saw an old lady bow down before the ruins, touch her head to the ground, cross herself, and, with tears in her eyes, whisper a prayer. Religion remained a powerful force in a nation governed by atheists.

Kiev was divided roughly into three parts: the first one, Soviet and postwar; the second, centered on the cathedral, historic and impressive; and the third, possibly the oldest part, the Podol, the marketplace fronting the Dnieper. Having paid my respects to parts one and two of Kiev, I wanted to see part three. My cabdriver objected. "Why see that?" he asked. "There is nothing interesting there. It is old." I insisted, hinting a big tip would be his reward, and off we went. But he refused to stop anywhere, and when I saw the Podol, I understood his reluctance. In truth, I didn't know what to expect. Because my mother was born there in 1899, well before the Russian Revolution, I imagined from her stories that it would be a modest, middle-class community of merchants, artisans, and teachers. Now, it was anything but. In fact, I was "thunderstruck," as I noted in my diary, by the sight of "incredible poverty, filth and misery, slums unparalleled in my experience."

The Nizhny Val was the Podol's main street. It was dirty, crowded, cluttered with pushcarts and peddlers, and littered with garbage. I wrote, "Nothing that Dickens described in 19th-century capitalist London could hope to match the reality of the socialist Podol." I made a quick decision: I knew I would have to return, but I wanted to do so on my own. I asked the cabdriver to take me back to my hotel. "Yes, sir," he smiled, tickled to escape the Podol.

The following day, late in the afternoon, after exhausting hours of cathedral hopping, I left my hotel and slowly made my way down a steep, narrow pathway running a few hundred yards from the upper reaches of Kiev to the Podol, to the pit of Maxim Gorky's Lower Depths, a classic depiction of Eastern European poverty. The Nizhny Val was still overcrowded with pushcarts and peddlers. The odor everywhere was foul, and the rickety houses looked old and windblown. I heard many languages—Russian, Ukrainian, Armenian, Georgian; more than any other, I heard Yiddish. Most of the people were Jews. The Podol was the Jewish ghetto of Kiev. An elderly man, dressed in rags, told me there were more Jews in Kiev than anywhere else in the Soviet Union, and more Armenians in the Podol than in the Armenian Soviet Socialist Republic. I doubted his estimates but did not challenge him.

The Podol was a place of astonishing poverty. Many of the people I saw were barefoot, their feet wrapped in rags. Behind one stand stood an old women selling potatoes that looked rotten and vegetables that looked wilted. The meat on the adjacent stand smelled bad. Everywhere people pushed and poked in a Darwinian struggle for position—and survival.

Kiev had suffered severely, and it looked it. I suspected that my mother, if she were with me, would have been shocked by the Podol's shoddy appearance.

I stopped at a pushcart, where blankets were being sold.

"How much for this blanket, Yankel? It has holes in it, but how much anyway?"

"Seventy-five rubles, Moishe, the state price."

"I'll give you sixty-five."

"Don't be silly. You know it costs seventy-five. That's the state's price."

"Yankel, don't talk to me about 'the state's price.' How much?"

The negotiation continued for another few minutes. The buyer got the blanket for sixty-nine rubles.

The Podol used to have two synagogues. One was turned into a "theater for young audiences" in 1949 during one of Stalin's anti-Semitic rages. The other, small and sad, survived on Shcherbytsky Pereulok. A twenty-eight-year-old Jew, a native of Kiev, kindly escorted me to a Friday evening service. He had returned to Kiev in 1948 after fleeing the Nazi onslaught in 1941. He spoke both Yiddish and Russian and a "bit of Ukrainian." He told me that conditions had improved since Stalin's death. "If anyone calls me a dirty Jew now," he said, "I can turn him in to the authorities. Things have become much better since Stalin died."

Jews were gathering for prayer when I entered the synagogue. I became an instant celebrity, standing, so it seemed, a head taller than many of them. They gushed with questions:

"Where are you from?"

"New York."

"New York? I have an uncle who lives there. Maybe you know him."

"Are you married?"

"No."

"No? But what's wrong? Are there no nice Jewish girls in America?"

"What do you do?"

"I work at the U.S. embassy in Moscow. (I sensed a moment of caution.)

"But you are Jewish, yes?"

"Yes. Jews are allowed to work at the U.S. embassy? Yes."

"Where did you go to school?"

"City College and Harvard."

"They are good schools?"

"Yes, very good."

An old man approached me. He spoke surprisingly good English. "How is Harry Truman?" he asked.

"He's in good health," I replied.

"Oh good," he went on, "and can you please tell me how Margaret is? I mean, is she married?" I told him that she had only recently married Clifton Daniels, a prominent correspondent and an editor for the *New York Times*.

"Thank God," he said with a smile and vanished into the crowd that had formed around me.

Another man, also old, sidled up to me and, sensitively fingering the lapel of my jacket, asked where it had been made. "In New York," I said. "I bought it in a famous clothing store called Brooks Brothers." He turned to a friend and I overheard him say in Yiddish, "You know, thirty years ago, we made better suits than this right here in the Podol."

"Really?" his friend said.

"Yes, and better fabric, too. Of course, that was all before the revolution."

The rabbi intervened. Pointing to the ceiling—his way of saying, "Let's be careful. This place is bugged, you know"—he urged us to continue the conversation in the courtyard.

"Where were your parents born?" Many asked this question.

"My mother was born right here in Kiev."

With this personal revelation the mood changed, and what I would later come to appreciate as the highlight of my Podol visit began to unfold before me, one question, one answer after another:

"When did your mother leave?"

"In 1914, just before the war started." At the time, hustlers, for a hefty price, would arrange visas for Western European travel and, more important, for transportation to America, then, for many Eastern European Jews, the *goldene medina*, the blessed land.

The man with the wise fingers, who had melted into the crowd, reappeared. Looking up at me with eyes that had seen much of Kiev's recent history, he asked, "And what was her name? And what was her father's name?"

"Bluma," I answered, using the Yiddish translation of Bella, "and her father's name was Volf, Volf Portnoy."

"And her father—what did he do? How did he make a living?"

I paused, not certain how to describe his fur trading business. "He bought and sold furs," I said finally. "He was a furrier."

Something extraordinary, almost magical, then happened. "Volf Portnoy," the man sighed, old, old recollections forming around the wrinkles of his eyes. "Of course," he remembered. "Volf, the furrier—he left with two children, a daughter and a son." He smiled warmly. "We never heard from them again."

The daughter was my mother. I remember being overwhelmed, tears quickly forming. Was it possible? More than four decades had passed—from 1914 to 1956, four decades filled with war, revolution, collectivization, famine, more war and then the Holocaust, and this man remembered my mother, Volf Portnoy's daughter. I was serving as the human link between these two people. The Holocaust had claimed millions, but left these two.

Outside of Kiev, in a ravine called Babi Yar, the Russian poet Yevgeny Yevtushenko was soon to write of "heaving civilization," Jews not quite dead, still breathing below the surface of the earth. Now the heaving had stopped, and "over Babi Yar," he wrote, "rustles the wild grass. The trees look threatening, like judges, and everything is one silent cry."

As I left the Podol synagogue that evening, I felt like "one silent cry." There, I thought, but for the grace of God . . .

A Summertime Break in Central Asia

I had no idea how dreary Moscow could be in the summer. It was hot, smelly, and sullen. In August, Russians with connections (and money) would escape to their dachas on the outskirts of the capital. Others with still more connections would go south to Crimea—to Odessa or other spots along the Black Sea coast.

At the U.S. embassy many diplomats had already fled to Western Europe or the Mediterranean. The place seemed strangely deserted. I myself was restless for another trip. A month had passed since my memorable weekend in Kiev, and I set my sights this time on central Asia and the Caucasus. Ambassador Bohlen encouraged the journey, adding simply, "Be careful." Central Asia had only recently been opened to foreign travel, and the Russians were likely to be especially suspicious of American tourists and to assume that they were all spies.

A year or two earlier I had read Harold Lamb's romantic biography *Tamerlane, the Earth Shaker*, which at the time fascinated me. My itinerary included his glistening capital, Samarkand—at least, it glistened in Lamb's account. I would also visit Tashkent and Bukhara. My imagination raced back to the late fourteenthth century, when Tamerlane's empire stretched from the Mediterranean to Mongolia, from Russia to India. He was at the time a truly awesome figure, frightening to many, godlike to some. He stimulated the arts and left an impressive collection of monuments and museums, but he also slaughtered millions as he expanded his central Asian empire. He was called a "bloody butcher." If proof be needed that he had earned the title justifiably, it lay literally in the mountains of skulls that dotted his warpath, each a stark reminder of his brutality. When he raided a town, he often decapitated all of its inhabitants. Tamerlane, a direct descendent of Genghis Khan, was the last of the memorable Turco-Mongol warrior chiefs, his empire the last to flourish in central Asia, which then slipped into centuries of sandy nothingness.

As I prepared for my journey, I suffered more than a few bouts of jitters, as I noted in my diary. I wondered whether I was wise to travel alone to a region only recently opened. Foreigners could be made to disappear, never to be heard from again. But I found comfort in my diplomatic passport, which afforded a degree of protection, and I always felt, foolishly, I suspect, that since I had nothing to hide, I had nothing to fear.

And so, at 2:15 a.m. on August 25 (why Aeroflot, the Soviet airline, always chose to depart from Moscow at such ungodly hours escaped me), I set a southeast course for Tashkent in a pitifully small two-engine, twenty-seater plane. Like my flight to Kiev, this one to Tashkent was an awful experience: it was unrelievedly bumpy, the food was indigestible, and the other passengers all looked like overweight bureaucrats, drinking vodka from takeoff to landing and smoking foul-smelling *papirosi* cigarettes—those, that is, who were not already sick from the flight, doubled over in discomfort.

Four hours later our first refueling stop loomed on the near horizon. It was Uralsk, a small town in the northwest corner of Kazakhstan. It was a town of no distinction. It had a primitive airport, but there was no terminal building, no hangars, only wide expanses of desert sand rolling into the morning mist. While the passengers stretched their legs, the plane was refueled.

Our next stop was Aktyubinsk, two and a half hours farther east. It had a modern terminal that sported, much to my surprise, a moderately good restaurant. There I met an official guide from the Soviet travel agency, Intourist, who explained with pride that by doing nothing more daring than looking out of the window I could see Khrushchev's famous "virgin lands." It was one of the Soviet leader's most cherished projects—his way of demonstrating creative leadership, increasing grain production, and creating jobs. No doubt Khrushchev had flown into this desert metropolis on many occasions, which would explain why it had a paved runway and a decent restaurant. It was the modern equivalent of a Potemkin village. Khrushchev, like Catherine the Great, needed to be impressed.

Our third stop was Dzhusaly, another hot, dreary airport in the middle of the Kazakh desert. There were no other airplanes, no runways, no hangars, but there was the amazing sight of large photos of Stalin propped up one in front of another, extending from our plane to a ragged hut, where we could buy water, a precious commodity. An old Russian with a handlebar mustache explained, "Water to us is like gold to you." I asked him why there were so many photos of Stalin here in Kazakhstan when he was being criticized so sharply in Moscow. "Oh," he said, reflecting a widespread view in the Russian countryside, "Stalin was our great *vozhd*. He was a genius."

Finally, at 4:00 p.m., local time, fourteen hours after we had left Moscow, we landed in Tashkent, a city of a million, the largest in central Asia, described by Harrison Salisbury of the *New York Times* as "Russia's Number One Advertisement in Asia." But if indeed it was such an advertisement, it left much to be desired. I was there for only a few days, but it did not take long to see that Tashkent was a city without character—trapped, it seemed, between an old, enfeebled nomadic culture and an imposed, stultifying Soviet style of life. Tashkent was neither one nor the other.

After dropping my bag at the hotel, I set off for a quick walk around town before dinner. Prospekt Pravda Vostoka, or Avenue of the Truth of the East, one of the main streets in Tashkent, led to Gorky Park, an inevitable destination in any Soviet city. I bought an admission ticket (required in all parks) and entered what a young Uzbek later described to me as "the only place in town where one can have a good time." The park had everything—games, movies, dancing, even a free concert. Near the center, a lottery was being held, the winner to receive 300 rubles. I saw a young woman pull at her boyfriend's arm. "Don't buy a ticket," she whispered. "It's all fixed." Uzbeks were mixing freely with Russians. Couples walked arm in arm, very proper, almost as though their parents were watching. Here decorum reigned, so unlike in Kiev, where couples were openly hugging, kissing, and more.

I approached a large, fenced-in area reserved for dancing. In one corner a four-piece orchestra was playing Western music. I thought I heard "Stompin' at the Savoy." Courtships were brief. Boys approached girls, a question in their eyes, the answer soon in their arms. The dancing was graceless and awkward, but everyone seemed to be having a good time.

Under the rubric "Weird Things Can Happen Anywhere at Anytime," an MVD officer decided this was the moment for a lecture on Soviet hydroelectric power. Ten or fifteen young people gathered around him. As he looked at the dancers with obvious disapproval he proclaimed, "All of this energy could better be invested in building a hydroelectric power station, rather than wasted here on a dance floor. This is nothing more than a polite form of hooliganism." Most of the young people nodded in apparent agreement, but when the officer left they giggled.

I asked a Russian, "Where is the best restaurant in Tashkent"? He burst into laughter. "Maybe in Moscow, but not here." I figured it was time to test the one in the hotel.

A sickly odor of ammonia, apparent the moment I entered the large dining room, killed my appetite. The waitresses, heavy, wearing blotched uniforms, essentially indifferent to normal courtesies, did nothing to improve it. The dining room was crowded. I joined a young Russian who was alone at a table for two. He said he was a fourth-year student in a textile institute. Tashkent, he explained, was the center of an active needle trade. In front of him was a bottle of vodka, and he appeared to have been drinking heavily. "There is nothing else to do in Tashkent," he grumbled. "I go to the park, but one can quickly tire of the park. Nothing of interest here. Nothing to do. Here everything is *skuchno*—boring." He used the word *skuchno* several times, as if he were a character in a Chekhov play complaining about life in a village and yearning one day to visit Moscow. Then, realizing he might have spoken too candidly to a foreigner he had just met, he belted back another vodka, asked for his check, and left. I said good-bye, but he ignored me.

In the hotel lobby, a shabby kiosk was the place for the latest news, at central Asian speed. Copies of the Khrushchev speech were piled high. The title for this edition was "Overcoming the Personality Cult of Stalin and Its Consequences."

I asked the clerk, "When did you get copies of the speech?" In Moscow I had been told it was widely circulated shortly after Khrushchev delivered it in late February.

Here, six months later, the clerk excitedly responded, "This afternoon. It arrived here this afternoon."

I asked, "Is it selling well?" The clerk examined me with sudden suspicion. He did not answer my question, turning his attention to other customers.

The following morning, after a spartan breakfast of tea, toast, and cheese, I headed for the old city, which the Intourist travel agency vigorously discouraged me from visiting. "Nothing there," insisted one clerk. "Absolutely nothing there. Uninteresting." I went anyway. I didn't think I was being followed, but couldn't be sure. At a street corner, I asked for directions from an Uzbek woman dressed in a long, black *khalat* (a long-sleeved outer garment), her face covered by a dark veil. "The trolley," she replied in Russian, "the number four trolley ... to the very end." She pointed to a trolley rumbling to a stop across the street. I raced toward it, jumping over a rut filled with water. I saw a little boy urinating in it.

The trolley ride cost thirty kopecks, or a few pennies, cheap for an eye-opening spin through time and cultures. I started in the Soviet half of the city (paved streets, tall buildings, Gorky Park) and ended, an hour later, in the Uzbek half. It was like leaving one country and entering another. As the trolley car noisily bounced through Tashkent, I saw the streets becoming narrower, dustier, dirtier, with fewer automobiles but more donkeys and camels. The sun seemed to get hotter and the people poorer, their skin dark, their eyes slanted, their cheekbones set high on broad faces. Buildings were of clay, some of brick. Life here in the old city moved slowly—out of step, I thought, with the rhythm of the mid-twentieth century.

At the end of the trolley ride was Komsomol Square. I found myself facing the ruins of a large mosque. "Closed for repair" signs were everywhere. Like so many other mosques, it was also closed to prayer. Off a main street was the marketplace of Tashkent. It was extraordinary, covering a whole neighborhood with commerce and traffic. Masses of people swarmed through the small, crisscrossing streets, ready to sell or buy anything, from threads to furs. In Soviet society, prices were officially regulated. Theoretically, you were supposed to be able to buy a pound of butter for the same price in Leningrad as in Tashkent. In fact, however, every purchase had its own price. A buyer could scout the available merchandise, spot a possible purchase, and then haggle over price for long stretches of time. Every kopeck was like a gold coin. I heard an old man argue with remarkable passion, pointing his finger and yelling about a twenty-kopeck difference between his offer and a seller's price for half an hour—and then dramatically walk away. The seller lingered for a few minutes and then raced after the man, knowing that in a bazaar the negotiation never ended. Ultimately the seller yielded, the difference between their prices now dropping to five kopecks. The deal was struck.

In this marketplace, everywhere, leaning up against walls and checking the passing parade of potential buyers, were the sons and grandsons of the famous Basmachi, Islamic fanatics who opposed communism before and after the Russian Revolution. When Tsar Nicholas II tried to conscript central Asian Muslims into the Russian army during World War I, many went into rebellion and under the leadership of Enver Pasha, a former Turkish minister of war, formed a guerrilla army of 16,000 rebels. Enver Pasha, who looked to Timur the Lame as a model, dreamed of establishing a Pan-Turkic confederation encompassing all of central Asia. In a series of vicious battles in the early 1920s, the Russian communists beat down the insurgent Basmachi, and by the early 1930s the Islamic movement fizzled, having run out of both drive and energy, even though nostalgic tales of Basmachi courage could still be heard in hushed conversation in shady corners of the Tashkent marketplace.

Language was crucial to communist governance in central Asia. In the early 1920s, during the hot years of the Basmachi insurgency, the Uzbek language was written in Arabic script, leaving communist overlords feeling decidedly uncomfortable. They could not exercise total control if they could not read Uzbek script. Making matters worse, the Turks had just changed their script from Arabic to Roman, as they sought to modernize their society. Soon thereafter, the Uzbeks followed suit—they also changed their script to Roman. For the Russians this was a step too far. They angrily ordered that henceforth the Uzbek and other central Asian languages would be written in the Cyrillic script, like Russian. And so it has been since the late 1920s: every word in central Asia was written in the Cyrillic script. Because I knew Russian, I could read headlines in newspapers and street signs in the old city, but because I did not know the Uzbek language, I could not understand a single word.

I decided in mid-afternoon to walk back to the hotel. It was a three- to four-mile journey. It was hot, and with each step I felt that I was picking up part of the pavement, softened by the relentless sun. As I started, I spotted an old woman riding an even older donkey. She was not wearing a veil, which surprised me, and she looked like a queen, sitting atop the donkey in regal fashion. From her bearing it was clear she had survived the communist takeover with her personal dignity intact. Most others could not claim such distinction, walking slowly, shoulders bent, faces drawn with daily worries. I could not have imagined seeing a prouder figure in all of Tashkent than the old woman on her donkey.

A huge statue of Stalin dominated one small square. It made him look like a Greek god, muscular and omniscient. People walked around it, as I did, but they paid no attention to it. I did, taking a picture of it and in so doing attracting quizzical stares from Uzbeks passing by. In another square I took a picture of an Uzbek man sitting in a small cart and snapping a thin stick across his donkey's backside. He saw me but did not object. In fact, he asked, "Did you get a good shot?"

"I hope so," I answered.

"You from Moscow?" he wanted to know.

"Yes, I'm from Moscow, but I'm not a Russian. I'm an American."

The Uzbek seemed incredulous. "An American? Here? I guess things are really better, like they say, if you can actually meet an American in Tashkent these days."

Slowly, block by block, the old city began to slip out of focus, replaced by images of the new Soviet half of Tashkent: paved streets, brick buildings, cars, buses, a woman in shorts carrying a tennis racket, young men on motorbikes. And, everywhere, statues of Stalin, far more than statues of Lenin. In the Museum of Art, near the hotel, two favorites from Russian history were on display. One was Peter the Great, who launched Russia's imperialist drive into central Asia in the early eighteenth century, and the other was Stalin. Dozens of paintings and statues of him, large and small, were everywhere, the ubiquitous portrait of Kremlin power. Khrushchev had taken a hammer to the late dictator's reputation, but obviously it was going to take a long time for the first secretary's startling message to spread, and be accepted, throughout this vast country.

After I returned to the hotel I noticed a plaque to the right of the main entryway stating that the hotel had been headquarters in 1920 for the Russian army sent to central Asia to establish communism and demolish the Basmachi.

During my last night in Tashkent, prior to my departure for Samarkand the following morning, I had the uncomfortable feeling that I was being watched. It was as if the walls in my room had sprouted eyes and ears, and every creak was the footstep of a Soviet cop, coming to arrest me. This was, for me, a new feeling. In all my travels in the Soviet Union I had never felt anxious about my safety. But that night in Tashkent was different.

In the morning, when I left my room, a man in a dark suit was seated a few feet from the door. He had not been there the night before. Two militiamen waited downstairs in the lobby. They watched me pay my bill, pick up my bag, and head for a taxi waiting in front of the hotel. They followed me but did nothing more.

At the airport a young English-speaking Intourist agent met me and suggested that I follow her into the waiting room. "May I go to the souvenir shop first?" I asked. "I want to buy a few gifts."

"Maybe later," she replied. "Now I think you should sit here." She pointed to a chair in a corner. I followed her advice. "And don't go anywhere without me," she added.

Three Russians in dark suits stood about five feet away. Their eyes were fixed on me. I felt as if I was one step away from being arrested. All I had to do was provide them with a pretext. I caressed my diplomatic passport, sighed deeply, and waited for the boarding of the Samarkand flight. My Intourist hostess returned just in time. "Come back again," she said, unpersuasively.

███

I was relieved to join five other passengers on this flight over an amazingly white desert to Tamerlane's historic jewel, nestled in an unexpected rim of mountains, which in the flatness of central Asia looked like the Swiss Alps. The mountains afforded protection and time against enemy assault. Beautiful museums, monuments, and mausoleums crowded the inner circle of the city. Samarkand was an impressive fortress.

Marco Polo, when he stopped in Samarkand in the late thirteenth century, described it as a "very large and splendid city." For a traveler on the fabled Silk Road connecting China with the Mediterranean, it was a valued and luxurious stop. A hundred years later, the famous Moroccan Arab traveler, Ibn Battuta, was even more excited. "It is one of the greatest, the fairest, and the most magnificent of cities," he wrote in his journal. "It stands on the bank of a river called 'Potters' River,' covered with water mills and canals that water the gardens. . . . Here there are balconies and sitting places and stalls, where fruit is sold. There are also large palaces and monuments that bear witness to the high spirit of the inhabitants."

The question on my mind as we approached the Samarkand airport was "Will this once 'splendid' and 'magnificent' city have a similar, captivating allure in the mid-twentieth century?" Part of the answer caught my eye even before the twin-engine plane came to a stop. Across the runway stood twenty-four jet fighters, a rather impressive show of Russian military power in central Asia. A more meaningful part of the answer came in the ride from the airport to the hotel. It cut through two Samarkands.

Once again, as in Tashkent, there was an old and a new part of town. The old Samarkand, the original capital of Tamerlane's empire, looked tired and tattered at first glance, but it was obviously being primed to attract tourists, many of its historic landmarks being renovated. Meanwhile, the new Samarkand reflected both the Russian and Soviet styles of architecture and political control. The first Russian military units arrived in 1868, the vanguard of an imperialist drive through central Asia. The communists arrived in 1917, determined to retain czarist control over the entire region. If that meant slaughtering tens of thousands of Uzbeks and Tajiks in the process, then so be it.

My hotel was in the new Samarkand, and my Intourist guide was a trained archeologist. He made no effort to propagandize me; quite the contrary, he seemed happy to show the historic wonders of old and new Samarkand to a visiting American.

Old, first. Among the many architectural wonders was an ancient observatory constructed under Ulugh Beg's direction in the fourteenth century. Ulugh Beg was Timur's grandson. More than anyone else he was the loyal warrior who built on his grandfather's vision of an extraordinary capital. The observatory sat on a hill overlooking the city. The top two-thirds had disintegrated with neglect over the centuries, but the bottom third survived, thanks to recent excavations by Russian archeologists. Now a huge ring of restored instrumentation could be seen running around the lower base, no longer capable of being used to read the stars, as long ago it had, but a remarkable reminder nonetheless of the exceptional scientific achievement of an earlier age.

From the observatory we drove to the Street of Kings, the scene of a succession of monuments and mausoleums whose turrets glistened with blue, white, and green ceramic tiles frozen in irregular patterns captivating to the passing eye. An odd sight was clumps of hay sprouting between the tiles, as though soil and a seed or two had gotten trapped in the clay.

In the back of one mausoleum I was surprised to see a quorum of Uzbeks absorbed in prayer. They sat cross-legged in an otherwise empty room, communicating with a spirit said to live in the bottom of a deep well set behind a thick stone wall at the far end of the room. A mullah welcomed me, and together, saying nothing, we watched this unusual religious service. What, I wondered, did a spirit in a well have to do with Islam? After ten minutes or so I left, expressing gratitude to the mullah for allowing a stranger to observe this unusual rite of faith.

No monument was more appealing (at least, to me) than the Registan, which Ulugh Beg envisaged as a graduate school of Muslim teaching. Behind a sparkling white front loomed a complex of buildings, each one with a tall spire graced by pale blue ceramic tiles. The courtyard was crowded with students from nearby communities. A docent told them that the repairs would be completed within a year.

Not too far from the Registan stood Tamerlane's tomb, a magnet for tourists from near and far. Its blue ceramic tile walls gave it a special glow. Here Timur was buried, though he actually died during a military campaign in China. Ulugh Beg decided that it was only proper for his body to be returned to the capital of his empire. He built a large tomb and left orders that on his death he was to be buried there, too, along with Timur's son, father, and favorite wife. A modern-day plaque with an inscription in Arabic script read: "This is the resting place of the illustrious and merciful monarch, the most great Sultan, the most mighty warrior, Lord Timur, conqueror of the earth." Fifteen years previously, I was told, Russian archeologists had opened Timur's casket and confirmed that Timur was indeed very tall and had a lame foot.

I enjoyed my day in old Samarkand, soaking up the legends of Tamerlane, but by late afternoon I was ready to return to the hotel. Dinner beckoned, and the restaurant was supposed to be the best in the region. Why bother looking for another one? The head waitress, a Russian by appearance, seated me at a table for four but with a place setting for one. Apparently her orders were that foreigners were not to mix with locals. They were to eat by themselves. On this evening, though, a young Armenian joined me, and when ordered to leave he simply refused. He ordered a bottle of vodka and told me the story of his life.

He said he did not care what happened to him. "They could come and arrest me, but so what?" He had no job, very little money. I had rarely met anyone so unhappy. When I asked him how he got into this fix, he would not tell me. Instead he asked whether I liked the music the band was playing.

"It's okay," I answered, not wishing to offend him or anyone else. It was, in fact, a dreadful rendering of the same "Stompin' at the Savoy" I had heard in Tashkent.

My dinner companion screwed up his face in disbelief. Dismissively he muttered, "There is an old Russian saying, 'If you don't have meat, eat fish.' Like everything else in this country, it is second rate." He then poured another drink for himself, belted it back, and left.

The next morning I went to the marketplace. Unlike the one in Tashkent, the marketplace in Samarkand was a wide, open square. Peasants from surrounding villages brought large watermelons, cantaloupes, and grapes to market, and they seemed prepared to sit there for hours waiting for a customer. One of my favorite products, though, was not to be eaten, but worn—the small, native Uzbek hats, which are called *tubeteiki*. They were handmade and cost 150 rubles. I could not resist.

Now, for the "new" Samarkand. It dated back to czarist times but had been interestingly updated during Soviet times. I visited the Historical Museum, probably one of the best, if not the best, in central Asia. I was especially impressed by the archeologists' research and restoration work, much of it proudly displayed. One expert was assigned to explain each project. The history of the Uzbek people was traced, not with disdain for a "backward" folk but with respect, which surprised me. When the czar's army, and then the Red Army, invaded central Asia, they regarded the local people as either a nuisance or a threat, and killed them either way. Respect was the last thing on their minds. But now, in this special museum, Uzbek history and culture were subjects that seemed to attract serious scholarly interest. Even old *khalats*, trays, plates, and lacquered boxes, the work of craftsmen who had spent a lifetime beautifying a single plate, were treated with a courtesy rarely seen in other Soviet museums.

When my guides were explaining the past, they were in their element. But when it came time to explain the present, they were embarrassingly trapped in a political dilemma created by the Khrushchev speech. At least half of the museum was devoted to the history of Soviet Uzbekistan, from its founding to the day of my visit. Not surprising, then, was the fact that paintings and photos of Stalin were on almost every wall. He had been the boss from day one. None of the pictures had yet been removed, even though the legend of Stalin was now under daily attack in national newspapers and magazines. Many museums in Moscow faced the same dilemma. What was my guide to say about a hero, a god, a *vozhd*, who was no longer in good standing? He decided to say nothing, not a single word. He went on endlessly, it seemed, when comparing the wonders of Soviet Uzbekistan to czarist-controlled Uzbekistan, but he refused to say anything about the dark, mustachioed face staring down at him and us. My guide retreated to time-tested clichés about the glories of Soviet manufacturing.

Fingering a new *khalat*, he said with unpersuasive pride, "This design took Soviet Uzbeks five minutes to make by machine." Then, pointing to a delicate, intricate design on an old *khalat*, finished three hundred years before, he said, "Now look at this *khalat*. Do you realize it took this man a whole lifetime to weave it? But is there really that much difference?"

There was, in fact, a world of difference. Did my guide appreciate the difference? I doubted it. Time and again, as he compared uninspired and sloppy Soviet craftsmanship to old Uzbek craftsmanship, he seemed unable to appreciate that one was awful and the other beautiful.

In one room I was quite astonished to see a very large painting of what looked like Russian soldiers killing Uzbeks. Why would Soviet authorities choose to remind Uzbeks of these slaughters? I asked my guide, "Who are the Uzbeks being killed?" He looked around and, lowering his head, whispered, "They are the Basmachi, rascals who raised trouble during the early twenties." He again looked around, and dropping his voice still another octave, continued, "They were counterrevolutionaries who had to be wiped out. They were regressive forces. They held up the imposition of Soviet authority, which is an advanced form of government. In opposing the Soviets, they became regressive, anti-Soviet and hence anti-revolutionary." On an opposite wall was another large painting of Russian troops storming a Samarkand fortress in 1888 and killing the Uzbek defenders. It was beyond me why museum authorities continued to feature paintings of Russians killing Uzbeks.

During my stay in Samarkand I had no trouble with my Intourist guides. While not friendly, they were all helpful. I told them that I would like to visit the Pushkin Library, the Uzbek State University, and the Friedrich Engels Cotton Collective Farm. For what reason, they asked. "I'm interested in Timur and the people of central Asia," I answered. Whether they believed me or, more likely, suspected me of some hidden but surely nefarious scheme, I had no way of knowing. But they arranged the visits, as requested, and I was grateful.

The Pushkin Library was actually the one-story home of a former czarist governor of central Asia. It consisted of five rooms, one large, the others small, but all filled with dusty books that looked as if they had not been opened for many years. The garden in the back was crowded with Uzbeks and Tajiks, many catching forty winks on rugs stretched out in the shade of a big tree. A few were actually reading. One was tickling a girl's feet as she pretended to sleep.

The director, a Russian woman, asked, "Why are you interested in Timur?"

"Because," I answered, "he was a great man." For the director of the Pushkin Library in Samarkand, it was the perfect response. What could she say? Off she went to find a book or two, while I deliberately loitered in the garden, hoping my presence, that of a very tall foreigner, would attract attention. And it did. Slowly, a dozen or so teenage girls began to gather around me. They were short, thin, and very pretty. They wore brightly colored skirts, blouses, and kerchiefs, and their hair was in long braids trailing down their backs. Once they learned that I was an American, they bubbled with questions, their curiosity over the top. They wanted to know about everything from Eisenhower to Harvard.

"Can we take a picture of you?" they asked.

"Yes," I said, "and may I take pictures of you?"

Yes, indeed.

"If you send me a copy of this picture," one youngster said, "I shall treasure it all my life. I love Americans."

The director returned with two old books and many apologies. There were no other books on Timur in the city where he was buried. I was puzzled. She tried to explain. "These days, one finds out all about central Asia in Moscow," she said. "Go to the Lenin Library. There are many books on Timur there."

"Isn't it strange," I remarked, "that there are so few books on Timur in Samarkand's major library?"

She seemed embarrassed, yet held to the safe party line. "No, not at all. All information about central Asia's past is in Moscow. Years ago, all of this material was removed from Samarkand. Our best students now study Uzbek history in Moscow."

I was late for my appointment at Uzbek State University. My Intourist guide had mysteriously vanished, and one of the teenage girls, seeing my predicament, raised her hand. "Do you know where the university is?" she asked.

"No, but I'll find it."

"No, I shall escort you there. May I?"

"Please, I'd be delighted."

We set off down the street and took a short cut, as she put it. I saw an old, fenced-in brownstone building. It instantly sparked a memory. I had seen it before, in the painting of the fortress where the Russians had killed so many Uzbeks in 1888. My teenage guide said, "It's now an MVD base."

"I know the history of that building," I said softly.

"We all know the history of that building," she responded, even more softly. I had a feeling she had deliberately taken this "short cut" so she could show me the infamous building. And having showed it to me, she vanished.

Uzbek State University was located on Maxim Gorky Boulevard, which was broad, leafy, and very attractive. The university, which had recently celebrated its twenty-eighth birthday, looked older than that. An Intourist guide, all smiles, greeted me with an invitation to see the rector, who, he explained, had taken time from his busy schedule to welcome me.

I expressed my gratitude but added, "I do not want to be an imposition. I'd be happy just to wander around and meet with students." But that was precisely what they did not want me to do.

"No," he repeated firmly, "the rector has taken time from his busy schedule to welcome you." I again expressed my gratitude.

The rector's office was surprisingly plush. His desk was large, the rugs were thick, and on the wall behind his desk were two immense photos, one of Lenin and the other of Stalin. Sitting on a hard-back chair, the rector, a short, trim man wearing a white tunic and trousers, resembled the caricature of an Asian despot trying desperately to exude an image of authority. But when he spoke, I could hear an accent in his Russian, and I knew immediately that his authority had to be limited. As in many institutions in central Asia, he was the ethnic front man for the inevitable Russian deputy who made the important decisions.

His assistant, a young Uzbek, placed a tray of tea, cookies, and candies on a table near the rector's desk. Everything was to follow proper protocol. The rector explained that there were 4,000 full-time students at the university and another 3,000 who were part-time and attended evening classes. All courses were taught in the Uzbek language. A thorough knowledge of the Russian language was required. If a student could not read, write, and speak Russian fluently, he or she would not be accepted at the university. Courses in dialectical materialism and communist ideology were mandatory. Most interesting to me was the rector's explanation of how Uzbek history was taught. It was never taught as an independent subject, standing on its own. Rather, it was always taught as an integral part of pre- and postrevolutionary Soviet history. Likewise with Uzbek culture and language, which were always submerged in a greater Russian culture. As I noted later in my diary, this pedagogical approach was an "attempt to smother the dignity and value of independent Uzbek studies and to mold—at the risk of rewriting—Uzbek history into the totality of Soviet history, regarding everything prerevolutionary as 'regressive' in a Marxist sense and everything postrevolutionary as 'progressive,' in this same sense—thereby inflicting upon every student the impression that he is involved in the wave of the future, having freed himself absolutely from the shackles of the past."

I raised the subject of a linguistics conference that had just been concluded in Tashkent. It focused on how to teach the Russian language more effectively in schools with non-Russian students, such as those in central Asia. I asked the rector whether this issue posed a problem at his university. It was obviously a sore point, because he abruptly switched topics to biology, which was his field of study. I insisted on an answer, and he obliged reluctantly. There was no need to study this subject at his university, he said as though on automatic pilot, reciting a line from a political fairy tale, because there were "indissoluble bonds" linking Uzbekistan to the Soviet Union. The Tashkent conference was simply addressing the problem of pronunciation. Apparently Russian was difficult for Uzbeks and Tajiks, because it contained sounds not found in their own language.

"Is it not possible," I asked "that the Uzbeks and the Tajiks were actually resisting the imposition of the Russian language?"

"Absolutely not," the rector answered.

Gently I changed the subject to one he was certain to find equally problematic. Khrushchev had insisted on destroying Stalin's personality cult (at that very moment Stalin's face was staring down on us), raising Lenin's ideological profile and focusing more on technical courses than on the humanities. "What has been the impact of the 20th Party Congress on the university's curriculum?" I asked.

The rector answered flatly, "We have made no changes in the curriculum, and none are planned."

At which point, arriving at just the right time to include his own point of view, the chair of the Humanities Department burst into the room. A bright, enthusiastic, talkative Russian, he plunged into the "difficulties" and "shortcomings" of his department in responding to the Khrushchev challenge. "With Stalinism gone and Leninism resurrected, this was the time for action!" he shouted, as if from a soapbox, "But none has been sanctioned."

The rector squirmed, and the Intourist guide tried to change the subject; but the chair was not to be deterred. He continued his highly unorthodox critique. "Western philosophy must again be taught," he cried. "Locke and Montesquieu must again be studied, especially *The Spirit of Laws*, which is Montesquieu's classic treatise on democracy."

Then came a sudden and surprising display of power by the Intourist guide: he turned on the humanities chair and, with a fake smile, screamed, "Shut up! Our visitor has little time for such unnecessary pronouncements."

My name having been invoked, I thought I had the right to intervene in this intra-university squabble. Of course I sided with the humanities chair.

I told them about the American system of checks and balances, about a free press, about elections, about state and federal representatives.

I could have continued, but I suspected I would be hurting the poor chairman, not helping him. Besides, the rector was clearly in anguish and the Intourist guide in high dudgeon.

"I'm late for my ride to the cotton collective farm," I announced. It was as good a reason as any in the Soviet Union for ending a conversation. Before the rector or the guide could raise an objection, which they would not have done, I shook hands with both and left the room, leaving behind only a smile of support for the beleaguered humanities chair.

In the afternoon, still brutally hot and dry, I joined another Intourist guide, Pyotr, for a thirty-minute ride in a ZIS limousine to the Friedrich Engels Cotton Collective Farm on the outskirts of Samarkand. The streets of Samarkand were almost deserted, the only exceptions being a straggling donkey or horse from a nearby collective farm, and I could not help but wonder why Tamerlane had not chosen a better location for his capital. (Of course, we complained endlessly about the icy Moscow winters.) Our driver, an Armenian, asked a few questions about Armenians in America. A college friend was Armenian, I told him, and he lived very well, as did his friends. The driver said he had read in *Pravda* that they all lived poorly. I answered as diplomatically as possible that truth (*pravda* in Russian) did not always reside in *Pravda*. He looked at me as if it was the first time he had ever heard so outrageous a thought.

Most of the ride out of Samarkand was on a paved road, but then, after a sharp turn to the right, we suddenly found ourselves on a bumpy dirt road. The ZIS's tires kicked up a dust storm for the ages, but looking from side to side, I could still see an endless field of cotton. "We've still got ten days to harvest, ten days before the cotton is in full bloom," Pyotr explained. I would not have known whether it was ten days or twenty— this was my first time anywhere near a cotton field. We continued for another few minutes until I finally made out a small building in the whiteness of the cotton field. It looked lonely.

"This is the center of the collective farm," Pyotr announced. There was not a soul in sight, only the full sun against the chalk-white sky. No one was in the cotton field. I heard the barking of a dog, nothing more. Then, disturbing this silent emptiness, a heavyset Uzbek emerged from the building. As he approached he put his right hand on his heart, the traditional sign of hospitality in central Asia. He introduced himself as the farm's bookkeeper.

"Welcome," he said, smiling. "We were expecting you."

In a reciprocal gesture, I put my hand on my heart and thanked him for his hospitality. "I was hoping I could see the workers in the field," I said.

The bookkeeper nodded. "Let's go," and he led our modest procession of me, Pyotr, and the driver into the cotton field.

We walked along a narrow path. On either side was a dry ditch. "We will soon have water," the bookkeeper said, as though in prayer. "For us, water is gold." It was the same phrase I had heard earlier on the flight into Tashkent. I noticed that the cotton buds were small and, up close, not as white as I had expected. They came up to my knees, and many drooped under the blistering sun.

Up ahead, like a mirage in a desert, appeared a circle of clay huts, an oasis in the cotton field. Dogs began to bark. The bookkeeper put up his hand, a sign of caution. "These dogs are vicious," he said, "especially with strangers. Wait here." He went ahead while we stayed behind. The barking only got louder. A few minutes later the bookkeeper returned. "I had the dogs locked up. It's safe now." We entered the circle of huts and found about twenty Uzbek men sitting on rugs in the blessed shade of one tree, which stood like a throne in a castle room of the grateful faithful. Children, bareheaded and barefoot, played in the sun. Women, their heads lowered, waited on the side.

These Uzbeks represented one brigade of many on a collective farm of 20,000. Each brigade had an elected leader, and each leader was responsible to the farm chairman, deputy chairman, and bookkeeper. Presumably the leaders were all members of the Soviet Communist Party. When I sought confirmation, the bookkeeper pretended not to hear or understand my question.

All of the huts looked the same. "May I see one?" I asked. The book-keeper had been waiting to hear that question. A hut had already been prepared for us. A woman waiting at the door welcomed us, her right hand to her heart. The hut consisted of two small rooms, both Spartan in appearance. One, furnished in Uzbek style, had a single bed pushed against a wall and many rugs scattered on the floor and carefully hung on the walls. The other room had only a hammock. I wondered whether she lived there alone. Unlikely. But if others lived here with her, where did they asleep? Where did they eat? There was no table. The woman herself seemed friendly. She offered green tea and grapes. Before I could accept, the bookkeeper, speaking in Russian, said we were on a very tight schedule. "Maybe next time," he said with a nod to diplomacy.

I asked the woman, "May I take a picture of you?" She shook her head no, and the bookkeeper, relieved, ushered us away from the peasants and back toward our limo.

We drove about ten minutes in the opposite direction to the Dom Kultury, the House of Culture, which served as school, library, theater, propaganda (agitprop), and general amusement center. I had the impression it must earlier have been two huts, now rolled into one. Miraculously, it was located in a heavily wooded area, possibly the only such area in the Samarkand *oblast* (region). The bookkeeper pointed to a shady spot behind the house, where we headed. Two Uzbek women, dressed in bright skirts and blouses, rushed to spread rugs on the ground and then quickly produced two trays of beautiful black and yellow grapes, the largest I had ever seen, delicious flat bread, and many pots of green tea. After a few minutes the women added figs and watermelon. A feast for kings, I thought.

As we sat, enjoying the food and the rest, we began to talk, and we quickly found ourselves talking about everything, in particular, much to my surprise, what Pyotr referred to as "the glories of America."

To these citizens of the Soviet Union, nothing seemed more fascinating than American cars. Not just the Armenian driver—they all loved them, Chevrolets in particular.

How many different car companies existed, and how many cars were actually produced?

How many models were there for each car?

And, most amazing, how many different models of the different cars were produced every year? I did not have exact figures, but they seemed content with my enthusiastic generalizations.

I told them I had once owned a 1952 Chevy convertible.

"Really!" "How much did it cost?" "You didn't need government permission to buy one?" To them it was all new and breathtaking. We discussed express highways and thoroughfares, which also intrigued them. How many were there in Washington? I had no idea. We talked about jazz music. Pyotr confessed that when he was a student in Moscow, he listened to the Voice of America every night and often danced with fellow students till dawn. We spoke about the Empire State Building, and the other skyscrapers that defined the New York skyline. The Russian word for "skyscrapers" was the verbal concoction *skayskreperz*, and every Russian knew it.

Most touching to me was our conversation about my family. They were astonished that my father was a tailor, a workingman, and my mother a housewife. How could I be a diplomat, working at the U.S. embassy in Moscow, and my father a workingman? How could that be? I tried to explain that my job, translating the Soviet press, was not really important—it was way down on the totem pole of power and authority—but they didn't believe me.

They were even more astonished when I told them that my mother and father owned their own home and their own car, and that it was not that extraordinary for a workingman to own his own home. Many did.

"How many?" Pyotr demanded.

"I don't know," I said. Pyotr smiled—he thought he had caught me in a fib.

"How many suits does your father own? One or two?" asked the bookkeeper.

"Five, I think." They looked at one another with knowing skepticism.

"And how many dresses does your mother have?" asked Pyotr, the number one skeptic.

"I'm not sure, maybe five or ten." Pyotr wanted to believe me, but could not.

The bookkeeper, somewhat flummoxed by my description of my family, which obviously did not fit his image of the oppressed American worker, decided on the spot that we should talk about Russia. Enough about America. And we should talk about Russian casualties and suffering during World War II. That, he hoped, would explain why most Soviet workers did not have their own home or car. "The ordinary people of Russia hate war," he said soberly. "We want peace."

It was time, I thought, for me to invoke Khrushchev's call for "peace and friendship." I raised my cup of green tea and toasted "peace."

They all joined me.

The driver shot a hard glance at Pyotr. "Isn't this better than hating Americans? Why can't we just get along like this always? Why must we always be told about 'inevitable war'"? He had not yet been told about Khrushchev's new formula of "peaceful coexistence." We all agreed that peace would be better than war, and we should all strive to achieve a world where "peace and friendship" prevailed.

That evening I noted in my diary: "I had a wonderful time today, and driving back I felt I had known these two men all my life. They were good people, who would much sooner get along with me than carry the torch of enmity."

After dinner I walked over to Gorky Park, bought an ice cream cone, and sat on a bench, watching the people of Samarkand walk by. No more than a minute or two passed before two Uzbeks joined me. One was talkative, the other silent but clearly interested. They worked on a nearby collective farm. They came to Gorky Park almost every evening.

"Where are you from?" the talkative one asked.

"America," I answered, and watched as his jaw dropped.

"I want to travel to America," he said with excitement. "Now we can, you know. Now we can do many things we couldn't do before." He grinned with satisfaction. "Oh, things are much better now. Things are much better." He repeated his last sentence, almost as if he was trying to convince himself that indeed they were much better.

I asked, "So you are now confident that things will get better?"

He answered, "They must. We cannot go back again. There have been too many going-backs. Now we must go forward to better things. The 'pope' is dead, and now things have to be better."

He paused, and looked up at me. "Don't you think so?" he asked in a plaintive tone.

"Of course," I replied. "Of course."

"Oh, God, I hope so," he said.

His friend, looking at his watch, leaned over and whispered something in his ear. "Oh, I forgot," the talkative one exclaimed, "we're going to the movies tonight." They both shook my hand, looked me in the eye and, with a friendly wave, left.

I had asked myself when I arrived in this historic city whether twentieth-century Samarkand could somehow match the allure of fifteenth-century Samarkand. My answer was no. The beauty of old Samarkand had an unmatchable allure, if it was fully restored, and the Russians were making a good-faith effort to do this. But the effort, in my judgment, would ultimately fail, because everything imposed by communism ended up being corrupted by the underlying injustice, arbitrariness, and cruelty of the system. Old Samarkand, even if restored, would probably look like an artificial tourist trap, a prop against the cheap reality of the new Samarkand.

It was a short plane ride from Samarkand to Bukhara, but it took me to a backwater town that was clearly not a priority concern for Soviet authorities. Why it had recently been opened to foreign tourists and diplomats was puzzling. It was not ready for prime time. If Tashkent and Samarkand could charitably be described as "Soviet" in appearance, a mix of old and new, Bukhara was only old, an apparently untouched relic of a much earlier time. Even the usually bright red communist posters urging fulfillment of the sixth five-year plan, which were everywhere, had already faded to a pale pink. The airport lacked a paved runway and the terminal building looked withered, hardly a welcoming mat for an arriving tourist. The road to the city was also unpaved, and the city itself was old and tired, like the donkeys that meandered through the central square. My hotel, the best in town, I was assured, resembled a large outhouse, or so I wrote in my diary at the time. The odor was oppressive, and the rooms felt cramped. None had a bathroom. Near the city center was an old mosque that had been converted into a pool room with three tables. Another mosque now housed the directors of the political indoctrination center.

If Peter the Great had been on my plane, he would not have been surprised by the city's sagging skyline. I had the impression that not much had changed since 1717, when the ambitious czar sent his army to central Asia in an unsuccessful effort to conquer the Khanate of Bukhara. The Khanate, though backward, proved to be an agile and stubborn foe. Not until 1868, when General Konstantin von Kaufmann led the Russian army in attacks against both Samarkand and Bukhara, did the czar succeed in extending Russian power into that corner of central Asia.

In his book *Eastern Approaches* (published in 1949), Fitzroy Maclean, a Scottish writer, diplomat, and explorer, described Bukhara as an "enchanted city" whose edifices rivaled "the finest architecture of the Italian renaissance." He had visited Bukhara in 1938. Could Bukhara have changed so drastically in eighteen years? I had my doubts. Maclean must have been a very generous guest, whose imagination was constrained by the requirements of British diplomacy.

The streets were dirty and dusty and ran in odd patterns. Women adjusted to the heat by wearing dark, heavy *khalats*, their faces hidden behind veils, their heads down. The men wore white turbans wrapped loosely around their heads. Everyone was going somewhere, and yet seemingly nowhere. I had hoped that Bukhara might be another Samarkand, but I was wrong. One was a city of promise, the other a city forgotten in the desert sun. The marketplace had none of the outdoor charm of the Samarkand market. Here the marketplace was indoors, functioning under three round, hollow stone covers, looking from a distance like three huge walnut shells placed upside down near the center of the city.

Nothing I saw in the architecture of Bukhara reminded me of the Italian renaissance. Near the marketplace was the blue-bordered Kalyan minaret, built in 1120. Its nickname was "the tower of death" because criminals were executed by being thrown from the top. "It was more than a 'tower of death,'" my guide said. It also served as a watchtower to alert Bukharans to a foreign attack, a dust storm, or an approaching trade caravan. Now it stood as a mute symbol of a dead culture.

Nearby was another Registan, desperately in need of a facelift but easily the most impressive building in town. Like its parent model in Samarkand, it was built during Ulugh Beg's rule to serve as a madrasah, or religious school, for roughly forty-five students at a time, each admitted for eight years.

"Can one study Islam now?" I asked.

"Of course," the guide answered.

"Where?" I asked.

"Somewhere," he replied. "Somewhere in Bukhara."

"Can we go there now?"

"No," he said, looking at his watch. "No time for such a visit." As we walked away from the Registan, I noticed that Uzbeks were playing basketball in the back. In an adjacent building grain was stored.

I had heard much about the rug weavers of Bukhara, but for some reason, they, like the religion students, were "somewhere in Bukhara" and unavailable.

"What about the Jews of Bukhara?" I asked. "I have been told they are a thriving community here."

My guide, uncertain about the party line on the Jews of Bukhara, mumbled, "Maybe tomorrow. Maybe tomorrow we can see the Jews."

I realized that my guide was not the most courageous Uzbek in town. If I was to see the Jews, I would have to make my own arrangements. I pretended to be tired and returned to the hotel, a decision so pleasing to my guide that his face broke into a wide grin. "Yes, and one must be careful about the sun," he observed. "Too much sun, no good." When we got to the hotel, he vanished, assuming, I guess, that I was going to take a nap.

But instead, after a half hour or so, I left the hotel and walked down Lenin Street, crowded with Uzbeks and Tajiks, Armenians and Russians, Germans and Jews, all hustling either to the market or home. I was at least a head taller than everyone else, and I was looking for a sympathetic face, someone who could tell me where the Bukhara synagogue, known to be one of the oldest in the world, was located. In this swirl of humanity, one such face miraculously materialized: it was dark from the sun but European in shape, and its eyes were amazingly blue. I looked at him, and he looked at me, and he seemed to beckon for me to follow him. Not a word was exchanged. I followed him for a few busy blocks, all of them lined with brown clay buildings.

Then Blue Eyes stopped, turned to me and asked, in Russian, whether I was searching for the synagogue. "You are Jewish, aren't you?" he asked.

I was absolutely stunned by his question. "Yes," I replied, "I would like to visit the synagogue."

"It's right here," he smiled, pointing to a nondescript one-story building consisting of three rooms around an open courtyard. "I knew this was where you wanted to go." Blue Eyes's eyes twinkled with special delight. He led me inside. Carved into the courtyard wall was a large Star of David. On both sides of the star was Hebrew script. I also saw three pages, apparently ripped from a prayer book, nailed to another wall.

"You see," explained Blue Eyes, "we have only three prayer books in the whole community, and only very old people come here to pray."

"What about younger people?"

"They rarely attend services, and we have no real rabbi, only an old man who has memorized all the prayers. He worries that soon there will be no Jews in Bukhara."

He told me that there were two groups of Jews in Bukhara, one group that came here centuries ago and another that came in the early 1940s to escape the Nazi onslaught. They would all like to leave the Soviet Union, he said. "They are very, very unhappy."

"What about you?" I asked. "Would you want to leave?"

"Oh, yes" he replied, "I would love to go to Israel, and now it's possible." His blue eyes teared up. "Maybe one day, maybe one day."

Later, after dinner, I walked from the hotel to the park near the city center. What I saw blew my mind. Everywhere people were drunk, and hooliganism was widespread and unchecked. Gangs were fighting against other gangs, blood was being shed, but militiamen, observing the brawls, did nothing to stop the fighting, maybe because they were afraid to intervene. Drunks were staggering down Lenin Street, punching bystanders and fondling women. Everyone was singing and cursing. I wanted to watch this incredible scene like something out of Dante's *Inferno*, but not get into any trouble myself. I sat down on a park bench. Nearby, on another park bench, a man was making love to a woman. A Russian sitting near me, possibly offended by the sight, tapped the man on his back. "There is a foreigner here watching you. Have you no shame?" he asked. "So what?" was the man's response. "I'm a foreigner here, too." He continued his lovemaking, and no one passing by seemed to pay any attention to it. It seemed as if everyone was letting off steam, and no one, most especially the militiamen, cared one bit.

By reading, rumor, and through the stories of other travelers, I had heard a lot about the Bukhara bazaar, an unusual marketplace about twenty minutes from the city center, and I wanted to visit it. Maybe I could see the city's famed rug weavers there. I didn't have much time. Later that morning I was scheduled to fly westward to Baku, the capital of Azerbaijan, and then on to Tbilisi, the capital of Georgia, by train; but because nothing in the Soviet Union ever went directly from one place to another, I would first have to fly eastward, back to Tashkent, before being allowed to fly westward to Baku. It was Intourist's maddening way of distracting passengers from sensible pursuits and earning more money. The director of the hotel, who had unhappily learned of my discovery of the Bukhara synagogue the previous day, wanted to make sure that I would not wander off by myself once again. He assigned an official Intourist guide to be with me at all times and to make sure that I got to the airport in plenty of time for my Tashkent-bound flight. The director's aim was to get me out of town as quickly and uneventfully as possible. It did not work out quite that way.

Instead of walking to the bazaar, we took a bus. The bazaar, with many broken-down stalls of fruits and vegetables, was open to the blazing sun. I asked the first tradesman I met if he could direct me to the rug weavers. His first instinct was to help, but the minute he saw my official guide he decided to say nothing. He just frowned and moved on. I turned to my guide. "Can you please help me? You know I don't have much time." Clearly under orders to be helpful, if necessary, he nodded and went looking for directions. While waiting, I pulled my camera out of my traveling bag and started taking pictures of the peasants selling watermelons and grapes. Almost immediately, as if waiting for a pretext, a militiaman approached and asked for my identification. I had no official document with me, because my passport was still back at the hotel. I told him that I was an American tourist. I told him he could check with my guide, who would be back in a moment. I continued taking pictures. The militiaman put his hand in front of the lens and then, rather abruptly, held my arm and "suggested" I go with him to police headquarters. Instinctively I pulled loose of his grip and informed him that I was about to leave soon for the airport. I did not have time to go with him. But suddenly I found myself surrounded by a dozen other militiamen, who must have been waiting nearby.

"You will come with me," repeated the lead militiaman, who was a sergeant.

"Are you arresting me?" I asked.

"No," he replied, shaking his head.

"Then why must I go with you?"

The sergeant explained that until he verified who I was, I would have to obey him. I realized that I was on the brink of a possible "incident," which the U.S. embassy always tried to discourage, and I urged him to call the hotel. I did not want an incident. I knew the hotel director would confirm that I was an American tourist (indeed, one with a diplomatic passport) and the sergeant would then have to let me go. But for reasons beyond me, the sergeant refused to telephone the hotel, telling me that instead he was going to call his immediate superior at police headquarters and tell him that he was holding a foreigner who had no identification and who, in addition, was taking pictures. A large crowd formed around us. We all waited while the sergeant called to get instructions.

After a few minutes he announced in rather somber tones that I would, in fact, be detained (he avoided using the word "arrested") and brought to police headquarters. I knew that eventually, after his superior had checked with the hotel and learned that I was an American diplomat, I would be released. But by then I would likely have missed my flight and thrown my schedule into a mess, a situation that was not that easy to resolve in central Asia. I decided on the spot that I had no option but to stand my ground. I was guilty of no wrongdoing. I told him, and everyone who had gathered around us, that I was an American diplomat traveling through central Asia for pleasure and learning; that I had the permission of the Soviet Foreign Ministry; that the sergeant was in clear violation of international rules governing the treatment of diplomatic personnel; and that I intended to submit a formal protest to Moscow authorities.

"What is your name?" I demanded.

The sergeant, who had earlier conveyed an air of authority, seemed now to look uncertain and, I thought, afraid.

What would Ambassador Bohlen do? Try diplomacy, he would advise, and so I did. I suggested, with a gentle smile, that there was a way out of this conundrum—that the sergeant really ought to call the hotel, as I had asked him to do before, verify that indeed I was an American diplomat, inform his police superior what he had learned, and then let me catch my flight. I added, in a serious tone, that if he refused, I would definitely submit an official protest in Moscow and he and his superior would both be responsible for what I called "a gross violation of diplomatic norms." The sergeant, trying desperately to reestablish his authority, especially as the crowd got larger by the minute, grabbed me by the arm and announced that he was going to take me to police headquarters, and that was final. I again pulled loose and refused to go with him. I urged him, please, to call the hotel. I understood that he needed a way to save face, and I had to catch a flight and wanted to avoid an "incident." I decided to tell him in a loud but polite voice that I was "wrong" to have taken pictures without asking permission. Then I placed a cherry on top of my apology, telling the crowd that I had had a wonderful visit to Bukhara, that I loved the people and looked forward to my next visit. Many people smiled and applauded in Soviet style. A few actually shook hands with me. Whatever tension was accumulating seemed magically to disappear.

The sergeant, on his own, then called the hotel, learned officially of my diplomatic status, informed his superior, and, his lower lip trembling, told me that he was sorry and hoped that I would return to Bukhara. I assured him I would. At which point, my Intourist guide reappeared, rushed me into a waiting taxicab, which took us first to the hotel, where I recovered my passport and my bag, and then to the airport, where I caught my flight to Tashkent, but with not much time to spare.

Central Asia had been interesting and, on occasion, even compelling, but I was happy to leave. Because of Intourist's uniquely idiotic way of arranging a travel schedule, I knew I would have to spend the whole afternoon and evening in Tashkent before my 1:35 a.m. flight to Baku—again, why 1:35 a.m., and not 1:35 p.m., a more reasonable hour?

I decided to attend a play—*Sixth Floor*, an amusing French production, even if translated into Russian—and I enjoyed three chance conversations. In Theater Square I met a Volga German. Since the outbreak of World War II, he had been forced to live an exile's life in a small town on the Chinese border. Now, in the wake of de-Stalinization, he could move to Tashkent, but not back to the Volga region, where his family had lived since the time of the Catherine the Great, who had invited German colonizers to the area. He volunteered, without my asking, that in his judgment 60 percent of Volga Germans would return to Germany if given the chance.

I encountered a Jewish man from Kiev, who had been living in Tashkent since 1942. He operated a small shoe-repair booth—too small to be described as a store. He told me, "Here in Tashkent we all envy the baker. At least, he's got his loaf of bread." He estimated that 80 percent of European Jews living in central Asia would leave the Soviet Union, if given the chance. Most would go to Israel. He looked unhappy. After polishing my shoes, he held my hand and whispered, "Don't ever forget us."

At the airport I met a young Korean history teacher, a Soviet citizen born in Tashkent. When he learned that I had once taught Russian history, he said, beaming, "We historians share one thing: We both speak the truth. We both seek the truth." The first topic on his agenda was how African Americans were treated in the United States. That was no surprise. The subject came up often, especially with Soviet citizens who were members of the Communist Party. I told him that after a recent U.S. Supreme Court decision banning segregation in state schools, the last barrier to genuine equality between the races had been blasted away. I said, "The issue of racial prejudice was a live issue only in some southern states. I think in time the issue will lose its significance even in those states." (How wrong I was!)

He asked me, "Do you think true freedom exists in the Soviet Union?"

I responded, "No, in my judgment, it does not," and added, "Communism has become a bloodless ideology, and it will wither away in time." (How right I was!)

"But we have elections, free and secret, just as you do," he said. "How then can you say that we do not have freedom at least equal to yours?"

I told him that where there was no choice, there was no freedom.

"I thought you would say that," he said, "and, you know, I can't help but agree with you. Our freedom is a paper freedom." He looked around, wondering, I guess, whether he had been talking too much.

I was left with the impression from my visit to central Asia that de-Stalinization had had only a limited impact on the people. Life had eased a bit, but it had not really changed. I suspected I would find that it had had a much deeper impact on the people living in Tbilisi, the capital of Georgia, Stalin's birthplace.

CHAPTER ELEVEN

Where Stalin Is Still Worshipped

Bukhara was hot and dry. Baku was hot and humid, certainly on the day I got there. It was like Washington in mid-August. From the moment the plane door opened, I could feel the moist heat rushing in, and this mix of heat and humidity dogged me during my stay in Baku, the capital and commercial hub of Azerbaijan, then one of the fifteen Soviet republics. Intourist had assured me that "Baku" meant "city of winds," and the temperature would never climb higher than 78.

Like Bukhara, Baku had only recently been opened to foreign travelers. In fact, I was to learn, only a small parcel of downtown Baku had been opened. Most of the rest of this sweltering city, sprawling along the western coast of the Caspian Sea, was still off-limits. When, on my first encounter with Intourist in Baku, I requested a tour of the whole city, my guide could only smile grudgingly, his attempt at official humor. "Little Baku," he called it. "I can show you only little Baku. The rest of the city is really—he paused, searching for the right word—uninteresting."

In Sovietese, the word "uninteresting" generally meant "interesting," probably "very interesting," and for that reason tourists like me were barred from it.

The ride from the airport to the accessible heart of Baku took longer than an hour—seventy minutes, to be exact. The Caspian Sea glittered in the morning sun. The city skyline was uneven: a long pier reaching into the Caspian, a series of rundown houses two to four stories tall, and the ubiquitous oil rigs on both land and sea, hundreds, perhaps thousands, of them, slowly rising and falling as though they, too, had had to adjust to the heat. The rigs looked rusty but seemed effective, steadily extracting from beneath the earth or sea what the locals called black gold. Baku and oil were inseparable: one a location, the other an invaluable source of energy and always a magnet for greedy investors. I could see that the city was divided into two parts: "black city," where oil was the only industry, and "white city," where many of the oil managers and workers lived. There seemed to be little else.

During World War II the Germans had made a frantic push toward Baku's oil fields, assuming that if they could reach Baku, they would be in an excellent strategic position not only to crush the Soviet Union but also to open the door to Persia and the Middle East. But the Russians, fully aware of Baku's critical importance, stopped them and eventually beat back Hitler's panzer divisions at Stalingrad and won the war.

Baku has been of critical importance to Russia ever since the early eighteenth century, when Peter the Great, having more than oil on his mind, drove his army toward the Caspian Sea and the provincial Islamic city of Baku. If one of his key lieutenants could be trusted, Peter had targeted India and possibly China for imperial plunder. "The hopes of His Majesty were not concerned with Persia alone," the lieutenant wrote. "If he had been lucky in Persia and still living, he would of course have attempted to reach India or even China. This I heard from His Majesty himself." In 1723 the Russians conquered the eastern rim of the Caucasus, including Baku, throwing a Christian Orthodox flag over this region of bubbling Islamic pride. Two years later Peter died and the Russians were forced to abandon much of this region, but they kept an eye on Baku, which after many battles they seized and formally annexed in 1806, possessing it until 1991, when the Soviet Union disintegrated and Azerbaijan, like the other Soviet republics, took advantage of the moment and declared itself independent.

In recent times the history of Azerbaijan has really been the history of oil: its discovery, its exploitation, and its sale on the international market. For many hundreds of years, traders and travelers knew about the abundance of oil in and near Baku. The first well, using percussion drilling, was built there in 1846, the first oil refinery, in 1858. Within two years Baku was producing 4,000 tons of oil per year. By 1900 it was producing nearly 8 million tons per year, a rather impressive output for the estimated 3,000 oil wells in Baku, which produced half of the oil needed in the rest of the world. The Nobel brothers and the Rothschilds were among the early investors in the Baku bonanza. Stalin largely depended on the oil reserves of Baku to keep the wheels of war turning during World War II.

Now, eleven years after the war's end but only eight months after Khrushchev's bombshell at the 20th Party Congress, Baku was beginning to show signs of a post-Stalin thaw in culture and politics. But it would clearly need more time before the thaw could affect the life of the average Azeri. In the meantime, life meandered from one day to the next, meaningful change still more a hope than a reality.

Compared to my hotels in central Asia, my hotel in Baku was luxurious. My room was large and clean and had its own bathroom. From a picture window I could see the harbor, one of the most beautiful in the Soviet Union. It sparkled in the sunlight, and I thought it resembled Plymouth Bay in Massachusetts, a horseshoe of land washed by the sea on three sides. Here, though, were oil wells. No matter how far my eye wandered, I still saw them.

When I went on my tour of Baku, I was kept close to the hotel. Everything was off-limits except the old city. The old city itself was on a high hill overlooking the harbor. The guide pointed with pride to the cobblestone alleyways and to a decaying mosque that had served as a fortress hundreds of years ago.

"Against whom?" I asked, already knowing the answer.

The guide said he did not understand my question.

"Why would you need to turn a mosque into a fortress? Who was attacking you?"

The guide, realizing that an honest answer could only lead to trouble, suggested instead that I see the remains of an underground Moslem bath house that had been accidentally discovered in 1941, when a cover of earth collapsed, revealing this ancient site.

But that was it—the guide had nothing more that he could show me. I asked whether there was a history museum I could visit, assuming every Soviet city had one. The guide looked troubled, explaining that he had to check whether the Baku Historical Museum was open for visitors. It had been shut for "remont," one of the most popular words in the whole country. He called headquarters, we waited, and finally he got permission to take me to what turned out to be a very impressive building, once the home of a Persian oil merchant. We could have walked to the museum, but he insisted we go by limo, eliminating the possibility that I could have seen something along the way that was "uninteresting."

The museum was impressive in one respect, disappointing in most others. In one large room it traced the history of the Azeri people back to the Stone and Bronze Ages. It was a superficial review. In another room, Azeri history as presented ran up to the seventeenth and eighteenth centuries. Again, truly superficial. Finally, the jewel in the museum's crown: the Azeri people living under Soviet rule. This was fascinating for only one reason: the way Azeri history was shoehorned into the Soviet experience. My guide used every cliché in his communist handbook to paint Azeri history in Soviet colors, stressing especially how "progressive" Azeris unshackled themselves from "regressive" capitalism and embraced the "glory and wonder of Marxism." Paintings showed starving workers fighting fat millionaires. It was a dreadful presentation. If there was a saving grace, it was in the beauty of the building.

After a shish-kebab dinner, which was delicious, I went for a walk along the promenade fronting the Caspian Sea, and surprisingly my Intourist guide made no effort to stop me. I was not alone, of course. It seemed as if everyone else was also out for a walk. As I noted later that evening in my diary, "They too undoubtedly have nothing else to do." Hundreds watched a young daredevil wearing a parachute jump from a rooftop to the promenade below, a jump of over fifty feet. He landed safely and everyone applauded. Apparently this was his way of earning some extra cash because he ran around with his *tubeteika* in hand collecting coins. I gave him a ruble, and his eyes lit up. "Big tipper am I," I muttered to myself.

Tied to the pier were two sightseeing boats, one named *Druzhba*, "friendship," and the other *Mir*, "peace." I chose *Druzhba*, and another dozen or so passengers and I chugged into the bay for about a half hour, watching one another when we were not watching the oil wells, which never broke their up-and-down, twenty-four-hour-a-day routine. We passed a yacht club. I was told that it was private, guarded, and reserved for "rich people." One passenger kept staring at me, and I had a feeling he wanted to talk. So I approached him and in Russian asked whether he lived in Baku and what he did for a living. By this time we were already returning to the pier. As we left the boat, he started talking about his life in English. It turned out that he was Armenian, and his English was excellent. I bought each of us an ice cream cone and we sat down on a park bench. He said he was born in Palestine and lived there until 1948, when, as he put it, "I made the greatest mistake of my life." He decided to return to Armenia, the land of his ancestors but a land controlled by Russia. "All Armenians love Armenia," he explained. "Once we were a great people. I think we still are. I thought that the communists had given us a chance to build an Armenian life once again. I found out in one year that I was wrong, that such a life under Soviet rule was impossible." He never gave me his name. Nor did he explain why he was now in Baku. "Since then I have been trying to get out," he continued. "But this, I now know, I cannot do. I am hopelessly their prisoner, here so close to my own home." Armenia borders on Azerbaijan.

Even as he spoke of himself as a prisoner, he showed no emotion. It was as if he had finished crying long ago. Now all he wanted to do was practice his English. All I wanted to do was listen.

"Baku is a crazy kind of city," he said, matter-of-factly, his voice flat, betraying neither approval nor disapproval. "There are many nationalities here—Armenians, Jews, Georgians, Russians, Ukrainians. But the Russians are a minority only in number. They run Baku. They call the Azeris *zvery*, wild animals. The Azeris call the Russians onionheads. But between them there is no hostility, none you can see anyway." He paused, as if struggling for the right words. "During the day, they smile at each other. At night they hate." Three Russian sailors happened to stroll by at that moment. My friend looked away, as though searching for something that had dropped behind our bench.

"Are you frightened of them?" I asked.

"No, but it is not good to be seen with foreigners. Actually, I don't care. But still it is not good."

I asked him whether, in his judgment, Russia had changed since the Khrushchev speech denouncing Stalin.

"Yes, this cannot be denied," he said. "Things have eased up considerably. Now people will not be arrested as much in the middle of the night, and people talk a little more, but only among their best friends. In the presence of some who are not trusted, no one says anything but 'the weather is hot' and 'when do you think it will cool off?' The communists are like sheep. If the top man says boo, all below him will jump. They do not think independently, and why should they? They have it so good here now." My friend again looked behind him, as if he was afraid of someone or something. "I only make five hundred rubles a month working in a plant, but my wife earns three hundred, and we get along. I must go, but thank you for listening to me. I feel like a person again." He shook hands with me, his face breaking into a polite smile, and off he went into the night. As he walked away, I later noted in my diary, "he seemed so completely without spirit, so lifeless, so corpse-like."

I decided that I would leave Baku the next day, but first I was determined to see "Nina," who at fifty still had the ability to tickle my intellectual curiosity about her special role in Russian history. I had read about her, and wanted to know more.

"Nina," a favorite of any student of Russian history, had lived for many years in an old one-story house, number 102 First Parallel Avenue, in a slum neighborhood that had recently been opened to foreign tourists. Why would such a neighborhood be opened? It was obviously an embarrassment. There could be only one reason: "Nina" had played a key role in seeding the ground for the Russian Revolution, and Intourist wanted foreigners to be impressed by it.

When I informed my guide that I wanted to visit "Nina" before I left later that afternoon for Tbilisi, he could not have been more delighted. "A ZIS limousine will be waiting for you in one half hour," he said.

"No," I objected. "I'll walk."

"No," he insisted. "You'll ride in a limo."

We both understood that he did not want me to dawdle along the way and see the sorry mess that most of Baku still was—and, worse, stop and talk with people, who might want to share the story of their lives. I agreed to the limo. The ride was short and uneventful.

"Nina" was the nickname of a historic printing press in the early days of the twentieth century. In czarist Russia, such a press was illegal. It spread the message of communism and revolution, and it did so in newspapers called *Iskra* (*Spark*) and *Borba* (*Struggle*). *Iskra*, the more famous, harked back to an optimistic phrase associated with Alexander Pushkin: "From the spark will come the flame." For Lenin the "flame" would be the Russian Revolution.

At Nina's home, I was greeted by three MVD officers and the docent of the museum, who escorted me into a small room where the walls were covered with portraits of Lenin and Stalin. He explained Nina's history with enormous pride, telling me of its central, controversial role in disseminating Lenin's vision of revolution.

"Sir," I said, impatiently, "where is Nina?" I was conscious of my tight schedule. I was to board a train to Tbilisi in a few hours.

"Just a moment," he said. "Just a moment." Slowly he led me to a tiny kitchen in the back of the house. It had a stove, a window, and a few cabinets. I did not see Nina.

"Where is Nina?" I repeated. At which point, the docent pulled a string, and, as in a magic show, the curtain covering the window dropped, revealing an opening to a small underground room lit by a naked light bulb. There in the middle stood Nina, an old printing press with many stories to tell.

"Nina began to function in 1901," said the docent, making conversation as he and I made our way down a few treacherous steps into a dim cellar. "She played a very major role in the revolutionary movement, not only here in the Caucasus, but throughout the Russian empire. In September 1901 she began to roll off *Iskra*, the best illegal Marxist newspaper inside Russia." The docent stressed that I was not to touch the press, which, he noted unnecessarily, was precious to him and historians. "There is only one Nina."

"When it was printing, it made noise," I said. "If anyone heard the noise, that would give away the whole show."

The docent agreed. "The person most likely to hear this noise was the man who lived next door to Nina, the owner of this house. Fortunately he was drunk most of the time and only thought that he imagined the noise."

"Why put up with this stressful situation?" I asked.

The docent had a simple answer. "These people had a mission. They did not like tyranny. They knew that to overcome tyranny, they had to endure great suffering, which they did. But they worked hard for their cause." Their cause was revolution, and they needed newspapers to sell their message to the public. They needed Nina to produce their newspapers. Before the revolution, Lenin wanted and needed a free press, one free to publish his message. After the revolution, once in power, he banished freedom of the press.

The docent, who looked tired, sat down on a bench, caught his breath, and suggested I return tomorrow. I told him that by tomorrow I would be in Tbilisi.

From Baku the train ran south for almost four hours, by which time the sun had fallen behind the rising rim of the Caucasus, and we had begun our westward ascent to Tbilisi, nestled among the highest mountain peaks of Georgia. It was a capital city of warm springs, passionate nationalism, and an adoring pride in the dictator, Stalin, a native son whose legend was being brutalized everywhere else in the Soviet Union but not there. The train ride, though long, was thoroughly enjoyable, largely because my compartment mate was a chubby young Azeri woman named Maria, who unashamedly admitted that "pull" was the key to a satisfying life in the Soviet Union.

Her father was a prominent doctor in Baku who knew everyone and readily exchanged favors with other bigwigs in Azeri society. Her mother was a housewife who had never had to work, and her sister was in her second year of studies at Baku University. Maria was a French-language teacher in a small town in southern Azerbaijan, and she felt she needed a change.

"There is no fun there," she said, her head shaking slowly from one side to the other. "What is a young girl to do? After work, I like fun, but there is none there. In Tbilisi, there is a lot of fun." Her father's friend, a communist with connections, was at that time using his clout to get her shifted from this small town to Baku. At least that would be a step up. She was confident he would succeed. "I know that someone must live and teach in such small towns, but it doesn't have to be me."

"Have you no guilt feelings?" I asked.

"Not at all," she replied. Her tone was even, unemotional, like the Armenian's the night before. "If I didn't use pull, someone else would. Pull is the best way of getting anything in Russia. I think it is the only way." She told me that corruption was "rampant" at the university. Students gained admission not because they deserved it but because their parents enjoyed special privileges resulting from their social rank or political position. "They bought admission, like buying an apartment," she said. "Many of our young people are this way. I admit this. I am not ashamed. I have no conscience. I do not believe in God. In our family, we do what is good for us. That is the way it is here."

When we arrived the following morning in Tbilisi, the sky was dark gray and the temperature was in the low seventies. After weeks in the merciless heat of central Asia, I was thrilled, but Maria was unhappy. "Tbilisi needs sun," she grumbled. "It is beautiful only in the sun." She was right, as I was to learn during my time in the Georgian capital. In fact, Tbilisi was picture-postcard beautiful. It was situated on the banks of the Kura River, which ran through a valley surrounded by the skyscraping peaks. Many stone bridges crisscrossed the Kura. Small houses looked as if they had been chiseled into the face of the mountain. Georgians seemed taller than Russians or Ukrainians, certainly taller than the Uzbeks or Tajiks. Most men sported mustaches, and women appeared stylish, well dressed, confident of their looks. Trolley cars clanged up and down hills, little different from those in San Francisco, and private cars honked incessantly on the main streets, unlike those in Moscow, which made their way timidly through the comparatively thin traffic. It was obvious that the standard of living was higher here than in the Soviet capital.

At the railroad station in downtown Tbilisi, I was surprised when I was greeted by a smiling Intourist face rather than the usual frowning one that had accosted me in other Soviet cities. A ZIS limo was waiting, and it whisked me to the Intourist hotel, where I was ushered into a giant suite with a gorgeous view, at the modest price of $15 a day, meals extra. The Intourist guide told me there was one other American in the hotel, a photographer from California named Max. He had scheduled a trip to Mtskheta, Georgia's ancient capital, a thirty-minute-drive from Tbilisi along a narrow mountain pass. "May I go with him?" I asked. Maria had urged me to see Mtskheta, which she described as "exquisite" and "romantic." Fortunately the photographer welcomed company, and off we went. He had a specific assignment—to photograph the ancient icons and frescoes; I simply wanted to see the city.

The ride to Mtskheta was instructive. Farmhouses dotted the landscape. If there were any collective farms in the neighborhood, I did not see them. Fat, healthy-looking cows mooed as we drove by. In Mtskheta we could see clouds hugging the mountain peaks, a gray mist making everything look unreal. A large church, the largest I had ever seen in the Soviet Union, stood incongruously on a small square in this very quiet town. The church was built in the eleventh century on the ruins of a smaller church built in the fourth century. Mtskheta was Christianized in A.D. 337, almost 700 years before Prince Vladimir of Kievan Rus decided to Christianize the people who would later be known as Ukrainians and Russians. In the smaller church was an icon of Christ, brought there by Georgian pilgrims who had returned from the Holy Land centuries earlier. Another icon, hanging on a bare wall, showed Christ's eyes watching you at all times, no matter where you were in the church. I could not help but notice that the icons in Mtskheta were more beautiful, more sophisticated than any of the Russian icons I had seen (at least until Andrei Rublev arrived on the artistic scene in the fifteenth century).

Mtskheta was the capital of Georgia for 300 years, but in the fifth century, after it was leveled and many of its citizens massacred, it was decided, for reasons of security, to move the capital to nearby Tbilisi, which has remained the capital ever since. Tbilisi has always been considered a jewel of a city, a rich marketplace at an attractive intersection between Asia and Europe and a strategic hub for warriors from Mongolia, Persia, Russia, and the Ottoman Empire, at different times a prize for Tamerlane, a Persian shah, or a Russian czar. Looking around on that rainy day I could understand why. It was indeed a jewel, measured by everything from location to scenery, culture to art, beauty to people—most of all, people, who strode through their history with unparalleled pride. I asked a Georgian professor whether he had ever been to Western Europe, or China, or America, and he said no, adding with bewilderment, "What is there to see there that isn't better here?"

After a lunch of veal shashlik accompanied by Georgian wine, my new photographer friend and I visited the Chavchavadze Desyatilyetka (*desyatilyetka* means "ten-year school," mandatory for all Soviet students). Wherever I went in the Soviet Union I always tried to spend a little time at schools with students. Since they represented the future of their country, I wanted to understand their thinking.

There were 1,000 students in this school, half at the elementary and half at the secondary school level. Roughly 250 students had been graduated the previous year. Half of the graduates went on to university, the other half directly into the workplace. All classes were conducted in the Georgian language, but everyone had to study Russian eight hours a week.

We spoke to the principal, an attractive Georgian woman who spoke Russian with a distinct accent. She was especially absorbed with the educational mandate of the 20th Party Congress: to place greater emphasis on teaching technical subjects without lowering overall academic standards. "This is part of our desire to raise the technical proficiency of our youth," she explained. Khrushchev wanted more engineers and physicists, and this was his way of achieving that goal. I had read about another new goal—increasing the number of boarding schools.

"Will the Chavchavadze Desyatilyetka be one of the new boarding schools?" I asked.

She replied, "Not likely"—there was no room for expansion. But she was nevertheless convinced that within ten years all Soviet schoolchildren would be housed in boarding schools. Already 285 such schools had been opened in the last year. In four years, by 1960, she estimated, the number would theoretically skyrocket to 1 million boarding schools. The Kremlin's point was to indoctrinate young people with a communist-centric view of the world. That had not yet been achieved, and my own guess was it never would be.

"Would you like to see our classrooms?" the principal asked.

"Yes, of course," we said.

The classrooms were clean, and every one had a large photo of Stalin (the offices, too). Stalin looked young, vigorous, intelligent, and even handsome, like a Hollywood movie star. The latest school newspaper, a weekly, featured a photo of Stalin on its front page, even though there was no news-related reason to put one there. Beneath the photo was a poem about freedom that Stalin had supposedly written when he studied religion at a Tbilisi seminary (a building that was later converted into the Georgian State Museum). Stalin was born in 1878 in a village called Gory. His mother was a hardworking housekeeper, and his father was a drunk who often beat his wife. Stalin was a bright, promising student who one day might have become a priest—that was his mother's dream—if it were not for his after-hours dedication to the rising revolutionary currents then sweeping through the Russian Empire. His seminary teachers kept warning him that he would be expelled if he did not stop his subversive activity, but Stalin either could not or would not stop, and he was soon expelled, much to his mother's distress. From then on, Stalin devoted himself to Lenin's revolution, ultimately riding his coattails to absolute power in the Kremlin.

Intourist must have alerted the Georgian State Museum of my impending visit, because a small team of docents backed by two MVD officers was waiting for me. "Welcome," said one of the docents, an elderly man with a V-shaped beard and an elaborately etched cane. "We have something special for you." Much to my surprise, he and the officers led me to a locked room in the basement, which when the doors opened proved to be a treasure chest of Georgian icons. I had never seen a collection so enchanting anywhere. The icons, crafted in Georgia, dated back to the seventh and eighth centuries, graphic evidence of a once-flourishing civilization. When we got to examples from the thirteenth and fourteenth centuries, the quality of the icons seemed mysteriously to dip. The docent, sensing my unasked question, explained the dip with one word: "Mongols." There was one other noticeable dip in quality. This time I could figure out the reason myself. When the Russians seized Tbilisi in the early nineteenth century, the Georgian craftsmen "lost" their creative passion.

I had one more question for the docent. "Why did you bring me here?"

He smiled broadly. "Three years ago Ambassador Bohlen visited our museum. He identified part of one icon we have here as the sister part of an icon in the United States. He was very excited, and so were we." He leaned on his cane. "You see," he went on, "we are now brother and sister." When he learned that a visiting American diplomat wanted to see the

Georgian State Museum, he remembered the Bohlen visit. I was the lucky beneficiary. I got to see this exceptional collection of Georgian art. The docent told me, his voice filled with pride, that a new generation of Georgian artists was studying this ancient art and hoping in this way to recapture the greatness of the Georgian renaissance, which he placed in the tenth through twelfth centuries. "That's two hundred years before the Italian renaissance," he noted with a broad smile.

After my visit to the museum I asked my Intourist guide if I could walk back to the hotel alone, and, miracle of miracles, he said yes. The guide went one way, and I another. I knew what was going to happen. Within a few minutes, I was positive, a young Georgian student would engage me in conversation, and so it happened. He was, like most other Georgian students, relatively tall and well dressed, and he had a thick mustache. He was a student at the Pedagogical Institute, and he had a special interest in America. He said someone at the hotel had told him an American was in town. "I was following you, waiting for you to be alone," he said in good English. He did not give me his name, but in every other respect he seemed to be uninhibited. We sat down on a park bench, and we talked, and talked, and talked.

He asked me many questions about the United States, and I answered them with honesty and candor. Only when I sensed he was beginning to run out of questions did I ask him a few of my own about Georgia. I focused on the student uprisings that rocked Tbilisi in early March after Khrushchev's startling denunciation of Stalin at the 20th Party Congress. I told him that in Moscow we had heard unconfirmed stories that thousands of students, many armed, had demonstrated against the government, that about a hundred had been killed, and that the Red Army had had to be called in to contain the crisis.

"That's all true," he said, "only it was worse. At least 150 students were killed, and hundreds more were wounded." What happened was that on March 4, a day before the third anniversary of Stalin's death, a student delegation asked the rector of the university for permission to stage a pro-Stalin demonstration on March 5, the day of his death. The rector's response was no. According to a 1955 decree, such demonstrations could only be held on birthdates, not death dates. Nevertheless, groups of students began to gather around the huge Stalin statue in Tbilisi's central park, more of them with each passing day. Police were brought to the scene in case of trouble. On March 8, two students were killed. No one was quite sure how.

The following day everything changed. Anger turned to violence. While the Georgian Communist Party, on orders from Moscow, staged a counterdemonstration, ostensibly to honor a new statue of Lenin, hundreds of Soviet troops entered Tbilisi. The main streets were lined with tanks and the main square was cleared. Students began to clash with troops, throw stones at passing cars, and disrupt communications. Troops opened fire. Many students were killed. Later that evening thousands of other students marched toward the main post office, which was one block from the headquarters of the council of ministers. Both buildings were now being guarded by troops with machine guns. The commanding officer, speaking through a bullhorn, pleaded with the protesting students to disperse and go home. One student shouted back, saying they wanted to send a telegram to the United Nations asking for help to fight the Russians. Another student said they wanted to send a telegram to Moscow, specifically to Molotov, a known supporter of the Stalin legacy, demanding an end to Khrushchev's de-Stalinization drive. But the troops had their orders, and the students had only their anger. They resumed their march on the post office, and the troops again opened fire.

In Moscow Khrushchev kept a close eye on the student uprising, hoping that by the end of the day they would have "kick[ed] up a row and then calm[ed] down." But when it became obvious that the student uprising was continuing and its message was spreading throughout Georgia, "we intervened very sharply," Khrushchev's son, Sergei, later recalled. Khrushchev feared that a successful anti-Soviet uprising in Georgia could quickly spread to other regions of the Soviet Union and threaten the regime itself.

For the next week Tbilisi was held in an iron grip, my student friend told me. A midnight curfew was imposed. Armed troops, supported by tanks, patrolled the streets. Schools were shut. Only the funeral parlors and the churches were busy, burying the dead. Tbilisi was the scene of the bloodiest uprising against Russian rule since the Basmachi awakening of the early 1920s.

I asked my new friend whether Georgians were still angry about the de-Stalinization drive. "We feel this very deeply," he replied. "You are an American. You might not understand our feelings. But we are a proud people and a good people. When Stalin ruled Russia, we felt secure. Now our security has been shattered. We have never liked Russian rule. We don't like it now. Only we are small, we are few in numbers. Will the Russians listen to us? They are so many. They don't have to. But one thing I can assure you. They will not be able to treat us the way they treat others. We won't allow it."

"But surely," I said, "you can see that things are improving now. Right?"

"Yes," he conceded, "we all feel that a change is taking place, a definite change. How far it will go, where it will lead—we don't know. I don't think that even Khrushchev knows."

When we finally said goodbye hours later, my student friend was crying. He embraced me. He asked, with tears, if I could please promise him that Georgia one day would be free of Russian control, and that America would help Georgia. I wanted to say yes, if only to make him feel better, but I said no—I could make no such promise.

In the hotel lobby after dinner I met a group of Czech tourists, and we went for a walk around town. No Intourist guide accompanied us. The Czechs spoke with amazing candor, as though they were not from a country that is a member of the Warsaw Pact, the military alliance controlled by the Soviet Union. We spoke in English. They did not know Russian and seemed in no rush to learn it. They said they had to travel in groups; individual travel was strictly forbidden. They did not need passports to travel to the Soviet Union, and they were surprised that Soviet citizens needed internal passports to travel from one republic to another, from Russia to Georgia, for example.

It was a short walk from the hotel to the central square, but it did not take long for the Czechs to express their "shock at the poverty, misery and unhappiness" of the Georgian people. They described Tbilisi as "shabby." I disagreed. I thought it was one of the best-looking cities in the whole country.

"In comparison to Czechoslovakia," one tourist said, "the Soviet Union is a very poor country." In the last few years, since Stalin's death, the standard of living in Czechoslovakia had improved "100-fold," I was told.

"Look," another tourist remarked, "we are here now. This we could not do two years ago. Now we want to travel west. We want to go to Paris or London. We want Prague to be a part of Europe again. Now we have the feeling it is a part of the East, and not the West, and Prague is the West." Bluntly they stated that their government was an "Eastern imposition." In parting they said, "Let us pray that times will get still better, and we can even travel to America. We all know what Wilson's call for national self-determination did for us, and we never forget the kindness of America."

———

I sat on a park bench near the hotel. An old woman was seated nearby. She looked at me once and then twice and asked, "You are a Russian *stilyag*?" *Stilyag* was the unflattering name for a sharply dressed Russian.

"No," I said and smiled. "I'm an American."

"Good," she replied, obviously pleased. "We don't like Russians here, and we certainly don't like those two fat fools."

She seemed proud of her candor. I assumed that the "two fat fools" were Khrushchev and Bulganin.

———

I was determined on my last day in Tbilisi to ride the old trolley up a mountain to the very top, 650 feet from ground level. When my guide and I left the hotel at 8:00 a.m. the sky was still gray and the clouds heavy over the surrounding peaks, but the city was already active. The trolley had been a Tbilisi landmark for half a century. The seats were rickety, but the conductor, a nice-looking woman with a ready smile, seemed perfectly competent to get us to the top and back. Halfway up we saw an attractive white church standing solitary on a mountain perch. I realized immediately that it was the place where Stalin's mother, who died in the early 1930s, was buried, as well as the Russian poet Alexander Griboyedov. The conductor promised that we could stop there on the way down. At the top was a restaurant and, behind it, a lovely park. "In the evening," my guide told me, "many young people come here. It is so dark, and so quiet, and so beautiful, that we lose track of time, me and my girl friend." He blushed.

The view was spectacular, even on a cloudy day. I could see the Kura River twisting through the city, stone bridges arcing from one riverbank to the other. The old part of Tbilisi, carved into the mountainside, came into stunning relief, the newer part much less so. From this altitude the cars looked like beetles and the people like ants. "This is truly a pretty city," I said, turning to my guide. "Yes, it is," he replied. "It is also a city of legends."

"Legends?" I said. "Tell me one."

"What the old women say, including my grandma, is that many years ago, in the fifth century, the king of Mtskheta was hunting in this area. One day he spotted a stag and fired an arrow into his chest. Blood spurted from the wound. The stag rubbed up against a tree, got the arrow out of his chest, and then leaped into one of the warm springs around here. A few minutes later, the stag jumped out of the water and raced into the woods. There was no sign of blood, no wound, nothing. The king was amazed and decided to move his capital to Tbilisi, the city of miraculous warm springs." He then added, "The Russians, when they came here, could not pronounce Tbilisi very well. They changed the name to Tiflis, but now it is once again Tbilisi."

We walked over to a mound of heavy rocks. Water trickled out of them. "Another legend," the guide continued, "is that deep in the night blind people come here, and let the water from these rocks drip, drop by drop, into their eyes, and then they can see again." He must have seen a look of skepticism on my face. "It is the legend," he assured me. "The Georgian people are a simple people who believe in legends and superstitions. Not so much in the city, but in the countryside."

On the way down, as promised, we stopped at the white church. Up close it was not as beautiful as it appeared from afar. Built in the twelfth century, the church hid a small graveyard. Side by side were two tombstones, romantically linked—one to the poet Griboyedov, the other to his young bride. Griboyedov, serving as Russian ambassador to the Persian court in Teheran, was killed by an anti-Russian mob, and his bride arranged for his body to be returned and buried in Tbilisi, the city he loved. On top of his coffin was the figure of a young woman leaning against a cross, tears in her eyes. Beneath her was an inscription in which the unhappy bride asks an unanswerable question: "Your works and deeds are immortal in the memory of Russia. Then why has my love outlived you?"

Buried nearby was Stalin's mother. Her gravestone was simple, made of black marble. A small crowd had gathered around it, a tribute as much to her son as to her. Apparently this was a common sight.

■

With the clock ticking down on my stay in Tbilisi, I wanted to visit one more place, Tbilisi State University, where the pro-Stalin rebellion had originated the previous March. I took a cab to the handsome, tree-lined campus. Classes were just then beginning for a new academic year. Girls entered the large courtyard, walking arm-in-arm with other girls, pretending to ignore the glances of the young men standing to one side and whispering to one another. I heard only Georgian with an occasional Russian expression thrown into a conversation. Everything seemed perfectly normal, a campus like any other, yet the previous March it had sparked a bloody rebellion against Soviet authority. Anti-Soviet resentment lingered among many of the students, I was told, but they appeared to be corralled behind a common need to be practical and get on with their lives.

My experience on Soviet campuses was that, like the Pied Piper in the Robert Browning poem, I would be quickly surrounded by a crowd of students and pummeled with questions. I walked around the campus for a few minutes, to see and be seen, and then I sat down on a bench and waited for the inevitable to happen. Five, ten minutes passed; fifteen, twenty minutes passed, and nothing happened. I noticed groups of young men gathering nearby, looking at me, but no one approached me.

Finally, one young man, apparently betting I was not a Georgian, called out a question to me in his native language. I shrugged my shoulders. I did not understand him. The young man then shouted something to his friends that must have been the equivalent of "I told you so," and a crowd quickly began forming around me, dozens of young men firing questions at me about Stalin and Marx, baseball and football, housing and clothing, Eisenhower and Stevenson. This extraordinary Q and A ended five hours later, and it ended then only because I had to catch a train to Sochi, my next stop. Otherwise, it could have continued through dinnertime.

Later, on the train, I reflected on the differences between Russian and Georgian students. First, the Georgians were so nationalistic they took offense at any criticism of their country. They defended Georgia as if it were heaven on earth, though they knew better. Most Russians, on the other hand, invited criticism of their country and its communist system. If they thought your criticism did not go far enough, they would rush to fill in the blanks. Second, for Georgians criticism of Stalin was unacceptable. He was sacred, untouchable, a god. For Russians Stalin was suddenly a juicy target for all forms of criticism. He was evil incarnate, a political and ideological curse to be expunged from Soviet society. Finally, Georgian students seemed cocky, self-confident, unafraid, much more so than Russian students. The Georgians conveyed the impression that they controlled their own destiny. Russian students seemed to know better.

One subject—the "Negro question," as it was often framed at the time—was on the top of their minds that day. *Pravda* had run a disturbing story about riots in Clinton, Tennessee. These Georgian students were convinced that America was a racist country. Their questions were sharp, their attitude confrontational. In my responses, I tried to be honest. I acknowledged the problem and provided some historical context. I told them about the 1954 Supreme Court decision desegregating public schools, which they knew nothing about. I told them about Lincoln, the Civil War, carpetbaggers, and Truman's integration of the armed forces. Again they knew little about this history.

My candor seemed to disarm them. When our conversation shifted to their next big question—fingerprinting in the United States—their questions were less pointed.

"Why did the United States insist on fingerprinting Soviet exchange artists and students?" they asked.

"It's the law," I said. Just as Soviet law prescribed internal passports, American law insisted on fingerprinting foreign visitors. "That is the law," I repeated, adding, "If a Russian really wanted to visit the United States to understand us better, he would not permit the fingerprinting issue to stand in his way." I described Khrushchev's blistering criticism of the American practice of fingerprinting Soviet visitors, which I had heard at the Queen's birthday party at the British embassy a few months earlier. I thought they would like to hear that the Soviet leader agreed with them.

"Don't mention that man's name in this country," a student snapped. Khrushchev, by attacking Stalin and his legacy, had become persona non grata in Georgia.

No matter what the subject, whether it be "the Negro question" or American fingerprinting, we always somehow returned to Stalin. "Tell me," asked another student, standing in the rear of the crowd, "what do Americans really think of Stalin?"

I told him the truth. "Americans don't think much of Stalin," I replied, "and when they do, they disagree with his policy."

"But certainly you consider him a great and noble person?"

"No, actually they consider him to be a cruel dictator." The students gasped in disbelief. "When the history books on the twentieth century are written," I continued, "Stalin will play a major role. But we do not think he was a noble person, nor that he was a good person."

"Well, what do they think of Marx?"

"In truth, I must say we do not even think about Marx." The students laughed, breaking the building tension. "Marx was a major political theoretician," I went on, "but we believe that his system has been disproved time and again by the facts of history."

Still another student interjected, "One must admit, whether you are a capitalist or not, that Stalin made many, many creative additions to Marxism and Leninism."

I shook my head. "You may consider them creative," I said, "but few others do."

The student continued, "Well, but you must admit that reading Stalin on linguistics is a truly fascinating experience. He was so brilliant. He could write on anything. He knew everything." I almost choked on the thought of having to read Stalin on linguistics. "He certainly was interesting," I said, trying to soothe ruffled feathers. "Interesting, indeed."

"Do you think Stalin was guilty of creating a personality cult?" another student asked. "Some people even say that pictures of Stalin are being removed throughout the Soviet Union." He looked at me incredulously. "These things they cannot do. These things they must not do."

When I told the students that I myself had seen pictures and paintings of Stalin being removed from museums, they angrily said no, they did not believe me. "That is not true," one shouted. Another added, "You simply can't remove Stalin without also removing Lenin. Both were inseparable in life, and Stalin was faithful to Lenin. In many ways, he was even better than Lenin. After all, he built the Soviet Union, not Lenin. A Georgian did this, not a Russian. No, this is quite impossible."

The students stood united behind Stalin, leaning on his close association with Lenin as backup support. I thought I saw an opening. "Russians are once again the rulers of the Soviet Union, and they are returning to Lenin and Leninism. Even here in your own *Zarya Vostoka* [a Georgian newspaper], they write about the harm done by the personality cult."

The student responded, "Those who write about the harm of the personality cult are toadies, who keep thinking that our fate is tied in with Russia. The Russians came here in 1801. Since then, nothing creative has taken place here. Now it is my opinion that we are starting to think again. Even in the arts." He mentioned that Georgians are again studying their history and trying to rekindle the flames of their renaissance. With a mournful air, he concluded, "But yes, we have a lot of catching up to do."

I made a point of shaking hands with every student in the small crowd around me, expressing the hope that one day they would all be free, and then I raced to the hotel for my bag and then to the train for Sochi.

Why Sochi? Because, from the moment I started planning this trip, I put Sochi in the must-see category. My reasoning was simple: it was close to Tbilisi; it was on my way back to Moscow; and, most important, it was Stalin's favorite resort. He rarely missed a chance to vacation in Sochi during the brutal Moscow winters. He pumped hundreds of millions of rubles into this stretch of beachfront on the edge of Russia closest to Georgia, his birthplace. More than anyone else, Stalin turned Sochi, once an unimportant beach town, into one of the best resorts in the Soviet Union, a place on Russia's riviera where the new true blue bloods of communism could spend their holidays. Foreign diplomats and businessmen would also want to vacation there, partly to rub shoulders with Soviet bigwigs and partly to enjoy Sochi's incomparable beauty. Temperatures in the summertime rarely rose higher than the mid-eighties, and in the wintertime they were always in the moderate range. It was Russia's Camelot, and I wanted to see it.

I knew the broad outlines of its history. After a Russian-Turkish war in the late 1820s (there were many such wars during the eighteenth and nineteenth centuries, as both nations struggled for control of the Black Sea coastline), Russia ran its flag, famous for its two-headed eagle, up the Sochi flagpole. It has remained there ever since, even though throughout much of this time Russia has had to battle local Muslim tribesmen for actual control of the city and the region. Not until 1874, for example, did the Russians feel comfortable enough to build an Orthodox church in Sochi. Normally that would have been at the top of their to-do list.

Soon after entering my train compartment, where I was hoping I would be able to type up my notes on my Tbilisi visit, I met my compartment mate, a friendly, talkative, middle-aged assistant economics planner for the Georgian republic. At first I thought that he would be the perfect companion: quiet, self-contained and cautious with a foreigner. I was wrong. Within minutes he was telling me his reason for traveling to Sochi (he was going there to pick up his wife and son, who had been there for the summer), his narrow, negative judgment of America, and his bright vision of communism. He was not a communist, but he talked like one, never more noticeably than in his description of America, which sounded like it had been lifted from a tired editorial in *Pravda*. Why, he started like a rocket off the launchpad, the "persecution" of Paul Robeson; the "murder" of "innocent Negroes"; the "hounding" of Jews; the "growing impoverishment of the working class"; the "forced imposition" of private cars and homes on workers, who, unable to pay the high fees, become "enslaved" to their "bosses," whom he compared to the "ancient warlords" of China; the "inability" of young Americans to get a proper education; the "need" of the American government to start "wars of aggression" to save their "failing economies" from total collapse; and, finally, the "fact," as he put it, that Americans soldiers were "unleashed" on the public to "rape women in the streets and chew gum."

By the time he completed his nutty assault on America, I was ready to scream, punch him in the face, denounce Soviet communism, and move to a new compartment, if one was available, but—not wanting to create a diplomatic scene—I stuffed my temper into a duffel bag and softly suggested that since we were approaching the midnight hour, it might make sense for us to go to sleep. My companion wouldn't hear of it. He ordered two glasses of tea and cookies and resumed his assault on the United States.

When he paused for a moment to sip on his tea, I leaped in. "Look," I said, "we are not going to agree on anything. Listening to you, I think I am listening to a very bad *Pravda* editorial. Enough. Let's take a nap."

He responded, "No need for such sharp words. We are just talking."

What I found interesting was the tone of his voice—level, unemotional, sounding like a parent patiently explaining something to a child who was not very bright. Finally, unable any longer to contain my anger, I erupted. I used Khrushchev's own denunciations of Stalin and the Soviet system to make my point.

My companion seemed to wilt for an instant. "True," he admitted, "we have made mistakes. But"—his eyes lit up—"now we are correcting them." This open admission of mistakes was now the official fallback position. He continued, "Communism is the wave of the future. It will triumph everywhere, even in the United States."

I told him that he was misreading history. "Communism will never come to the United States," I said. My companion laughed at me; he seemed completely sincere, and there was no rancor or bitterness in his manner. He believed that what he said was true. He had seen the future, and it belonged to him. The zigs and zags of today were only bumps on the road to communism tomorrow.

The hours dragged on. I fell asleep twice during his rhetorical flirtation with history. At 4:30 a.m. I appealed to his better nature. "Let us get a few hours of sleep, please." He agreed, reluctantly.

I awoke close to 8:00 a.m., and my Georgian commissar was already up and ready for combat.

"No," I pleaded with him, "Let's talk about Sochi. What should I be sure to see when I get there?"

My companion was disappointed. "Don't you want to continue our talk?" he asked.

"No," I said. "I would rather talk about Sochi, baseball, or literature, but not politics. There is no common ground in our thinking. There is just a big gap, and every time you spout the communist line straight out of yesterday's *Pravda*, this gap only grows wider and wider."

My companion literally scratched his head. "I don't understand you," he said. "You defend a system that is dying. You justify racial terrorism, and you deny that communism will conquer the world."

I begged him. "Please, let us just sit quietly, not argue about politics, and watch the scenery."

To my surprise he agreed, and for the next few hours, until we reached the Sochi railroad station at 10:30 a.m., we looked out the window in silence as the train descended from the mountains to a rail line along the shore of the Black Sea, deep blue under the rising sun. To my right the Caucasus seemed to leap from the landscape to the sky, disturbed, it seemed, only by an occasional cloud. Along the way we passed fishing villages, and I could see people lounging on the beach, others swimming in the sea.

The closer we got to Sochi, the more sanatoriums I saw. This was the place for sanatoriums. Every ministry, every industry or enterprise, had a right to build a sanatorium for its workers, and they all built them along the Black Sea coastline. Every worker therefore had a theoretical right to go to a sanatorium for his or her vacation, assuming of course that there was room, which was not always the case. The Red Army sanatorium was among the largest, built into the mountainside and looking out over the sea. It took no genius to understand why Stalin would choose to spend so much of his time here and why Khrushchev and Bulganin (the "two fat fools") would vacation here too. Why not? It was lovely.

No Intourist guide was at the station to meet me, which I found refreshing. I took a cab to the Primorskaya Hotel, set on a high hill overlooking the crowded beach. It was the hotel for foreign diplomats. The ride there took thirty minutes. Sochi was small and charming. Semi-tropical trees grew everywhere. The stores were crowded, the restaurants were filled, the streets were clean. The women, in Soviet-style bikinis, were buxom and bronzed—all in all, quite a sight.

After checking in, I walked down to the beach to take a swim, and there stumbled upon my first disappointment. The beach, though breathtakingly beautiful, was covered with a rug of rocks and pebbles, and though Russians had no problem walking on the beach, I had a huge problem, which made it difficult for me to get to the water. But I did anyway and loved my first swim in the Black Sea.

At dinner, shared with a number of visiting Americans, I met two Soviet students, a lovely young woman from Kuibyshev and a young man from Rostov. Both were finishing a two-week vacation before returning to school. She was in engineering, he in economics. I asked her whether there were many women in the engineering field. Her friend jumped into the conversation. "Of course," he said. "Women in this country do the same work as men, and get paid the same."

At first, the woman nodded in agreement, but then after a moment of reflection, flatly contradicted her friend. "Actually," she said, "only 15 percent of the students at my oil institute are women, and most of them, when they finish, get desk jobs and rarely go out into the field." The economist decided there was no point in getting into an embarrassing argument with his friend—he knew she was right—so he raised a toast to "peace and friendship," his way of changing the subject. I thought his suggestion was diplomatic, and his timing perfect, and we happily joined him.

He did want to make a point, though. "Last night we met a young American in this restaurant, and he told us that everything in the Soviet Union was bad, that women dressed poorly, that the food was terrible. And we began to think that all Americans were like him. This is very bad. If he does not like us, why does he come here? Why doesn't he just go home? To us, this is the finest, the best country in the world. Granted, we have seen no other country, but we have this confidence. Maybe we are right. Maybe we are wrong, but this is what most of us believe. He is a guest here. He should respect our feelings." I told him that I fully agreed with him, and that I hoped he would be able to meet many more Americans. We raised another toast to "peace and friendship."

I remembered what an embassy colleague told me about the courtesies Americans ought to show while traveling in the Soviet Union these days. "Every American tourist," he cautioned, "is a kind of poster child of American life. This year and next, they ought to be handpicked. It's that important." He believed that 1956, the year of the thaw, was potentially historic, perhaps in his judgment the beginning of the end of Soviet communism, and every American had to be especially careful to let history take its course and not rock the boat.

I spent the next day as the perfect tourist. Immediately after breakfast, no matter how rocky the beach, I made my way cautiously to the water's edge and did what any self-respecting Soviet vacationer would do—I plunged into the Black Sea. The water was cool, and I thoroughly enjoyed my swim. I then dedicated myself to the worship of the sun, hoping that in an hour or two I could become as bronzed as the Russians—an impossible task, but that still didn't discourage me from trying. In the afternoon, after a quick lunch, I rented a car with a driver for a ride to the highest observation point in the region. The view of the mountains, rolling, deep green, was awe-inspiring, and the Black Sea looked blue near the shoreline and purple farther out. Mother Nature had done a splendid job, creating a nest of beauty.

My plane back to Moscow was scheduled to leave the following day at 11:40 a.m., a proper time for departure. My monthlong summertime journey through central Asia and the Caucasus was rushing to an end.

The plane made two stops. The first was Rostov-on-Don, where the sky was beginning to cloud over. The second was Kharkov, where it had begun to rain. Moscow, when I got there, was cold, rainy, and dreary, and once again I needed my coat, scarf, and hat, which I found in my duffel bag and which sent me into uncontrollable laughter. In the morning, hot and lovely Sochi; in the evening, cold and dreary Moscow. The Soviet Union was a very large country, filled with dozens of different tribes and nationalities. Once it began to crumble, warned my Harvard professor Richard Pipes, it would be hard, if not impossible, to put the pieces back together again. It had not then begun to crumble, but after this trip I understood, perhaps for the first time, how inherently fragile this seemingly cohesive and powerful nation was.

CHAPTER TWELVE

Back to a Familiar Chill

Very quickly I returned to earth. The glorious scenery of Sochi, the mountain legends of Tbilisi, and the sandy, troublesome history of Samarkand and Bukhara receded reluctantly into my memory bank as a vacation well spent. The moment I got back to the Kremlinology of JPRS and the U.S. embassy, I realized that the "thaw," which had generated so much hope for meaningful change, was now in retreat. Ever since Khrushchev at the 20th Party Congress had delivered his historic attack on Stalin's policies and personality, the country had been in a state of dizzying confusion. Could one really criticize the party and its leaders with impunity? How much freedom would Khrushchev actually allow? Could a dictatorship be dismantled, step by step, and still be a dictatorship? In short, had the "thaw" gone too far? And if it had, was it not time to throttle back? Left unanswered, such questions fueled deeper doubts within and outside the party. At the embassy it was assumed that a climactic battle had erupted in the Kremlin between Khrushchev on one side and such hard-liners as Molotov on the other. Which side would ultimately prevail? Bets were placed, but no one could yet collect a kopeck. One sensed that de-Stalinization might be rumbling off the rails, Russia might be losing its guiding compass, and something had to be done. But what?

Rummaging through old papers from October 1956 while preparing this memoir, I came upon clear examples of a country in modest retrenchment, yet clinging to the hope that greater freedom was still possible, including better relations with the West, especially the United States:

- Fifty American millionaires arrived in Moscow to explore increasing trade and investment opportunities. They were well received, optimistic, and determined to do business.

- Two students at Moscow University were expelled after voicing criticism of government policy at a meeting called expressly for that purpose. They later disappeared. No explanations were offered.

- Shortly after Khrushchev's de-Stalinization speech, the Kremlin circulated two letters to all party officials, which stated that open criticism of party and state "shortcomings" and "high-handedness" was not only to be tolerated but also encouraged. Then a third letter was circulated that contradicted the message of the two previous letters: now such criticism was to be discouraged. Criticism of the party and its leaders needed to be constrained.

- Molotov, who had opposed Khrushchev's de-Stalinization policy and, as a result, lost his job as foreign minister, was just appointed to a new job: head of a state commission to determine the acceptable cultural and ideological limits on the new "freedoms" marking the Khrushchev era. Everyone assumed Molotov had just been given authority to cut back on those freedoms.

☙ An old, sad feature of Stalinism was the widespread practice of snitching on family members and neighbors. If you heard anyone criticize Stalin, the party, or the state, you had an obligation to inform your local communist cell. One out of every ten workers in a factory had that responsibility. At the 20th Party Congress this practice was publicly denounced and most Russians breathed a sigh of relief. It has now been brought back. Apparently, the party did not appreciate the avalanche of criticism generated by the 20th Party Congress.

☙ I heard this story from a Russian friend. At a recent party meeting at a Moscow factory, where workers were told that criticism was officially encouraged, a worker rose and criticized his foreman. His courage was applauded, even by the foreman. The following week, the worker's norm—the amount of work he or she was expected to do—was arbitrarily tripled. Every worker had a norm, which had to be fulfilled. This worker was already working at peak capacity, but according to his new norm he was producing only one-third of what was expected of him. As a result, his salary was effectively cut to one-third of what it had been. The net effect of this worker's criticism: (1) his salary was cut; (2) his status as a top-flight worker was undermined; (3) he was forced into a position where he had either to recant or quit (he recanted). Result: no further criticism.

Strung together, these vignettes suggested a regime edging toward a major crackdown. By the late summer of 1956 the Kremlin learned that freedom of speech in the form of criticism, even sanctioned criticism, was intoxicating and could, if unchecked, undermine the foundations of a modern totalitarian state. Although Khrushchev continued to believe in his policy of de-Stalinization, he also realized that it had a dangerous, corrosive effect on his own power base and therefore had to be contained. In fact, in a short time Khrushchev faced a Molotov-led challenge that came close to ousting him from power.

"Religion is the sigh of the oppressed creature," wrote Karl Marx, whose work inspired the Russian Revolution, "the heart of a heartless world, and the soul of soulless conditions. It is the opium of the people." In Russia, no force except perhaps nationalism was more powerful than religion, which made official communist preaching of atheism so foolish and counterproductive. During World War II, when Stalin needed to galvanize the Soviet peoples to fight Nazi Germany, he soft-pedaled atheism and, with drums and flourishes, returned the Russian Orthodox Church to its central role in the life of the Soviet people, a role that it has never lost since the war. (Up to that time, Stalin never spent a kopeck to rebuild mosques or resuscitate Islam, which he and other Russian leaders always distrusted.)

In October 1956 I paid a visit to Zagorsk, home of the famous Trinity Monastery. I saw the continuing power of the Orthodox Church in Russian life. On October 8, a special day of prayer in the Russian Orthodox Church, thousands of Russians young and old crowded into Zagorsk to celebrate the 650th anniversary of the death of St. Sergius. To gain admission to the Troitsky–Sergieva Lavra monastery, whose fourteenth-century walls were covered with golden icons honoring the revered saint, they had to wait for many hours, and they did so with remarkable patience. Once inside they were enveloped in both melodic prayer and incense wafting from colorful censers being swung by priests wearing gold and purple robes and dark stovepipe hats, called *kamilavki*. They sang a prayer known to anyone who has ever been in a Russian church, "*Gospodi pomiluy*," "God have mercy," repeatedly crossing themselves and listening to church bells ringing with enchanting regularity, like background music for their prayers. Hundreds of candles burned on small altars, and in a private chapel, opened specially for this occasion, was a delicately sculptured water fountain. A priest stood to one side, with one hand blessing the believers, the other dispensing holy water to many in the crowd appealing for help to cure incurable ailments. Some came with cups. Those so blessed with drops of holy water seemed rapturous, as though each drop was a personal gift from God.

Outside, large groups of schoolchildren in gray uniforms waited for their turn to enter the church. They talked among themselves. They, too, waited patiently. Even the weather was in a festive mood, the sun shining brightly on this scene of religious observance with an unusual warmth for early October.

Watching this impressive spectacle of religious devotion, evidence of a total failure of the state's official policy of atheism, I recalled a scene at a Moscow church a few blocks from the Kremlin only a week before. It was not an unusual scene. A small group of young Russians was being baptized. Parents beamed with pride and pleasure. As a visiting American with more than a passing knowledge of Russian history I watched and observed, and asked myself: "Could this have been much different fifty years ago, one hundred years ago, even two hundred years ago?" I did not think so. There are certain constants in every society. Religion was a constant in Russian society.

I also recalled a conversation with Valya, a twenty-seven-year-old Russian who worked at a Western embassy in Moscow. She told me with a mix of pride and joy that for the first time in her adult life she had attended services at her neighborhood church the previous Sunday. She and her husband had never attended church services. "We saw no reason to," she explained. "Our friends never did either." But her four-year-old son, Volodya, once asked her a question she could not answer. He usually went to church with his grandmother, Valya's mother, a very religious woman.

One Sunday Volodya returned from church services to find his mother sitting in the kitchen in her nightgown. "Momma," he said, "why don't you go to church? Everyone I know does. And Granny goes; so why don't you and Poppa?" Valya felt she could not tell Volodya that she did not believe in God—that would have raised too many questions. So she promised that she would go to church with him and Granny the following Sunday.

On that day she got up early, dressed, and with her mother and son attended services at their neighborhood church. "And do you know what?" she said, a broad smile on her face. "I enjoyed every minute of it. It was like when I was young all over again. I liked it, and I am going to go again. All thanks to my little Volodyushka." A moment later, she added as an unhappy footnote that her husband did not attend services, and would not. He remained the family's atheist, arguing privately that it was better that way if he wanted to maintain his privileged position at his factory.

I met Katya at the Lenin Library during one of my many visits to do research on my favorite minister of education, Sergei Semyonovich Uvarov. She was not only the librarian but also the deputy director of the local chapter of Komsomol, the Soviet youth organization. She was tall and pleasant, with a warm, welcoming smile, and she invited me to a Komsomol ball, one of several sponsored by the library in anticipation of 1957 World Youth Festival in Moscow. I was surprised and delighted to accept. I arrived at the new wing of the Lenin Library at exactly the right time.

The entryway was crowded and festooned with balloons, and on the walls surrounding an enormous stairwell leading to the second floor hung the flags of the Soviet Union and the fifteen Soviet republics. Hundreds of young Russians ignored the flags as, looking forward to the dance, they hurried upstairs to the ballroom. The women wore very tight, transparent blouses, the rage in Moscow at the time, and the men wore the uniforms of neighborhood military academies. A four-piece band played American jazz, and many danced to the quick, exciting tunes. Those who for whatever reason did not dance stood, watched, and gossiped on the sidelines. It was not uncommon for women to dance together, but men never did. Katya had organized the dance and entertainment with Teutonic precision—she was a very impressive young lady—and everyone seemed to be having a delightful time, even though, in their conversations with me, they could not conceal a deep inferiority complex.

They kept asking me, "Do you like our ball?"

"Do you like the way we dance?"

"Do we dance as you do in America?"

"Is our clothing nicely tailored?"

"Is the band all right?"

"Does it play like your small bands?"

"Is the vocalist good, up to your standard?"

"Does he sing the Latin numbers as you do in America?"

And always: "Please be frank and tell us what you do and don't like." There was no reason to be defensive.

When it ended, Katya found me in the crush and politely escorted me to the exit. "Good night," she said, shaking my hand vigorously, as though she had just completed a successful diplomatic mission. "I hope you had a good time."

"Yes, indeed," I replied, "and thank you so much." If I entertained the thought, for just a moment, that this friendship might blossom into something more personal, Katya killed it by spinning around and vanishing into the crowd.

Nikolai Pogodin was a Soviet playwright of no particular distinction. His play *Kremlyovskiye Kuranty*—roughly, *The Chimes of the Kremlin*—was popular, in part because it was being performed by Moscow's top theater, the Moscow Art Theater. The play was set in 1920, and the leading male character was Lenin, always courteous and compassionate, brilliant and kind.

A young Russian dressed in Western garb applauded wildly whenever the actor playing Lenin appeared on stage. He poked me in the ribs. "It's true, isn't it," he asked, "that Lenin was the greatest man of the twentieth century?" I paused, realizing there was no point in debating Lenin's role in history with a Russian so committed to the party line. He continued, content with his reverie, "Even the most biased Westerner must admit Lenin's genius, for he was indeed the greatest man of the twentieth century." The Russian, whose name was Kostya, short for Constantine, smoked American cigarettes and loved the new American monthly called *Amerika*, 50,000 copies of which had just been published and distributed. They sold out overnight. As we left the theater, walking into a drizzly night, he complimented me by calling me a *shtatny baron*, which in Moscow at the time meant a "classy guy from the United States."

Kostya wanted to talk. All I had to do was listen. We talked for a long time. He was a compelling character, with an interesting story, and I tried to remember every word. Later that evening I typed it all up. "I have had an easy life," he said. "My father is a topflight engineer, and he makes a lot of money. I have never been in need of anything. We have always had the two most important things in Soviet Russia: money and connections." He told me that during the summer he had spent three months in the "virgin lands" of central Asia "gathering in the harvest," as he put it. He was especially proud of his decision. "Most of my friends did not wish to go to Siberia, but I did." He wanted to help the people. "I want to see them live much better than they do now." Then, sounding like the nineteenth-century *narodniki*—the guilt-stricken, idealistic young noblemen who went to the countryside to educate the peasants, to teach them the virtues of democracy, only to see their efforts spurned by the "dark masses"—he explained, "I wanted to talk to the peasants, to tell them what is their due, what they should expect from the [communist] system. . . . We went to the people." I reminded Kostya that in their day many of the *narodniki* returned from the farms disappointed and despondent, believing the peasants to be hopelessly locked in their own small worlds, unable or unwilling to learn about the revolutionary changes rushing through their country. "I hope that will not be your experience," I said.

Kostya and I walked along Gorky Street, which was almost empty because of the dispiriting drizzle. Occasionally a woman covered in a heavy shawl would pop out of a doorway, look around, and then disappear. "Possibly, you are right," Kostya whispered. He seemed deep in his own thoughts. "You see, we have a society that is based on good, humanitarian principles, but that functions on base, narrow principles," he continued. "The entire administration stinks of bureaucracy. Fat bureaucrats with fat mugs and fatter rears sit around for weeks, months, years, simply fulfilling quotas." Kostya spat in disgust, stopping for a moment at the foot of the Pushkin statue.

"All my life my father has brought such people into our house. Are they interested in the principles of the revolution? No, they are interested only in themselves. They want more money and a second dacha and maybe a second car. These are the people I have seen all my life, and I must admit my father is the same way. I still believe in the principles, which I feel sure Lenin believed in. I want to see our people happy."

"How will they be happy?" I asked.

Kostya focused on the Russian peasant. "The way my friends and I view our country—Russia is still a peasant country. About 65 percent of the people are peasants. These are the people the government should be concerned about. But instead they push them into collective farms, which they couldn't care less about. They want their own little piece of land. They want to be masters of their fates and their harvests. They want to deliver grain to a person, a dealer, who they know and can talk to, not a collective agency. . . . And, you know, this is the strangest thing: from birth, people are taught to think and to act in a collective way. Yet the farmers only want their plot of land. They couldn't care less about the collective land."

Kostya felt he was speaking for his generation. "Our feeling, and I mean the feeling of the overwhelming majority of my friends at the institute," he continued, "is that the peasants, the ordinary people, must begin to get a fair portion of our national production and profit. This has not happened to date, and it is about time. The Soviet system has existed for thirty-eight years—soon we shall celebrate our thirty-ninth anniversary—and still there are enormous shortages. How many times can we be told to wait until tomorrow?"

"Well, how many times indeed?" I asked.

"I don't know. My friends don't know. And I'm sure that Khrushchev, 'the sorcerer's apprentice,' as we call him, doesn't know either, just as nobody in Russia these days has a real image of the future. Lenin had his image. His image was prosperity for all people, but his image has been distorted by Stalin and his friends, like the present collective leadership."

Kostya was an idealist, a kind, decent, and intelligent young Russian who tied his dreams of political and economic prosperity to a totally unrealistic reading of Lenin's policies and plans. Lenin wanted power to achieve revolutionary change in Russia and then the world. His vision was communist by design and universal in application. Kostya's was more modestly limited to Russia. He understood that something was profoundly wrong with Russia's system of government. He did not want to go so far as to repudiate the system, for that would have meant repudiating Lenin himself, for many young Russians an unimaginable idea at the time. But he did want to see fundamental reform. He did not know quite how to define the reform, nor how to achieve it, but he yearned for it with a passion he could not quite contain.

Kostya then told me about a recent meeting at the Institute of Art, where he studied. The meeting sounded similar to meetings I had attended at the Lenin Library. The meeting as Kostya described it was run by a "very sharp" communist leader named Ivanov. It started in a traditional way. The leader listed the "new tasks" facing students "today, tomorrow and the day after." In fact, they were not new at all—they were the usual tasks of yesterday and the day before. "We all knew them by heart."

Then an older student stood up, "a man of about thirty-five who had been wounded six times during the big war." He wanted to know "what he had fought for."

Ivanov answered, predictably, that the older student "had fought for Russia and the Soviet system."

"No," the student shot back, "I fought only for Russia. I did not fight for the Soviet system." Kostya said that he and his friends broke into loud cheers.

Ivanov felt the need to restore order. "The reason things are not really so right in Russia today," Kostya quoted him as explaining, "is that many mistakes had been made, but they are all now being corrected." Sighing, Ivanov said, "It is the fault of the Stalin tragedy."

One student yelled out, "That is no answer. A Marxist explanation demands that the system itself is at fault." Kostya continued, "All the students then stood up, stamped their feet and shouted that Ivanov indeed had not really answered the question which was raised." Ivanov decided at that moment that it would be the better part of valor to say nothing more. He hurriedly collected his notes, stashed them into his briefcase, and left the room. "Fled the room" might have been a more accurate description.

Kostya and a group of students then went to a friend's house and continued their discussion. "We ranged over the entire issue," Kostya disclosed. "Some of my buddies called for inciting an uprising. Others called for assassination of the leaders and the convocation of a representative government. But others, and I am one of these, thought force and violence would get us nowhere. If I thought that it would, I swear to God I would go to Red Square tonight with all my friends and stage an uprising. But it would yield no beneficial results." Again he paused, deep in his own thoughts. "The Russian people are a frightfully inert mass," he said. "They do not move easily. And we cannot do it alone. There must be a way, but so far we don't know the way. We have no image of tomorrow. All we want is a happy Russia where people get a fair share of a powerful industrial machine, but the bureaucracy stands in the way. What we need now is leadership. We need another Lenin desperately. He could lead a revolution. Without leadership, we are nothing, and our dreams remain dreams."

We continued our walk along empty streets, each of us absorbed in the power of Kostya's diatribe. We passed the Marx-Engels-Lenin Institute, which until recently had been called the Marx-Engels-Stalin Institute, which prompted Kostya to observe, "You know, we call this place 'The Institute for Black Magic.' Here anything can happen. Even Trotsky can be rehabilitated tomorrow morning. All of history can be rewritten. It is like black magic. It can do anything."

Kostya's face suddenly lit up. He remembered a relevant story. He told me he had recently attended a public trial of six Russians accused of illegally selling Western clothing. The prosecutor rested his case on the testimony of a few of the buyers, but the approach backfired. His first witness stated in simple Russian, "I was tired of dressing badly, of living badly. I had a chance to buy a good suit, and I bought it, and I would do it again if I could." Kostya smiled. "What was funny was that all the people who bought this clothing were wealthy Russians who belong to our new aristocracy, just like my father."

"Was there any conviction?"

"No, the trial is still going on. . . . Things happen today which no one thought imaginable when Lenin lived. Most people with money have become just like the bourgeoisie of old. They want material comforts. I guess I myself am no different, for I, too, am a product of this system. The system breeds the people, and I am one of the people. The only people who have not become contaminated by the system are the peasants, because they stand above the system. They are pure."

Kostya was indeed a modern-day *narodnik*, I thought, capable of believing all kinds of fanciful romances about the "pure" peasants and the inevitable improvement in Soviet society once the people rise up from their long slumber. He still believed in a fairy godfather named Lenin and was destined, in my judgment, to be deeply disappointed.

"Are there any great leaders in Russia today?" I asked. "Leaders who stand for the rights and interests of a majority of the people? Aren't Khrushchev and Bulganin able leaders?"

"Let me tell you what they are good for. Khrushchev would make a fine district party leader, and Bulganin, good Mr. Bulganin"—he used the English word "Mister"—"would be better off eating five meals a day, living in a suburban dacha, and reading Pushkin. They are the kind of leaders who met the needs of the Stalin era well. They killed, and slept well afterwards. But these are not the leaders who can meet the challenge of the modern times. Now they rule sort of in between the old and the new, but they don't realize that there is no going back to the old. There is no retreat possible at this time. Only forward movement, only change, and undoubtedly the people of Poland and Hungary have realized this too, for they don't want us there anymore, and I don't blame them."

By this time, Kostya and I had circled back to the Metropole Hotel, where I was certain I could get a cab. It was 2:30 a.m. The rain had stopped but our coats were soaked. We had talked about everything, it seemed, even the historic events in Poland and Hungary, which Kostya knew could affect his life. He was hungry for fresh information, as, I assumed, were his classmates. "What is the latest you have heard?" he wanted to know.

"Well," I began, "earlier this evening on the BBC, I heard—"

Interrupting me, he exclaimed, "We know all that. We also listen to the BBC and the Voice of America. We do so regularly. What I'm asking is, is there anything newer?" I had to disappoint him. I knew nothing newer.

In parting Kostya told me that Polish students at his institute had sent a letter to Wladyslav Gomulka, the new Communist Party leader in Poland, urging him to continue his reforms. They were thrilled by signs that a new nationalism was blooming in Poland. Kostya's friend, Yanka, now insisted on being called Jan, his proper Polish name.

■

If truth was not to be found in *Pravda*, then how would Russians learn the truth about what was happening in Poland, Hungary, and other hot spots in Russia's Eastern European empire? It would be very hard indeed. They could still read Soviet newspapers and try to translate the gobbledygook of Russian reporting from Warsaw and Budapest into something resembling reality. They could listen to Moscow Radio. They could keep their ears cocked, with sensitivity born of experience, to rumor and gossip, which was a full-time industry in Soviet Russia. And Russians with shortwave radios (and there were many) could listen to real news reporting from the BBC and the Voice of America, often late at night, after most of their neighbors had gone to bed.

It was not true that Russians had no information about the bloody riots in Poznan in June or the even bloodier revolt in Budapest and its brutal suppression in early November. They had limited information, much of it distorted, but they still felt shortchanged—they wanted much more, believing after the 20th Party Congress and the Khrushchev de-Stalinization shock that it was time for them to be told the truth after so many years of lies.

I had stumbled upon smatterings of this craving for truth during my many visits to libraries. One evening, in the main reading room of the Lenin Library, I found myself jammed into a rear corner by dozens, maybe hundreds, of Russians, who had come to hear a lecture titled "International Affairs" given by a young, nervous, paper-thin communist official wearing a black suit, with two medals pinned to the lapel of his jacket. The reading room, serving as a lecture hall, was located between the cloakroom and the manuscript room, where I would normally do my research. But on this evening I could not work my way through the crowd, nor did I really try; I let myself be squashed into a corner so that I could unobtrusively hear how the party informed young people about the big news of the day.

The lecturer, who seemed to have a nervous twitch in his right cheek, spoke for the better part of an hour, assiduously reading from his notes and hitting a single theme: that the Soviet Union would maintain a firm policy of peace and cooperation with all countries, regardless of their social or political systems. "Just today," he said, "the glorious Communist Party and Soviet Government expressed their unwavering devotion to the Bandung Conference [of neutralist nations] and the spirit of Bandung in a talk with Mohammed Daud, prime minister of Afghanistan." He continued in this vein, using the standard terminology of the Soviet press. Whenever he used a phrase such as "the glorious, mighty, genius-like Soviet people, who are building communism," everyone around me, without exception, either made sarcastic comments or continued to read their books, magazines, or newspapers.

Toward the end of his talk, the speaker reached for Socratic eloquence to make his pointless points. "Who," he asked, "consistently struggles for peace?" He answered his own question: "The mighty, genius-like Communist Party and Soviet Government, inspired by the great decisions of the 20th Congress of the Communist Party and its Leninist Central Committee." His audience fidgeted, yawned rudely, scratched imaginary bug bites, or restlessly shuffled from one foot to the other.

The lecturer then requested that if anyone had a question, it should be submitted on a small sheet of paper. Notepads had been left in convenient places around the lecture hall for this purpose. The lecturer now riffled through the questions. "They all concern one question—about Poland and Hungary," he announced, obviously disappointed. "Comrades, would it not be better if we discussed the meaning of the 20th Party Congress, or the denunciation of the personality cult, or the decisions of the July plenum of the Central Committee?" He was urging a safer plateau for discussion.

"No," everyone shouted.

"We want to know about Hungary and Poland," one young student said. "Tell us the truth about what's happening there."

The lecturer, twitching still more, responded, "Comrades, the Soviet press has reported the full facts about the recent events in both countries."

Everyone seemed to be shouting at once, "No, no, we have all read the Soviet press. What we want now are the facts, the truth." Near me a student whispered to a friend, "He's on the spot now. I don't envy him. He had better answer."

The lecturer looked down at his notes helplessly, but they provided him with only one answer. "I truly believe, comrades, that we must turn to the 20th Party Congress for answers. There lies the truth."

A student standing near the front of the lecture hall walked toward the lecturer and fearlessly proclaimed, "We are all literate. We read the papers. We know the official line. Now we want to know the truth. We want facts. We want to know what is happening there. Don't repeat for us what is in the press. Tell us what is going on there."

Almost as one, the students burst into applause, shouting, "Truth, truth, we want the truth." The lecturer looked desperate. He had clearly lost control of the meeting. He appealed for order, but the students ignored him. They kept shouting, "Truth, truth." Then, over the roaring crowd, the lecturer screamed a question, "Would any comrade here suggest that the Soviet press does not print the truth, that there is a truth outside the statements of the press?" His question was remarkably naive—no student any longer believed anything in the Soviet press. If in earlier years they might have believed some things in the press, now, after the 20th Party Congress, they no longer believed anything.

Another student seized a microphone and bellowed in a loud voice, "We asked for the truth. We did not ask for a recitation from the press. We all read. Give us the truth now."

The lecturer, in an unexpected burst of candor, seemed forced to admit, "I am here to give you the official line on these matters. Please hear me out."

Several of the students thought this was a reasonable request. "Let him speak," they said. "Let him speak."

Lecturer: "What are your specific questions? I'll try to answer them."

Student: "Where was Gomulka for the last five years?" Gomulka, released from prison only a few days before, had just been appointed head of the Polish Communist Party and had pledged to carry out a broad program of national reform, music to the ears of young reformers in Moscow.

Lecturer: "Comrade Gomulka committed many errors. Five years ago, he favored the kulaks [wealthy peasants]. He did not support the correct line of the party."

His answer was drowned out in a chorus of boos.

Student: "Does the Sejm [parliament] rule Poland, or does the party rule Poland?"

Lecturer: "The party rules, because it is the expression of the will of the people."

More boos, jeers, shouts.

Listening to this extraordinary outburst of anti-Soviet sentiment, I realized the scope of the changes in recent months. Prior to the 20th Party

Congress, such demonstrations of disrespect for a Communist Party official would have been unimaginable. The students might have been expelled from school, sent off to the virgin lands, even arrested. But no longer. It seemed I was witnessing episodes in the disintegration of a dictatorship, though at the time I tried to steer clear of such large pronouncements. I felt more comfortable noting what I saw and heard.

A student then rose, turned his back on the lecturer, and in apparent disgust exclaimed, "I've wasted enough time tonight. I came here for answers, and as usual I'm not getting them. I'm leaving." He made his way through the crowd to the back door, and as though on cue almost everyone else followed him. In two minutes the lecture hall was empty. The lecturer was alone, holding in his hand the fifty small pieces of paper, each with a question about Hungary and Poland.

As I left, I heard students mumbling, "What sort of answers is he giving us?" "What a waste of time!" "We can read the papers anytime." "It's time for the truth."

That evening I noted in my diary that although I had been witness to other outbursts of student skepticism about the party line, never before had I seen "such an astonishing exposition of cynicism and disbelief." Communism would never be built on their skeptical shoulders.

■

Throughout the historic summer of 1956, Khrushchev saw evidence of a fraying empire. With workers' demands for "bread and freedom," Poland had gone into open rebellion, and Khrushchev came close to crushing it with the Red Army. But at the last second he changed his mind, deciding instead on a political option that he hoped would calm the troubled waters of his Eastern European empire. Reluctantly he allowed the once-discredited Gomulka to return to power, even though Gomulka, with his brazen call for a "Polish way to socialism," still represented a mortal challenge to Soviet dominance.

Yet if Poland was a crisis that for the moment seemed contained, Hungary was a crisis that was boiling, and the subject was on everyone's mind, especially Khrushchev's. He understood that while Stalin lived, little Stalins ruled his Eastern European empire, fearful but powerful puppets totally subjugated to the whims and temper of the man in the Kremlin. Only one communist had dared to defy Stalin, Tito of Yugoslavia, and he had paid the ultimate price in the currency of communism at that time: expulsion from Stalin's privileged fraternity. Only once had a communist-controlled country rebelled—East Germany, in 1953—and that rebellion had been brutally crushed.

Now Khrushchev faced a new and frightening reality in Eastern Europe, and it was of his own doing. De-Stalinization, his pet initiative, had launched "the year of the thaw," and it opened new worlds of hope and opportunity not only for the people of the Soviet Union but also for the people of Eastern Europe. They wanted a better life, a free press, a parliament with genuine debate, and they wanted a form of independence similar to Tito's "national communism," meaning a genuine loosening of satellite subservience to Moscow. Tito's example was crucial: when Khrushchev began to improve relations with Tito—inviting him in June to a twenty-one-day visit to the Soviet Union and greeting him with full pomp and ceremony, like a founding father of communism returning to the fold—other East European leaders, such as Poland's Gomulka, thought they could follow Tito's example with impunity.

Over the summer, while traveling, I could see examples of Khrushchev backtracking on de-Stalinization at home. His daughter, Rada, said that her father "increasingly sought to limit the boundaries of critical analysis, lest it end up polarizing society." But he could not "limit the boundaries" of excitement then sweeping through Eastern Europe, although he tried. The potential for positive change was in the air. People could breathe its intoxicating power. Fear, the normal human response to living in a totalitarian society, began magically to vanish. It was a time for action, not words. Hungary overnight became the stage for what the Soviets would later denounce as a "putsch . . . by fascist, counterrevolutionary forces," the very same forces hailed in the West as freedom fighters. Russian students told me that when they saw the word "putsch" in a *Pravda* editorial, they knew for certain that an anti-Soviet rebellion was under way. They demanded to know the truth about what was going on in Hungary, and they knew they were not getting it. Khrushchev had profoundly misjudged the impact of de-Stalinization on Russia's satellite empire. His reaction was late, confused, and ultimately self-destructive. For months he had hoped a political solution could be found, even if that meant he would open much of Eastern Europe to Tito's "national communism," but in early November, after much hesitation and self-doubt, he looked in the mirror one morning and saw only one option—no matter the cost, he felt he had to crush the uprising in Hungary, just as Russia had crushed the uprising in East Germany in 1953. Khrushchev had gambled with de-Stalinization and lost. Unfortunately, Hungary would lose, too.

The summertime run-up to the Hungarian crisis started after the Poznan uprising with purges in Hungary's ruling elite. Matyas Rakosi, one of the "little Stalins" running Eastern Europe, was arbitrarily dismissed on July 18 and replaced by a faithful understudy, Erno Gero, who promised better days but at the same time warned that in Hungary there would be no "second Poznan." His program might have been drafted by Khrushchev himself. It included:

Reconciliation with Tito

The end of Rakosi's "personality cult"

The start of "collective leadership"

The abolition of terror in government

Freedom for Janos Kadar, a former senior official, jailed three years earlier, ironically, for "Titoism"

Several weeks later Gero welcomed Imre Nagy, another former senior official, back into the Communist Party. He had been accused of "rightwing deviationism," whatever that meant at the time. Gero, under heavy pressure to reform his country, also opened parliament to political debate, unimaginable until then, and allowed Catholic priests to return to their parishes in Hungary. Many priests had fled the country to avoid religious persecution.

Meanwhile, in late September, Khrushchev and Tito exchanged visits—not, as it turned out, because they enjoyed each other's company, but rather because they were trying to divide up Eastern Europe into a Titoesque sphere of influence and a Soviet sphere of influence. It was a cockeyed idea, probably Khrushchev's, and it had little chance of success. But in Moscow it was a serious topic of conversation, mostly among those Western diplomats and journalists who felt Khrushchev might be losing power to hard-liners. Theoretically the Tito scenario would have allowed Khrushchev to retain personal power and keep all of Eastern Europe in communist hands as it grappled with Western capitalism (read the United States and NATO) for control of the rest of the world. According to one report of the plan, Tito would acquire ideological control over Romania and Bulgaria while Moscow would solidify its control over Poland, Hungary, Czechoslovakia, and East Germany. Also, as part of the deal Moscow would loosen its financial grip over all of Eastern Europe, theoretically stimulating economic growth and trade. On September 30 Gero joined Khrushchev and Tito in Yalta, thus adding the weight of his opinions as a communist leader eager for reform but determined to keep his country in the communist bloc.

On October 23 the lid blew. Thrilled by Gomulka's ascension to power in neighboring Poland, several hundred thousand Hungarian students and workers took to the streets in Budapest in a massive show of solidarity with Gomulka and his Polish colleagues. Many marched on parliament to hear Nagy lay out his reform plans. Others demonstrated in front of Budapest Radio, demanding a Tito-style "national communism." Still others converged on the hulking, thirty-foot-tall statue of Stalin in a central square and, in their rage, tore it down. "This we swear," the rebels sang, chanting the words of a patriotic poem, "this we swear, that we will no longer be slaves." Later that evening, Hungarian security forces opened fire on the crowd in front of the offices of Budapest Radio, killing one, wounding many others, and igniting a clash between the demonstrators and the police that ended with many of the police switching sides and joining the demonstrators. They probably didn't know it at the time, but they had just started a revolution that would send shivers through the Kremlin and, for this reason, among others, send tens of thousands of Russian troops and tanks into Hungary in an effort to crush it.

The same evening, in Moscow, Soviet leaders met in a frenzy of anxiety and fear. "Hungary is coming apart," cried Molotov. "The government is being overthrown," wailed Lazar Kaganovich. "It's not the same as Poland," observed Zhukov. "Troops must be sent." Everyone agreed, with the exception of the veteran communist negotiator Anastas Mikoyan. He argued for patience, suggesting that the Hungarians "restore order on their own." Khrushchev, fighting to protect his endangered policy of de-Stalinization, joined his other colleagues in their decision to send troops into Budapest and also to send Mikoyan and the Kremlin's chief ideologue, Mikhail Suslov, to Budapest to monitor the mess.

Very early the next morning, on October 24, Soviet troops invaded Budapest. A force of some 10,000 troops, supported by eighty tanks, rolled into the capital from their bases in the countryside. It was a rare show of Soviet efficiency, triggered by the fear that, as Molotov had warned, Hungary was "coming apart." Russian generals initially believed that their troops could contain the crisis, but after only a few hours it was clear that they had only inflamed it. Hungarian students threw Molotov cocktails at the tanks. The Russians fired at the rebels, starting a flow of blood that inspired those Hungarians sitting on the sidelines to take up arms and join the rebellion. The Kremlin quickly learned that the bonds of blood and nationalism were thicker than those of communist allegiance. According to one estimate, by midafternoon twenty-five students had been killed and 200 wounded. That was the estimate in Budapest. There was none for those killed in other parts of Hungary.

I noted in my diary that "Hungary had just ripped a page out of Poland's recent history and stolen the headlines from Gomulka." Just from the Soviet press, rarely a reservoir of reliable information, we learned that Hungarian rebels were demanding that Nagy replace Gero and press his plans for reform. At Moscow's direction Nagy did in fact replace Gero, but, like Gero, he also distrusted the student rebels. What were their true intentions? Nagy, as a Moscow-trained communist, wanted only to reform the Hungarian system of government, not to overthrow it, as many students demanded.

At JPRS and at the embassy we were being inundated with reports from Hungary, some reliable but many less so. One said that Soviet aircraft had opened fire on insurgent "mobs." At the time there was no confirmation of this. Another report, from Budapest Radio, said that Hungarian wives were appealing to their husbands to stay at home and "amuse" themselves with domestic "activities," which were left undefined. The point was to keep them from joining the student rebels. Still another report said that miners in two towns fifty to sixty miles from Budapest had joined the uprising, shutting down their mines and taking up arms against government troops. Again there was no confirmation, but the report strongly suggested that the rebellion was already spreading into the provinces.

We also heard that many rebels were now calling for "true national independence" and free elections—elections involving more than one party. Nagy, their hero in the early days of the revolt, took an interesting but puzzling approach to these rebel demands. While the demonstrators were hurling Molotov cocktails at Soviet tanks and troops, clearly seeing them as enemies of their revolt, Nagy appealed to the demonstrators to show "love and kindness" to the invading Soviet troops, suggesting that, even in these early days, the new prime minister was already losing touch with the fiery goals of the student-led uprising. Nagy favored the Soviet intervention, hoping it would restore calm. His goal was always reform; the students wanted revolution.

Often, when I got tired of official statements, even those uttered by American diplomats, I would turn down the embassy limo and jump into a cab for the ride back to American House. I wanted to hear a Russian discuss events in Hungary. Of course not all cabdrivers were talkative, but some of them were. On this evening the driver asked me whether I had "fresh information" about Hungary. Before I could answer, he launched into his own analysis. "Whose side are the Hungarian troops on?" That was the key to his analysis. "If you know anything about our revolution, you recall that success came to us when the troops joined the insurgents. This is the critical question." It was my pleasure to inform him that many Hungarian troops were in fact joining the insurgents; according to one report they had seized a Soviet airfield and burned the planes and hangars. When we reached American House, I tried to pay him for the ride. He waved his hand and shook his head, refusing payment. "Thank you," he said, with a smile, emphasizing the word "you."

One can imagine that Khrushchev had trouble sleeping for much of the next week. "Budapest was like a nail in my head," he later recalled. He had ordered troops into Budapest but the rebellion continued, the fighting spread, and Russian casualties mounted. (He did not care about Hungarian casualties.) Lenin's haunting question, *Chto delat'?*—What is to be done?—was the essential dilemma for Khrushchev. Indeed, what was to be done? He was in a quandary, uncertain about his next step.

The upshot was that his policy swung from one extreme to another, "lurch[ing] from surrender to bloodbath," to quote one of his biographers, William Taubman. One day he would urge his colleagues to "face facts." "There is no firm leadership there, either in the party or the government. . . . Their troops may go over to the rebels." He argued that the Soviet Union had "no alternative" but to support the wobbly regime in Budapest. Zhukov, after surveying military options, flip-flopped, stunning his colleagues by changing his position from intervention to withdrawal, stating, "We should withdraw our troops from Budapest, and from all of Hungary, if that's demanded."

On October 30 Khrushchev seized on the Zhukov proposal, using it as a military shield against political criticism. "We are unanimous," he proclaimed. "There are two paths, a military path, one of occupation, and a peaceful path—the withdrawal of troops, negotiations." He obviously preferred the peaceful path, at least at the moment he spoke. In this crucial week he was given to sudden changes of mind, heart, and policy. Surprising everyone, he even approved a remarkable TASS statement admitting "egregious mistakes" by the Kremlin, including "violations of the principles of equality in relations with socialist countries" and adding a pledge "to observe the full sovereignty of each socialist state."

Reading such an official admission of "mistakes" and "violations," in the midst of an anti-communist revolution in an East European satellite, what was the average Russian to think about his own government's policies? What was a communist official in the hinterlands to think? What was the U.S. embassy to think? At this revealing moment, all might have thought that the Khrushchev regime had been thrown into confusion and uncertainty by the startling events in Hungary and that it did not know what to do—and they would all have been right.

But then, in Budapest, as Nagy moved closer to supporting the rebels' ultimate demand for "true national independence," an anguished Khrushchev again changed his mind. He did not want to be seen as just another Stalin, using military force when political negotiations might have made more sense. In his memoirs he referred to the late dictator's prediction that without him, Russia would collapse into uncontrollable chaos. "You are blind like little kittens," Stalin had jokingly warned. "Without me the imperialists would strangle you." The imperialists were always a handy villain.

In Budapest a huge crowd had gathered in Parliament Square. Hungarian security troops demanded that the crowd disperse. The protesters refused. The troops opened fire and massacred more than 100 demonstrators, wounding many more. Even at a time of spreading violence, when bloodshed was no novelty, this massacre had a stunning impact, inspiring an angry mob to attack Communist Party headquarters, where they seized a handful of officials and, propelled by disappointment and hatred, lynched them by hanging them from city lampposts in downtown Budapest, a scene soon duplicated in other cities. The sight of hanging bodies was the lead item in newsreels around the world, including in Moscow, where Khrushchev now realized that he had to act, that continuing vacillation was an embarrassing symptom of Soviet (and his own) weakness, no longer acceptable in a Kremlin leader privately frightened by the prospect of the disintegration of Russia's Eastern European empire.

The following morning, on October 31, Khrushchev ordered what amounted to a second Soviet invasion of Hungary, only this time he sanctioned the use of overwhelming force. It was code-named Operation Whirlwind. The Red Army requested, and received, a few days for proper preparation. He also decided to brief his Warsaw Pact allies, all of whom would be affected by the news. He had never briefed them on his de-Stalinization speech, and they had been miffed. He did not want to make the same mistake twice. Accompanied by Molotov and Malenkov, on November 1 Khrushchev flew to Brest, near the Polish-Soviet border, to inform Gomulka, who was not happy about Khrushchev's decision but could do nothing about it.

The following day the Kremlin troika flew to Bucharest to tell the Romanians and the Czechs about the upcoming invasion, and then they went to Sofia to tell the Bulgarians. No one was happy but no one objected. Finally, Khrushchev and Malenkov flew through a violent thunderstorm to the Adriatic island resort of Brioni to inform Tito of the decision to invade Hungary, a decision the Yugoslav leader initially opposed but then supported.

On November 4 Soviet troops and tanks swooped into Budapest in a vast deployment of seventeen army divisions and crushed the Hungarian Revolution. In a three-column front-page editorial, *Pravda* explained the invasion, using rhetoric so ugly it would have satisfied the most demanding Kremlin propagandist. "Fascist, counterrevolutionary forces" had tried to control the "putsch," and "these elements, which are hostile to the people and alien to Marxism-Leninism," must be eliminated. To attain this goal, "huge concentrations of Soviet troops and forces" had been moved into Hungary "determined" to "crush" the Hungarian "putsch." There was never any doubt that they would succeed. The Hungarian Army was no match for the Red Army, and it was never in the cards, sympathetic rhetoric aside, that NATO would intervene in this Eastern European crisis. The cost in human life was high: 2,500 Hungarian "freedom fighters" and 700 Soviet troops were killed, most of them on the first day of the assault. More than 200,000 Hungarians fled the country.

The diplomatic cost was also high. The UN spent days denouncing the Soviet invasion, and the White House waved the "Captive Nations Week" banner, suggesting all workers laboring in communist-run countries were slaves and superpower relations could not be improved, despite Soviet protestations about desiring a foreign policy based on "peace, friendship and equality among nations." President Dwight D. Eisenhower expressed his sympathy for the Hungarian people, but his words lacked conviction. "I feel with the Hungarian people," he said limply. His secretary of state, John Foster Dulles, issued a statement that simply oozed with hypocritical sympathy. "To all those suffering under communist slavery," he intoned, "let us say you can count on us." But except for this lukewarm rhetoric, the United States offered nothing to the Hungarian people, who had expected more than words from the United States.

Just as the Red Army was smashing into Budapest in early November, British, French, and Israeli forces rolled into Egypt, creating a Middle East crisis that forced the suppression of the Hungarian Revolution to share the front page of world newspapers. What happened was that, in an effort to dethrone the Egyptian leader, Gamal Abdel Nasser, and reopen the Suez Canal to international traffic, Israel joined forces with Britain and France in invading the Suez peninsula in a daring operation timed to allow Britain and France to take control of the canal. But before they could complete this controversial and complicated operation, the United States, which had been kept in the dark by its allies, angrily interceded and forced the three invading armies to withdraw immediately, which they did, their plan an embarrassing flop.

Nevertheless, on November 6 the Kremlin plunged into a form of brinksmanship, sending sharply worded warnings to Guy Mollet of France, Anthony Eden of Britain, and David Ben-Gurion of Israel that Russia was prepared to intervene militarily in the Middle East, with or without a UN mandate, hinting at one point that unless the "aggressors" withdrew promptly, which they were starting to do anyway, the Russians would send an untold number of "volunteers" to Egypt. Bulganin then shot off a personal letter to Eisenhower proposing a joint U.S.-

Soviet force to accelerate the process, again threatening to demolish the "aggressors" if no action were taken. Foreign Minister Dmitri Shepilov urged the UN Security Council to take immediate action against France and Britain, adding that the Soviet Union would be willing to deploy its forces in such a UN endeavor.

Interestingly, the Kremlin agenda featured another, more immediate but not acknowledged objective—deepening this mood of gloom and doom about a possible big war in the Middle East in order to distract people's attention from the bloody slaughter of the Hungarian rebels. Russians were much more concerned about the rising casualty rates in Hungary than they were about "Zionist aggression" in Egypt. Moreover, deep down, they did not really believe that Khrushchev was going to send "volunteers" to Egypt. It was not a credible threat, not after their dismal experience in Hungary. No one at JPRS or the embassy thought the Russians would send troops or "volunteers" to Egypt.

But to drum up street-corner enthusiasm for a threat no one seemed to take seriously, the Kremlin resorted to another old propaganda ploy: it staged popular demonstrations in front of the Moscow embassies of the "invaders," the "aggressors," the "interventionists"—namely, the Israelis, the British, and the French—demanding an end to their "blatant aggression" in the Middle East. These demonstrations were intended to convey the impression both at home and abroad that the Soviet government was truly angry about the invasion of Egypt and would take drastic action against the "aggressors." For example, at the Anglo-American School children were sent home early, just to be cautious, even though everyone knew that the demonstrations were phony displays of popular anger. On the day of the demonstrations American embassy personnel were restricted to the compound for three hours, except for those on urgent business, and they needed to be driven in and out of the compound in embassy cars with diplomatic plates.

Pravda described the demonstrations as "spontaneous expressions of public anger," but in fact they were highly organized and coordinated to begin and end at a certain time. The demonstrators were bused to the embassies and then bused back to their factories, all as part of their day's work. They carried signs and posters, all painted and prepared on government time. MVD troops stood guard over the demonstrators, the troops and the demonstrators getting tipsy drinking vodka. Few were genuinely antagonistic, and they were mostly gathered at the Israeli embassy, where a door was smashed.

At one point a French journalist walked into the mob of demonstrators in front of his embassy.

A burly Russian demonstrator grabbed his arm. "Who are you?" he asked in belligerent tones.

"A French journalist," was the answer.

Suddenly the belligerence melted into a smile. "Good," the Russian said, releasing his arm and patting him on the back.

At the British embassy, where the demonstrating mob actually pushed open the garden door, the distinguished British ambassador, Sir William Hayter, walked up to the MVD colonel, who was "in charge of" the screaming, presumably angry demonstrators, and in a beautiful expression of British understatement asked, "Could you tell me please when these demonstrations will end?"

The colonel, apparently not thinking, glanced at his wristwatch and replied simply, "In half an hour."

On November 7 the Russians celebrated the thirty-ninth anniversary of the Bolshevik Revolution with the usual parade through Red Square. Standing atop the Lenin Mausoleum were Khrushchev, Zhukov, and other Soviet leaders, bundled up against the cold. I had opposed the goals of the Bolshevik Revolution for many years, but on this day there was another reason for resentment. To those members of the diplomatic corps wishing to observe the parade from privileged positions near the mausoleum, the Foreign Ministry made it clear that they had to be there by 6:00 a.m., before the troops, tanks, missiles, and other armor, needed for the parade, blocked access to Red Square. Needless to say I objected furiously—but only to myself in my otherwise empty room. I got to my place near the Kremlin wall well before the 6:00 a.m. deadline.

The parade itself started at 10:00 a.m., at the exact moment when the Kremlin clocks sounded the hour. The military marched through Red

Square, followed by the heavy armor, none of which, I was later told by the military attachés, was especially new or interesting. The "popular" part of the parade lasted until 12:30 p.m. Many Russians carried signs denouncing "Western" and "Zionist" aggression against Egypt. Zhukov spoke, and, consistent with the theme of the day, warned that Soviet troops were "available" to smash "Western aggression" against Egypt. By this time I was freezing but managed to jot down in my notebook his "warning" that Soviet troops were also "available" to "crush the Hungarian counterrevolution." Had they not already done that on November 4?

That evening I noted in my diary: "It snowed for the rest of the day, but this did not disturb the Russians who flocked into Revolution and Red Squares by the thousands, most of them drunk, dancing, delighted, and not in the least concerned about Suez or Hungary. This was their holiday. They did not have to work tomorrow, and the band played catchy tunes from an open bandstand opposite the Kremlin. . . . Many extra platoons of militia patrolled the streets. They were very severe with the drunkards, and there were many of them."

CHAPTER THIRTEEN

"Dark, Frightening, and Tragic Days"

Quite often on Sunday mornings I did a little extracurricular work for Dan Schorr and Irv Levine, the CBS and NBC correspondents in Moscow, translating articles from the Soviet press for them. Monday through Saturday they employed official translators, Russians who knew both English and Russian, either because they were superb linguists, which many were, or because they were born and raised in Britain or the United States and had been brought to Moscow by communist parents who wanted to live in the land of Lenin. They brought their fluency in English with them, too. For my Sunday immersion in *Pravda* and *Izvestia* and a few of the other Soviet dailies, I was paid $25 by each of the correspondents. Not bad, I thought.

It was the kind of work I did routinely on weekdays for JPRS. But even if there had been no financial reward I would have helped them on Sunday mornings anyway. They were my friends. We were in Moscow, and everyone seemed to be like family. In those years of the Cold War, we thought of ourselves as a band of brothers and sisters sharing a very special experience in communist Russia—one that we hoped we would be able to tell our children and grandchildren about someday. Every day had its own mysteries. Every day held us in awe of what we might behold tomorrow.

I felt closer to Schorr than I did to Levine, possibly because I was a CBS News radio listener. Schorr's was a more familiar voice. In my memory bank were other CBS voices, none more prominent than Edward R. Murrow's, although I could easily have recognized Eric Severeid's or Howard K. Smith's or David Schoenbrun's. While still in college I had started dreaming that one day I would be a network correspondent specializing in Soviet affairs, meaning that I would become what was then called a Soviet expert or a Kremlinologist. Such people knew the language, history, and culture of the one country in the world that potentially could inflict mortal damage on the United States. That was why I intensively studied Russian history in my senior year in college, why I had set sail for a doctorate in Russian history at Harvard as a graduate student at the Russian Research Center, and why I had happily accepted the job in Moscow as an interpreter-translator.

As I considered my next career step, I had a feeling that I was not wasting my time. Such a background could well open a door in journalism, in diplomacy, or in the academy. Every now and then, during a trip or a meal, I would share my thinking with Schorr, Levine, and even Anna Holdcroft, who always regarded diplomacy as my natural home. Schorr, especially, had other plans for me. Journalism, he advised, was my natural home, specifically a job as a Moscow correspondent for CBS News.

One Sunday in November 1956, when we were asking and answering the question of the day, "Whither Russia?"—a game all Muscovites played with increasing frequency as Russia bounced uncertainly from de-Stalinization to the invasion of Hungary—Schorr surprised me by raising a related and very personal question. Usually I sat in a chair next to his desk, he in front of his desk and typewriter: I would translate what I considered an interesting article or editorial in *Pravda*, and he would type the phrase or sentence that filled his journalistic needs, and then use it in one or more of his broadcasts.

"I've been thinking," Schorr said, with a smile forming around his lips.

"What about?"

"Well"—his smile widened—"what about you joining the bureau here, becoming effectively my number two?"

"Your number two?" I asked incredulously. "Come on. Be serious. What are you talking about?"

"I'm talking about you becoming effectively my number two," he repeated, the smile no longer on his face. "You'd run the bureau, do some translating, and of course reporting. I mean, if we had two stories one day, you'd do one and I'd do the other. If I was going out of the country, you'd be here representing CBS. With you here, I would be able to do more traveling inside the Soviet Union. You'd be what you have always wanted to be—a Moscow correspondent."

I wanted to respond, but I was momentarily at a loss for words. I looked down at the worn-out carpet on the office floor for a moment and then back up into Schorr's eyes. "Are you serious? Are you really offering me a job? As a Moscow correspondent? For CBS?"

Schorr nodded. "Yes, the job you said you always wanted. You'd be here helping to cover the Soviet Union."

I sat as silent as a Buddha for what must have seemed an eternity. Then I burst out laughing. "Let's go back to translating." That was safer, less challenging.

"No." Schorr was persistent. "What do you think?" I could hear his large office clock ticking. "What do you think?" he repeated softly, looking for my eyes, which were fastened on my shoe tops. "I checked with New York. Of course, they'd like to see you and talk to you, and all that. But I think the job is there, and it's yours, if you want it. And, by the way, I checked with the Russians, too, and they raised no real objection, but you can't tell and in any case that's for later."

I realized Schorr was serious. He had just offered me a superb opportunity, the job I had told him and a few others I truly wanted. "Let me think this over," I mumbled. "Let me think." I needed time. Suddenly I could not say yes. I could not say anything except "Tomorrow. I promise you an answer by tomorrow." Schorr had every reason to have expected an ecstatic yes, but instead he looked at me, understanding that I was in a state of shock, unable to say yes or no. He sat back, smiled, and lit his pipe. "Let's go back to the translation."

That night I did very little sleeping. The job I wanted was the job Schorr offered. Why not take it? It was for me a dream come true. And yet, I realized, after heated arguments with myself, that I could not take it, and the basic reason was a promise I had made to my mother. When Marshall Shulman offered me the chance to work in Moscow, I naturally checked with my mother and father. She was a reluctant no, and he was an enthusiastic yes. My mother's concern was that I would become so absorbed with today's Russia that I would forget about yesterday's Uvarov. All my preparatory research would go to waste. I would not get my Ph.D. I would not teach at Harvard or anywhere else, where a Ph.D. was the equivalent of a union card.

With my mother's concerns in mind, I had actually tried while in Moscow to do both my day job at JPRS and my evening research at the Lenin Library, and I thought that, to a very large extent, I had succeeded. As noted earlier, I had managed to gain admission and do research in Moscow's top libraries (an achievement in those days), and I had even gotten to admire Uvarov's singular contributions to Russian scholarship. But deep down I knew that if I took Schorr's offer, I would be working a twenty-four-hour day, learning the (for me) new craft of broadcasting, keeping up with a crackerjack professional like Schorr, and somehow continuing my research on Uvarov. Seriously, would I have enough time for both Schorr and Uvarov? The answer was obvious. Almost certainly not. At the end of the day, the minute-to-minute demands of CBS News would require my full attention, and Uvarov would have to wait. My Ph.D. dissertation would have to wait. And the promise I made to my mother would have to wait. That, I felt, I could not do. A promise was a promise, especially one to my mother.

By dawn's early light I understood that I would probably never again get an offer such as Schorr's; by declining his offer I might be crossing out journalism as my ultimate career. But I felt, then and there, that I was making the right call. And what the heck! I'd still have diplomacy and teaching on my dance card of career options.

At two in the afternoon of the following day I made my way to the Central Telegraph Office, located a few blocks from Red Square. That was where foreign correspondents gathered to write their news stories and have them cleared by Soviet censors. It was also where radio reporters such as Schorr and Levine transmitted their broadcasts directly to New York. When Schorr arrived, he spotted me, and I him. He plunked his briefcase down on an empty table and asked, "Well, what's up?"

I gulped. "Can I have a minute when you're finished?"

"Sure," was his quick response. Schorr then submitted his copy for clearance and turned to a few other reporters waiting for clearance of their copy and engaged in the Moscow equivalent of office gossip—generally who's leaving, who's arriving, the Bolshoi's latest ballet, the current Soviet screw-up, the weather. After a few minutes Schorr retired to a relatively quiet corner of the office, and I followed him.

"What have you decided?" he asked.

"I cannot accept your offer," I replied, looking at everyone except at Schorr. "I promised my mother I would finish my dissertation, and I have to do that before I do anything else."

For the next minute or so, Schorr said nothing. "Are you sure?" he asked.

I nodded. "Yes. I made a promise to my mother, and I feel I must keep it."

Schorr looked at me, a somewhat baffled look, and again asked, "Are you sure?" He was trying to give me more time.

"Yes, I'm sure."

Schorr then hugged me. He might not have agreed with my decision, but he respected it. He retrieved his cleared scripts from the censor and did his broadcasts. I stood listening outside his broadcast booth, tears running down my cheeks.

A Russian driver told me this story, giggling all the way. Three Hungarian officials meet in Moscow's notorious Lubyanka Prison. "What are you here for?" one Hungarian asks his former colleagues. "I supported Nagy," one of them replies. "And what are you here for?" he asks the other. "I was against Nagy." Then both prisoners turn to the third Hungarian. "And you, why are you here?" His answer: "I am Nagy."

After the Soviet crackdown of the Hungarian Revolution I spent a lot of my free time in Moscow libraries, assuming that if Khrushchev intended to restrict Soviet access to the West, and Western access to Russia, my own limited access to the Uvarov archives would almost certainly be curtailed. I thought it was only a matter of time before the Russians decided to cut off my access completely. But until then I was determined to study and absorb as much as I could about Uvarov. And so, as often as possible, I would return to the Lenin Library. Uvarov was always my stated reason, but I also had another reason, a secret yearning that I shared only with Ambassador Bohlen: to listen in on the clearly discernible dissatisfaction of Soviet youth with communism as their governing ideology. How deep did the dissatisfaction really run? Might it in time represent a threat to the Khrushchev regime? I was curious. Among the students at the library were the future rulers of Russia. What were they thinking? I had had some good luck months earlier stumbling upon library gatherings where students had raised questions about the limits of de-Stalinization, about the continuing relevance of communism, about their own sense of self. I listened to them then, and sympathized greatly, and I thought it was time for me to listen to them again, if and when the occasion arose.

One evening it arose, and then mysteriously vanished. I saw an announcement on the main bulletin board of the Lenin Library that a communist official would deliver a speech, and then take questions, on

"The Vigilance of the Soviet Man." He would speak on November 20. The use of the word "vigilance" was meant to suggest, in the Moscow mind of the day, that the "Soviet Man" lacked "vigilance" at a time when the Soviet Union, his motherland, was being tested by "capitalist encirclement" and "aggression," and this matter had to be addressed, and swiftly. "No time to lose!" was the between-the-lines alert. This was a lecture I did not want to miss.

But when I arrived for the lecture I noticed immediately that there was none of the hubbub that usually accompanied a major communist speaker. I checked with the information desk.

"Isn't there a lecture tonight?"

"No," the clerk replied, trying to appear nonchalant.

"But there was an announcement," I said, a bit bewildered. "I saw it on the bulletin board a few nights ago."

"No," the clerk continued, with a straight face. "There was no announcement."

"But I saw it," I protested.

"No, there was no announcement."

His insistence was not persuasive, and I decided to check with the librarian who handled my Uvarov file. We had become friends, sort of. "I saw an announcement a few nights ago about a lecture here tonight," I said. "But now I'm told there was no announcement. So I'm puzzled. What happened?"

The librarian began shuffling papers on her desk and looking everywhere but at me. "No," she said, "there was no announcement, and there is no lecture."

"But," I persisted, "there was an announcement. I saw it, several times. It was on the bulletin board."

The librarian, cornered, snapped, "All I can tell you is that this lecture was never scheduled. Never."

I quickly changed tactics. "When will the next lecture take place?"

"This I cannot tell you either."

She looked uncomfortable and excused herself, picking up a few papers and leaving her desk. She was obviously under orders to say nothing about the "vigilance" lecture, which probably had been canceled because the Communist Party feared another eruption of student skepticism about the official reason for the Soviet crackdown on the Hungarian Revolution.

A few days later *Pravda* published what amounted to an official explanation. The Communist Party newspaper lashed out at students who no longer "occupy themselves" with "socially useful labor." A "great many" students did no work at all. Absorbed with "abstract reasoning," they wasted their days. "Certain comrades," especially those at universities, the newspaper continued, entertained ideas "like a bourgeois ideology." The word "comrades" suggested that *Pravda* was fingering members of the Communist Party, who should know and act better. But in the aftermath of the Hungarian crisis, such "comrades" and students were demanding truthful answers to their questions, and they were not getting them.

In one case, a number of students at Moscow University in frustration took the unusual step of posting a daily wall newspaper, based not on reporting by TASS or *Pravda* about Hungary but on the BBC's reporting. This ad hoc form of student journalism became an overnight sensation. Many university students depended on it for information about the uprising and its suppression. A communist official, hearing about the wall newspaper's popularity, was outraged. He promptly scheduled a university-wide meeting at which he demanded that the student editor be dropped from the newspaper and expelled from the university. The students, defying the official, rallied behind the editor and continued reading the newspaper. The official reacted with rage, firing dire threats at the students, warning of mass expulsions, and insisting on the editor's ouster. Remarkably, the students held fast, refusing to comply with the party official's demands. The upshot: The editor retained his position and the wall newspaper continued to be published. Such student defiance would never have happened before de-Stalinization became the newly emerging principle of the Khrushchev regime.

Another example of exceptional defiance was not by student intellectuals at a university but by 450 workers at the Kaganovich ball bearing plant near Moscow. What they did was unprecedented. The embassy learned that on October 23 the workers arrived at their plant, checked in, as was required, and then sat down, refusing to work. In the West that would have been called a strike; in Russia there had not been a strike since the 1920s. The plant manager ranted and raved, threatening to fire anyone who did not return to work immediately. The workers refused to budge. They demanded a hearing to vent their grievances. The following morning, on October 24, the workers returned to the plant, checked in, but again refused to work. This time a communist official, no longer just the plant manager, insisted on behalf of the party that the workers return to their jobs. Immediately! They refused, again demanding a hearing. The party official, after many calls to more senior officials, agreed finally to listen to the workers.

Bravely, one man rose, a foreman obviously preselected by the workers. He told the party official that he had been released from a Siberian prison only six months before, one of tens of thousands similarly liberated from unjust imprisonment and trying to return to a normal life in post-Stalin Russia. For the last three months the plant manager had given only 200 to 300 rubles to his workers and kept the rest, measured in thousands, for himself. The foreman stated that the men would not go back to work until the manager was fired. That was their bottom line.

At first the party official described the foreman's demand as "outrageous," but then, after a few minutes, promised the workers that he would "consider" the foreman's demand. The foreman rose once again and in firm tones repeated his earlier demand for the manager's ouster. Otherwise, he warned, the workers would not go back to work.

Later that afternoon the manager was fired. The following morning the workers returned to the plant and resumed working. The strike, never called by that term, was over. For the next three weeks worker salaries shot up two to three times above the norm.

For the first time in more than twenty years, members of the Soviet working class had stood up to established power, demanding that a plant manager be fired. In this case, the party establishment caved to their demands. Before Khrushchev's de-Stalinization, it's safe to say that such a "strike" would have been unimaginable.

Change seemed to be everywhere in the fall of 1956. On some days it looked as though the whole system of communist rule was collapsing. The students were in rebellion. Workers were summoning up the courage to question party dogma, and even, apparently, to strike. Georgians, still loyal to their now officially disgraced Stalin, a hero in their eyes, were literally up in arms in bloody protest against Moscow's policy of de-Stalinization. And now, throughout Eastern Europe, Moscow's writ was being challenged and its domination questioned by restless satellites eager for greater autonomy and ready to challenge Moscow if necessary. Much to their surprise, Russians learned during the Hungarian uprising that, far from being the saviors of Eastern Europe, as *Pravda* had been trumpeting for years, they were actually seen as the oppressors of Eastern Europe.

Hungary had jolted the Soviet Union and the Soviet people, like an electric shock shooting through the entire nervous system. It raised profound questions, often forcing judgments without adequate time for reflection. One student told me that it had a "major impact on all of us." One casualty was his lifelong commitment to communism—it had been a central tenet of his upbringing, but now his commitment seemed to be withering on the vine. What was he to believe? Another student, Maria, a young woman I met at the History Institute, had a totally different take. "We may not be able to crush the 'fascists' in Hungary tomorrow, or the day after," she said, using the Kremlin's word for the rebels, "but we will. We will, eventually." Her faith in communism seemed firm.

We had met after a lecture at the institute. Maria was intelligent, well-read, talkative, and opinionated—on almost every subject. We discussed the Khrushchev speech. "How could he be so cocky, so certain that socialism would triumph over capitalism?" I asked.

"He was not cocky," Maria said. "He was simply stating the truth. He was repeating what all of us communists know. Socialism will follow capitalism. It's the law of social and historical development."

"But there is no such law," I said. "Anything can happen between today and tomorrow. You know that. I think it was Herzen who said, 'History follows no libretto.' And he was one of your own." Alexander Herzen was a nineteenth-century democrat who had fought czarism with his elegant pen, mostly from Western Europe. Had he remained in Russia, he would have been arrested and silenced.

Maria tried not to be condescending, but her explanation was patronizing and simplistic, and her approach to me was that of a mother to a six-year-old. "There are laws of social development," she began. "We can do nothing about them. They just exist. Even if I thought communism was bad, and wanted to fight against it, I'd be fighting against something that was inevitable. And that's just stupid, isn't it? Communism is the inevitable result of history. It is the culmination of historical development. It will happen, whether we like it or not."

For a moment I thought I had found a hole in her argument about inevitability. "If capitalism inevitably follows feudalism, and communism inevitably follows capitalism, and if everything in history is constantly in flux, then how do we know that another social system won't follow communism, another system that is better than communism?"

I saw a flicker of doubt rush through her eyes, but she recovered quickly. "I forgot to mention the 'class struggle,'" she said, smiling. "You see, in all other systems of government, there is a class struggle. It is never-ending, like workers fighting bosses. But under communism, or socialism, there are no longer any antagonistic classes. They are all harmonious. The class struggle is over, and communism is supreme." She folded her arms across her chest, a warrior after a triumph. "You do understand now, don't you?" she asked.

In frustration, I threw both hands in the air. "Maria, what can I say? You think you have discovered the single key to history. No such thing exists. There will always be change. Please, you must open your mind to change."

As I became more exasperated, she became more calm. "Change there will be," she said softly. "But at the end we will surely have communism, and with communism, an end to class struggle. It is simply a law of historical development, which will all end with the arrival of communism."

Sensing that our conversation had just come to an abrupt end, Maria returned to the book she was reading. As I left I looked over her shoulder. She was reading a Russian translation of Keats.

If Maria could believe in communism, then surely her leader could as well; and on November 18, in a speech at the Polish embassy designed to reassure his East European allies that Russia had no interest in military solutions to festering quarrels in Eastern Europe, Hungary notwithstanding, Khrushchev strongly supported the notion of "peaceful coexistence"—and not just among socialist countries. He also had his Western adversaries in mind, principally the United States. He wanted them to understand that his adventure in Hungary did not shake his belief in "peaceful coexistence" with the capitalist West.

One paragraph in *Pravda*'s edited translation of the speech, published the next morning, caught Anna Holdcroft's eye, and I translated it for the embassy. It could be seen as a personal message to President Eisenhower. "There can be no question of whether or not peaceful coexistence of the various states is needed," he said. "Coexistence is an acknowledged fact which we can see before us. We say to the representatives of the capitalist countries: if you wish, you can come and visit us; if you don't wish, you need not come. This will not grieve us particularly. But it is essential for us to coexist. The fact that the Great October Socialist Revolution was carried out, that the Soviet Union and the whole system of states of the socialist camp exist, does not depend on you, after all. Such is the law of social development. Furthermore, this law is operating in our favor. We Leninists are convinced that our social system, socialism, will be victorious over capitalism in the long run. Such is the logic of the historical development of mankind."

In Khrushchev's mind, the Hungarian repression was an unfortunate, unavoidable bump on the road to the ultimate triumph of communism. But it had saved his Eastern European empire, which to him was of fundamental importance. He hoped that it would not destroy the possibility of better East-West relations, but on his list of priorities, what came first was maintaining communist rule in Eastern Europe, a concept that many years later came to be called the Brezhnev Doctrine.

At the time, as fall slipped into winter and Khrushchev's "year of the thaw" started to refreeze, turning Moscow into an icy center of crackdown and controversy, I noted in my diary that I was living through "dark, frightening, and tragic days." At least that was how they struck me. The stories in the Soviet press were again filled with Western "plots," "aggression," and "conspiracies." In Gorky Park, where I often went to meet Russians with whom I could have casual conversations, I found fewer Russians willing to stop and chat, as if they too began feeling a familiar chill in the air. Cabdrivers, among my best translators of Kremlin policy shifts, were again turning their attention to the traffic, keeping their opinions to themselves.

At the embassy we were hearing stories of Russian atrocities in Budapest, hundreds of Hungarian rebels brutally slaughtered by Soviet troops. And at JPRS I came upon reports that Molotov, of all people, was the Soviet official charged with telling artists and writers, who had flirted with the concept of freedom, that this flirtation had to end, that loyalty to the "collective," to the Communist Party, was to take precedence over "individualist" tendencies.

What was happening in different corners of Soviet society helped Khrushchev realize that in his effort to ration democracy one liberalizing step at a time, he was losing control of his dictatorship. To retain personal power and reimpose the Soviet equivalent of law and order, he had to tighten the screws of party authority. But how tightly? Go back to Stalin's day, which would have invalidated his core policy of de-Stalinization? Or was there perhaps a middle ground, a place where a certain degree of democracy could coexist with a continuation of communist rule? That was Khrushchev's hope.

But by year's end he clearly had not found that place, and he retreated to the comfortable cliché that the party knew best, even when the evidence was overwhelming that the party was floundering in uncertainty, one day acting as though Stalin was back in the saddle and the next day acting as though de-Stalinization was still the name of the game.

Into this treacherous political swamp entered a thirty-eight-year-old Ukraine-born Russian writer, Vladimir Dudintsev, whose new novel, *Not by Bread Alone*, was quickly becoming a test case for the artistic limits of de-Stalinization. That was by no means Dudintsev's intent. Like many other writers, he had more modest goals in mind: most important, publication and praise—and the perks that would flow from being a successful writer. Had he written a book consistent with the traditional, sleepy norms of socialist realism, with its emphasis on dedicated, muscular workers, he might have achieved his goals. But with *Not by Bread Alone*, Dudintsev had created a main character, an innocent inventor named Lopatkin, who broke the accepted rules of socialist society by acting like an individualist, more absorbed with self than with the collective, which was forbidden in the harsh lands of socialist realism. In the uncertain climate of post-Hungary Kremlin policymaking, Dudintsev could easily be defined as a troublemaker, and so he was, much to his everlasting regret.

Dudintsev was a lawyer who became a journalist and then a novelist. In the 1930s, when Stalin unleashed his bloody purges, Dudintsev was a dedicated member of the Komsomol, the Young Communist League. He studied writing under Lev Kassil, a noted mentor who ran a literary circle in Moscow, and he studied law at the Moscow Institute of Jurisprudence. But before he got a chance to practice law, Nazi Germany invaded Poland and then the Soviet Union. For the Russian people this was the start of a horrible, costly war. Dudintsev joined the Red Army. Soon thereafter he was badly wounded. After his recuperation he was transferred to Siberia, where he served as a military prosecutor. (In *Not by Bread Alone*, Lopatkin is tried and found guilty by the same sort of prosecutor.)

Throughout the war, when he was not practicing law Dudintsev read a great deal, developing a special fondness for such writers as James Joyce and Marcel Proust. After the war he plunged into a study of the Russian masters, especially Ukraine-born Nikolai Gogol, determined to learn enough to be able to write a book about some of the major themes of Soviet life. In 1952 he started to write *Not by Bread Alone*. He finished four years later, shortly after the 20th Party Congress concluded its work. I was told by a Russian friend that Dudintsev had great difficulty finding a publisher, perhaps because the book was considered too controversial. He went from one publisher to another. Each praised the book and predicted that it would be a great success "one day" but refused to accept responsibility for publishing it "now."

In despair, Dudintsev turned to Konstantin Simonov, editor of the literary journal *Novy Mir*, or New World. Would Simonov publish *Not by Bread Alone*, perhaps in installments, dividing the 500-page novel into three parts? Surprisingly, Simonov said yes. In Moscow's literary world, Simonov was known to be an old party hack, not in any way an editor of excitement or daring. So why did he publish the first part in the August edition, the second in September, and the third in October, thereby making an eye-catching literary statement? Because, Simonov later explained, he regarded *Not by Bread Alone* to be the literary equivalent of the 20th Party Congress: big, bold, and promising. By publishing it when others declined to do so, he would be seen as the fearless conquering hero of Moscow's literary wars. His argument was that the 20th Party Congress condemned bureaucracy; so too did the book. The party congress favored initiative and drive; so too did the book. The party congress raised profound social and political questions; so too did this book.

When the first installment appeared, *Not by Bread Alone* was an overnight sensation. "Have you read this new book? Yes, by Dudintsev" was a commonly heard question among students at the Lenin Library. Among Russians literature has always enjoyed a special place. At that time, writers and poets, when reading their works, would attract huge crowds, numbered on occasion in the thousands. Was Dudintsev another Tolstoy? "No, of course not," I kept hearing, but another major writer had clearly surfaced on the literary scene and, with him, his sweet, eccentric hero, the inventor Lopatkin.

Like millions of others in the Soviet proletariat, Lopatkin works in a factory, where after eight years of toiling alone he invents a new machine for the centrifugal casting of iron drain pipes. "A what?" many asked, before bursting into laughter. Here was a character out of Gogol's imagination, so quirky and original, so much the loner, that he has never bothered to check with communist authorities—or with anyone, for that matter—on his road to the "centrifugal casting for iron drain pipes." He has done it on his own. When Lopatkin finally unveils his invention to factory managers and party officials, they are at first delighted and then weirdly appalled. They accuse him of divulging state secrets and send him to an Arctic prison camp. Here, then, was a story, whimsical in its approach, rich in detail, touching in its portrayal of Lopatkin, that described the deadening effect of the Soviet system on the creative powers of a human being. The book left the reader with many questions about the wisdom of the Soviet state and the unbelievably sad experience of a Soviet inventor.

If *Not by Bread Alone* had been published immediately after Khrushchev's anti-Stalin speech, it might have met a happier fate. But, published as it was in August, September, and October 1956, when Khrushchev was already facing powerful conservative pressures to scale back de-Stalinization, the book ran into an ugly and unavoidable buzz saw—which sealed its fate, at least for a time. Though many literary critics loved the book and hailed Dudintsev as a major writer, the Kremlin labeled it "unhealthy, tendentious, and noxious" and denounced Dudintsev as a writer who "one-sidedly and incorrectly understood the essence of party [read Khrushchev's] criticism of Stalin's 'personality cult.'" On December 2 the government newspaper, *Izvestia*, blasted Dudintsev, echoing the criticism leveled by Khrushchev himself—that Dudintsev felt a "narcissistic joy in describing the negative side of Soviet life." Obviously, in any battle between a writer and his boss in the Kremlin, the boss won. Dudintsev's novel was not published in book form until late the following year, and then only in a limited print run. Dudintsev, the man and the writer, was the subject of frequent assaults in the Soviet press. He stopped writing. He lived alone. His colleagues no longer called.

And yet, his book continued to send waves of excitement and defiance through the literary and political worlds in Moscow. One sign was that copies of *Novy Mir*, where it had first appeared, were impossible to find. Months later students in the Lenin Library were still arguing about the book. Many wondered whether Molotov, as the new literary czar, was cleverly using the book as a weapon against Khrushchev. Just as important, the Communist Party felt the need to defend its attacks on Dudintsev publicly, as though its criticism was not being accepted by the people, especially young people.

On the evening of December 11, I happened to be present at one such defense in the Lenin Library. The talk, "Latest Tasks of Modern Soviet Literature," was a serious party effort to ease student skepticism toward official criticism of Dudintsev. The speaker was identified in the announcement as a "literary critic of the Soviet Union" and a leading member of the Union of Writers. A tall man of supreme self-confidence, Grigory Brovman had a receding hairline accentuated by an already large forehead. He wore small, horned-rimmed glasses. His audience was not limited to students. Librarians, teachers, and professors also attended. This was a standing-room-only event. Everyone apparently wanted to hear Brovman, who announced strict guidelines for attending his lecture. No reading allowed! No talking allowed! "If you want to read, go outside now, before I start," he bellowed. "If not, sit still and listen." Literary critic Brovman was not to be messed with.

He began by admitting that much of his criticism might be wrong. "I shall try to be objective," he stressed, "but you may not accept my analysis." For several minutes he sounded not like a respected critic but rather like a party hack. He told a story about the year 1956 that might have been persuasive earlier but that now, after the Hungarian suppression, sounded stale. "A more objective approach to modern Soviet literature is the most outstanding feature of 1956," he said. Ilf and Petrov, the legendary writers of popular tales, were again being published. So, too, was Ivan Bunin, who had incurred Stalin's displeasure. The works of other writers who had been suppressed were again appearing in bookstores, especially those who were writing favorably about the "little person," rather than the "big man," so characteristic of an earlier time.

Then, as though building to a climax, Brovman proclaimed that the masses have again begun to be featured in novels, the proletariat again portrayed as the vanguard of the socialist movement. These were positive developments. In a loud voice, he added, "Those who continue to speak about old truths do not deserve our respect." A happy ripple of excitement flowed through the audience. To my right, a student muttered with satisfaction, "Maybe he's actually going to say something. Maybe he's different."

Brovman continued, hitting the same theme. "There have been many books published this year, comrades, which continue to echo old truths. These are bad books. One must regard literature as the expression of new, dynamic truths." Much to my surprise, students around the room rose to their feet, clapping and smiling with joyful anticipation.

"One writer of note," he went on, "is Vladimir Dudintsev, who wrote the book which has raised so much clamor and fuss and hullabaloo. *Not by Bread Alone*, published in *Novy Mir*, must be discussed seriously." Many in the audience nodded. "It is a fine piece of writing," Brovman continued, "and it has a provocative theme. Dudintsev is a writer of very considerable talent." The audience moved to the edge of their seats. It looked as though they were hoping that Brovman would change the party's critique of Dudintsev—indeed, perhaps praise him, which Brovman in fact proceeded to do. "Dudintsev is a very exceptional writer. His characters are varied and brilliantly portrayed. He paints a very good picture of Drozdov, the bureaucrat, as well as Lopatkin, the inventor. Some of his chapters are absolutely wonderful and rank with the finest in Russian literature."

Brovman was indeed complimentary of Dudintsev, and yet I feared there was going to be a "but" in his praise, even though he continued to sound positive. "Anyone who seeks to find a simple and clear solution to questions raised in this book will be disappointed," he said. No one could argue with that proposition. "There are no simple solutions in life," he continued, "and there are no simple solutions in this book. People simply are not that simple." The audience burst into applause, grateful for Brovman's positive tone and approach, and they did not let up for five minutes or so.

Summoning in his concluding comments the full majesty of the moment and the proper dignity accorded to his title and position, Brovman then dropped his "but" bombshell: "One thing, however, is clear, and in this respect we must all be keenly objective. The book has a major shortcoming of considerable importance. It is the fact that over the span of eight years Lopatkin did not once turn to the collective. We know that as a fighter Lopatkin can at times struggle alone, and this is satisfactory. But over eight years, certainly once, twice, he should have turned to the collective." Like a tire suddenly deflated, the audience seemed all at once to lose air, their sense of joy and hope gone, leaving them feeling once again that change, real change in the system, might in fact be impossible.

Brovman continued as though he had said nothing of special note. "Surely, comrades, in Lopatkin's place, would you not have turned to the collective at least once in eight years? Yes, of course, but Lopatkin does not, and this is a very bad feature of this book. One must in this country turn to the decisive truth of life, the party, once in eight years. It is only normal. By not having the character to do this, Dudintsev created a non-Soviet type, an egoist, an individualist of major proportion." Brovman understood that although he could not persuade the audience of the rightness of his argument, still, in his view, they had to realize that Dudintsev, as a writer and novelist, had to be approached in an "objective" manner. "Whether we say that *Not by Bread Alone* is written in the style of socialist realism, or not, is not very important. Large-scale discussions of whether a volume is socialist realism or not is child's play, for which we do not have the time."

Brovman seemed to be a very practical critic. What he implied was that he admired Dudintsev, but the writer could have bowed ever so slightly to the rules of socialist realism without sacrificing his principles, in this way avoiding the avalanche of official criticism. Lopatkin could still have been portrayed as an individualist while he was inventing his centrifugal gadget, but once or twice over an eight-year period he could have checked in with the collective, the party, and then in effect done what he wanted. In such circumstance the party would have been stripped of grounds for criticizing Dudintsev. "Play the game," Brovman seemed to be urging.

I always felt that though Khrushchev denounced *Not by Bread Alone*, he could have lived with it as a published best seller. Khrushchev, like Brovman, was not a stickler for form. He didn't care whether the book was written in the style of socialist realism or not. He was not much of a reader. For him as a communist leader, books such as *Not by Bread Alone* could be published as long as they did not jeopardize the communist system he ruled—a pragmatic, if short-term, vision. Apparently he did not really understand, nor did he want to understand, that over the long term books such as Dudintsev's did in fact jeopardize the communist system. When writers could write what they wanted, when books could be published on merit alone, when freedom could prevail in an open marketplace, then communism as practiced in the Soviet Union would not, indeed could not, exist. But such a scenario was for another day.

CHAPTER FOURTEEN

Uvarov, Sasha, and Stalin's Ghost

n January 1957, before leaving my assignment at JPRS, I spent two weeks in Leningrad The city, often called the cultural capital of Russia, was founded in 1703. It was christened St. Petersburg in honor of Czar Peter the Great, the name it retained until 1914, the start of World War I. Then it was renamed Petrograd to endow the Russian war effort with a special patriotic glow. In 1924, when Vladimir Lenin, the head of the Bolshevik Revolution, died, St. Petersburg became Leningrad, the name it was to hold until 1991, when the Soviet Union disintegrated. New postcommunist leaders arose, and they decided that the city ought once again to be known by its original name of St. Petersburg. So it was renamed, and so it has been ever since.

It was Peter the Great's favorite city, built in the early eighteenth century in the swamplands of northwestern Russia, where the winding Neva River flows into the Bay of Finland. St. Petersburg was Peter's "window on the West," as it was often called. Like no other city in Russia, it looked and felt

Western. Its narrow alleys and broad boulevards could have been transplanted to any Western European capital, and you would be hard-pressed to tell the difference. Inspired by Italian architects, many of the buildings, yellow and light green in color, decorated with tall classical columns, reflected the emerging imperial power of Peter's Russia and Catherine's later in the century. During my winter stay in Leningrad—just 450 miles from the Arctic Circle—the sky was often pitch black, except during the high noon hours, when the sun would occasionally peak through the charcoal-gray clouds. *Ne sluchayno*, as the Russians would say—"It is not an accident"—that many Russians were known to commit suicide during the winter months, so unremittingly bleak were the short days and long nights.

Despite the winter dark and cold, Leningrad had its magic. No matter the weather, the St. Nicholas Cathedral, with its aqua-colored walls and golden domes, inspired the people with song and prayer. On the first floor, small groups gathered around special candlelit icons; on the second, crowds of the young and old, huddled in heavy overcoats, listened to the melodious choir and the deep bass voice of the elderly priest. Together they composed a scene reminiscent of Dostoevsky's novels or Mussorgsky's opera *Boris Godunov*. Now many were deeply enveloped in prayer, but during World War II the people of this city were trapped in a merciless Nazi siege lasting 999 days. Many died, victims more of the bitter cold and hunger than of tanks and rockets, leaving deep memories.

Nevsky Prospekt, the Fifth Avenue of Leningrad, glistened with a sort of subdued excitement—for those with rubles to spend. The shops were open. Trading seemed vigorous. I enjoyed visiting the old Duma, the czarist parliament, and the Saltykov-Shchedrin Library (where Uvarov was once an assistant librarian), and I was amazed by the Russian crowds—how they maneuvered around the city's icy snow drifts in aimless panic, rushing somewhere or perhaps nowhere. The eye-catching statue of Peter the Great, brave and brazen on horseback, located in a vast park in downtown Leningrad, remained a magnificent magnet not just for the occasional winter tourist but for Russians as well, those who lived there and those who visited.

For anyone familiar with Russian history, Leningrad was a must-see stop. I could not have visited Kiev and Vladimir and missed Peter's "Window on the West." There was another reason, too, for me to visit Leningrad. A number of Moscow librarians, knowing of my interest in Uvarov, had told me that his private papers—letters, documents, family albums— were archived in Leningrad. Maybe, they hinted, I'd be given access to them. I felt I had to make the effort. I did, and I met with modest success.

One day, while hopping from one library to another, I spotted an advertisement on a poster in front of the Pushkin Drama Theater for Maxim Gorky's *Lower Depths* and immediately bought a ticket. *Lower Depths* was a modern classic, a controversial play written in 1901 but not performed in the Soviet Union since the late 1930s. Stalin did not like it, probably because its theme, similar in a way to Dudintsev's in *Not by Bread Alone* (1956), focused on the individual's indomitable spirit rather than on the collective's presumed strengths. It was again the individual against the collective, and it struck a powerful emotional chord among many in the audience. Time and again they interrupted the performance with sustained bursts of applause and shouts of approval. "Truth! Truth!" one man screamed, as he leaped to his feet. "Man is the only truth," another cried. "There never has been another truth, and there never could be." By implication, they were proclaiming their belief that truth, not the state and its know-it-all ideology, represented an ultimate goal of society. These were powerful words, and on this evening in Leningrad they apparently resonated with every man and woman in the audience. They stood up and applauded so vigorously that the performers returned for ten curtain calls. The actors blew kisses at the audience, and the audience blew kisses back. I left the theater feeling that Khrushchev's thaw had clearly planted deep roots in Peter's capital. Even as it was being rechilled in Moscow, it seemed to be warming to the moment in Leningrad. Or was it?

On the morning after the memorable performance of *Lower Depths*, while heading toward the Saltykov-Shchedrin Library, where I hoped to charm the docent into letting me see some of the Uvarov treasures, I passed the Central Lecture Hall on Liteiny Prospekt. A bell rang in my mind. The attractive old mansion, once the home of a Russian nobleman and his family, was the inspiration for many of Pushkin's most notable scenes from his short story "Queen of Spades." The building was now devoted to state-sponsored lectures. One was scheduled for 1:00 p.m., and I decided to attend. The sponsor was the Leningrad Division of the All-Union Society for the Dissemination of Political and Scientific Knowledge (the Soviets were masters at creating long, sometimes baffling, titles), and the subject was "The International Position of the USSR."

While waiting for the lecture to begin, I learned that the originally scheduled speaker, a local communist official named V. D. Smirnov, was being replaced by K. P. Voshchenkov, a more senior, presumably more trusted, party spokesman from Moscow. It was an important subject, and Moscow wanted to get it right. The audience seemed handpicked: although there were some young people, restless in their view that change was inevitable, most in the audience were older, probably members of the Communist Party, serious apparatchiks, the kind who took notes and applauded dutifully.

Voshchenkov started his lecture at exactly 1:00 p.m. He cited a glowing report by the Russian news agency TASS about a meeting, held from January 1 to 4, of the communist leaders of the Soviet Union, Bulgaria, Romania, Czechoslovakia, and Hungary on the "Hungarian situation." This summit meeting was proof, he said, that "good relations" existed among "all" socialist countries. Yugoslavia, East Germany, and Poland did not attend; no reason was offered as to why.

Voshchenkov spoke of a world divided into two camps: the "black forces of fascism" marked by "open American connivance" in the Hungarian rebellion, and the "peace-loving forces of socialism," which have given a "vigorous and decisive rebuff to the imperialist camp." He repeatedly referred to Lenin as the source of all wisdom. Stalin was not mentioned.

He asserted that the United States was "ugly," "evil," "responsible for insidious plots and conspiracies to bring capitalism back to Hungary. . . . They wish to destroy the great achievements of the socialist system in the Soviet Union and in Hungary. . . . They wish to establish military bases in Eastern Europe for use against the peace-loving Soviet Union. They are planning a Third World War." I later noted in my diary that Voshchenkov "castigated America in the most vicious terms I have ever heard since I came to the Soviet Union." And, reading the Soviet press every day, I thought I had heard quite a few.

Voshchenkov spoke with passion. He had a strong voice and a commanding presence. No one interrupted him. Hungary was clearly at the center of his concerns. "Many say that the events in Hungary have weakened the camp of socialism," he argued. "This is false. They have weakened the camp of capitalism. They have dealt a crushing blow to American monopolists. The camp of socialism, on the contrary, has been considerably strengthened by these events." But, he continued, "we have learned an important lesson." He paused, stared menacingly at his audience, glanced down at his papers, then again at his audience, suggesting that if they hadn't listened carefully before, they should now. "We thought we could get along with the capitalists, but we have erred." He again paused. "It is impossible to get along with capitalists." This seemed more the language of Molotov than of Khrushchev, more the language of hard-liners, who evinced no interest in "peaceful coexistence"— Khrushchev's policy—with the capitalist West. Were Molotov and his followers gaining so much power that they could press their line in public in Leningrad? I wondered what was going on.

"They will stop at nothing," Voshchenkov continued, pressing his argument. "They wish to restore capitalism in Hungary. But the putsch did not have a broad base. Only the fascists supported the revolt. [Admiral Miklos] Horthy and his men, equipped with American arms, took part in the revolt—not the honest workers. The Americans wanted to create a military base in Hungary, bring war very close, but we have stopped these vicious intrigues, and we will continue to crush these attempts. With the failure of the events in Hungary, the American monopolists have changed their tactics, but their aim remains the same."

A second theme pushed by Voshchenkov that day was the recent Anglo-French-Israeli attack on Egypt, which opened the door to aggressive Russian moves into the Middle East. Here was additional proof that the "imperialists" were seeking to roll back the "peaceful progress of the socialist camp." He painted a picture of the "capitalist encirclement" of the Soviet Union, a line out of Stalin's handbook and one that the 20th Party Congress was supposed to have supplanted with "peaceful coexistence." This was what he said about events in the Middle East (I took notes throughout Voshchenkov's talk): "The attack and aggression against Egypt is just another link in a major imperialist conspiracy against all peace-loving countries, against the Soviet Union, and the [neutralist] Bandung countries. Even in Indonesia, the Americans are trying to convert the country into an American military base. Churchill, who takes an active, backstage role in instigating the West against Russia, is just as bad as Hitler, and you all know what happened to Hitler! The Dulles-Eisenhower doctrine is nothing more than another American attempt to convert the Middle East into an American stronghold, taking advantage of the weakened position of the British and the French. There is a constant threat against the Soviet Union, and its purpose is a Third World War."

While in the Soviet Union that year I always had to remind myself that World War II had ended only eleven years before. Many cities, including Moscow and Leningrad, still showed scars of the Nazi assault. Many Russians still felt the pain of wartime losses—husbands, sons, children who died at the front. They did not want war; indeed, I thought they would instinctively oppose any policy that moved the world toward war. That was why the Kremlin always blamed the United States for any dangerous confrontation between the two rivals. The fault was never to be the USSR's.

When he finished, Voshchenkov was greeted with a tidal wave of applause that boomed off the walls of a lecture hall that had once been noted for aristocratic elegance, Viennese waltzes, and Pushkin's poetry. Because he was speaking in a lecture hall and not at a university, the questions were polite but still reflected the uneasy mood of the populace.

"Why weren't Poland and Yugoslavia invited to the summit?"

"How come UN observers were not allowed into Hungary? Did the Soviet Union veto such a move?"

"Was Nagy a counterrevolutionary?"

"Is Tito a good Marxist?"

"Why are the Jews such a warlike people?"

"Why did you allow some people to read newspapers while you were speaking?"

Voshchenkov's answers were rarely elucidating. He seemed eager to pack his papers and leave. His audience seemed content with his presentation; they accepted both his reliance on orthodox Marxist formulas to resolve complicated problems and his obvious unwillingness to provide honest answers. In his lecture I caught a glimpse of the real Soviet Union—among ordinary people a stunning lack of political sophistication, a shortage of reliable information, a willingness to live with obvious mendacity and mediocrity, and, despite the 20th Party Congress and the thaw it sparked, an underlying fear among many that a wrong word, a look of disapproval, could get anyone, even a member of the party, into serious trouble. Once again I felt sorry for the Russian people. They deserved better.

■

My first "official" visit to the Saltykov-Shchedrin Library was acutely disappointing. I had been led to believe that the head of the manuscript division would be both friendly and cooperative. He was neither. In a brief meeting, chilly though his office was overheated, he told me that the library had Uvarov's archives but he needed prior approval from his superiors before he could open them to my perusal. He was really hoping that I would just go away. "Perhaps it would be more convenient if you returned tomorrow. I might have word then," he suggested.

I answered that I would return later in the day, at about three.

"Tomorrow," he repeated.

"Three this afternoon," I insisted, stressing I had only a limited amount of time in Leningrad.

"More likely tomorrow," he said, sighing, and looked down at his papers. Our meeting adjourned on this sorry note of stalemate.

Undaunted, I made my way through the crowds to the Institute for Russian Literature, where I hoped my hunt for Uvarov's archives would meet with a happier end. And, miraculously, it did. An old man greeted me in the cloakroom with . . . a smile, of all things. He seemed like a pre-revolutionary relic—small, polite, curious, almost charming. When he took my coat, he paused to admire it.

"How much does it cost?" he asked.

"Seventy-five dollars," I replied, "or roughly three hundred rubles at your official exchange rate."

The old man seemed flustered. "No," he said, shaking his head, "impossible." He examined the coat more closely. "This would cost three thousand rubles here, at least, and in any case we couldn't get it. We couldn't find one like it. No, impossible." One of his friends, overhearing our conversation, approached and felt the material of the coat with experienced fingers. He joked, "I can get the exact same coat in Moscow for two hundred seventy-five rubles," at which point he and the old man snickered, each with a broad smile, knowing they could not buy such a coat in Leningrad or Moscow at any price.

I asked the librarian at the information desk if I could see—and study—the Uvarov archive. Like so many other librarians, she asked, "Why Uvarov?" I gave her my standard reply: I wanted to cover both sides of Russian history, the communist and the conservative sides. She nodded and asked me to wait in the vestibule. I waited, and waited, and waited, taking in large photos of Pushkin on every wall. After a while Pushkin's face seemed to change—he began to resemble an unappealing KGB agent. Ten minutes passed, and then twenty. After a half hour had passed, I grew restless and thought about leaving. Why not? I could always return the next day or try another library. But then, in the semi-darkness of the vestibule, a tall, graceful woman appeared. She was carrying an old file. My heart skipped a beat.

I rose as she approached. "Mr. Kalb," she said, shaking my hand. "I have a file of Uvarov's letters for you." I gulped. "You will, of course, have to fill out some forms, but first I have a question." I tried to contain my excitement. For a full year I had been trying, desperately, to get my hands on Uvarov's files, but time and again the Soviet bureaucracy would either act dumb or impose obstacles. Uvarov seemed unobtainable. Now, wonder of wonders, this tall woman with a dusty file appeared, and suddenly a treasure house of scholarly goodies opened before me—but, I had to admit, at a very inopportune time. In a single week my stay in the Soviet Union would come to an end. "Don't complain," I said to myself. "Smile, and be grateful." I tried.

Her question was the one I had come to expect from every Soviet librarian: "Why are you studying Uvarov?" My answer was the one I had fashioned over many months, one that was both truthful and, I hoped, understandable. I was a student of Russian history. The communist side of that history had been explored for decades, but the conservative side, shelved throughout the Soviet period, was largely ignored. It was about time its principal architect, Uvarov, founder of the famous slogan "Nationalism, Autocracy, and Orthodoxy," was rediscovered and brought to the bar of history. Not persuaded but gracious nonetheless, the librarian nodded. "I guess so," she said, shaking her head and sighing.

As I filled out the required forms, she sat opposite me and began to ask questions about American life, especially the prices of consumer goods—dresses, shoes, food, cars, apartments. Before long we slipped from consumer goods to a Q and A about the need for internal passports. I told her I found the Soviet practice of carrying internal passports on all domestic travel to be "offensive" and "demeaning."

She was amazed. "Surely you need some sort of identification in the United States," she said.

"Yes, of course," I replied, "a driver's license, a draft card, a library card, but not an internal passport. That's for foreign travel." Many Americans traveling in the Soviet Union, I told her, felt like criminals, having to show their passport at every turn in the road, their word never trusted.

"Well," she countered, "Russians feel like criminals whenever they have to be fingerprinted during visits to the United States. Fingerprints are for criminals, not for honest people."

"Look," I said, "I had to put up with the humiliation of showing an internal passport just to get into this library."

"I guess you've got a point there," she said and then quickly changed the subject. She wanted me to meet a "treasure house of a man, a genius, a gift of God, who also knows a great deal about nineteenth-century Russia."

"Absolutely," I said. "I'd be honored to meet him." The librarian vanished for a few minutes and returned with a short man with graying hair, Professor Alexander Berkov, knowledgeable, it was soon apparent, in many fields of scholarship.

The librarian invited us into her office, shut the door, sat down in the corner, and listened to our discussion of Russian and Soviet historiography. I was amazed at Berkov's familiarity with American scholars of the Soviet Union. He specifically mentioned Michael Karpovich of Harvard, George Vernadsky of Yale, Hans Kohn of City College, and Philip Mosely of Columbia. He also gave me valuable pointers on my Uvarov research. We spoke for about an hour, and I enjoyed every minute. We parted as friends. "Stay in touch," he said.

I promised I would, and with an extra measure of energy and excitement sparked by our talk, I opened the Uvarov file and started reading a letter Uvarov had written to his wife in 1842. It contained no nugget, no special insight into his family life, but I was thrilled. I read one letter after another, a few more to his wife and staff and many relating to his special interest in Greek literature. He was, it was clear, a careful, meticulous man, but I saw no evidence that he was a brilliant scholar. I filled my note pad with many quotes and impressions, all valuable in the writing of a dissertation. After three hours I returned the file to the tall librarian, thanked her, and promised to return the following day.

As I left the institute I realized that I was grinning with satisfaction. It was finally happening. I was doing what could only be described as original research in the Soviet Union. Finally, Uvarov would have his day in the sun.

At 5:00 p.m., the day's noontime sliver of sunlight long since gone, I made my way back to the Saltykov-Shchedrin Library. This time, instead of asking to see the sour, unresponsive head of the manuscript division, I asked to see the library's *uchenyi sekretar*, "academic secretary," the catch-all phrase for an institution's top administrator and sometimes its principal intellectual. Much to my surprise, he agreed to see me, and he knew about my earlier request for access to the Uvarov archive. When I asked whether I could actually see the archive, he answered matter-of-factly, "Yes, of course. Why not?" I almost collapsed in surprise. After so many no's, for the second time in one day I was getting a yes.

He could not resist the "Why Uvarov?" question, saying "Why anyone would want to study such a reactionary is beyond me." But we were soon on our way through a maze of corridors guarded by uniformed militiamen who at each turn insisted on seeing the *uchenyi sekretar*'s *propusk* and of course mine. When we reached the manuscript division he gave me a thick file of official letters and documents relating to Uvarov's time as Czar Nicholas II's minister of education. I wasted no time. I thanked him, sat down at an empty desk, and began reading the letters and documents.

At exactly 7:00 p.m. the *uchenyi sekretar* asked how much more time I needed. He had been sitting at an adjacent desk reading a newspaper. I told him I did not know. At 7:10 p.m. he asked me the same question, only this time with more urgency. I again told him I did not know. At 7:20 p.m. he made no pretense of politeness. He simply told me to stop working and return the file. I was surprised and puzzled and asked why I had to stop—there was still much more to do, and I wanted to get as much done as I could. With a smile of embarrassment, he whispered that he had a ticket to a movie at 8:00 p.m., and it was his responsibility to escort me out of the building, past all of the inquisitive militiamen. I understood immediately. I could never have gotten out of the building without him. As we left the library he assured me I would have no trouble resuming my work on my next visit.

I was to have one more exhilarating experience that day, when I was mistaken for a suave French singer. I hailed a cab, and the cabdriver launched into a rhapsodic report on Yves Montand's astoundingly successful swing through the Soviet Union. Like me, Montand was staying at the Astoria Hotel. As we approached I saw a huge crowd of Russian bobbysoxers. They swarmed toward my cab as it slowed to a stop in front of the main entrance. When I got out of the cab, they broke into a loud, sustained cheer.

"Montand," they shouted, screaming and swooning. "Montand," they cried. They thought I was Yves Montand! They mobbed me. They demanded my autograph. They kissed the hem of my coat. Young *stilyagi* grabbed my hands; others ripped away my scarf. I tried telling them I was not Montand, but they did not believe me. "Montand," they kept shouting. "He's so modest. Just like him. He says he is not Montand." Militiamen rushed to my rescue and escorted me into the lobby of the hotel. For a fleeting moment I thought of myself as the "False Dmitri," who 350 years earlier had raised a terrible ruckus in Russia by pretending that he was the czar.

But I could not resist the temptation to play the Montand role. At the last minute, just before I actually entered the hotel, I turned toward the crowd, still uncertain about whether I was the real Montand or a tall foreigner pretending to be Montand, and waved and blew them all a kiss. If asked—who knows?—I might have delivered an address on the hardships of singing in Parisian nightclubs. But then, rather unceremoniously, I thought, the militiamen pushed me into the lobby, and my moment of fame ended.

That evening, when I stepped into the busy restaurant, not waiting for the maitre d' to seat me, I spotted a man sitting alone at a small table to the left of a four-piece orchestra that seemed bent on butchering popular American songs. "May I join you?" I asked. The man seemed hesitant at first but then gestured toward the empty chair. For a half hour neither of us spoke, although I did order my dinner. Perhaps because he could hear an accent in my Russian, he finally broke the ice and asked whether I was an American. When I said yes, his face broke into a broad smile.

"I knew it," he said. "I just knew it." But then as quickly as he smiled, he suddenly looked sad. "How long it has been since I last spoke to an American." He filled first my glass with wine, and then his. We clicked glasses and toasted Khrushchev's mantra of "peace and friendship." Moments later he erupted with questions about America and me—about New York City, where I was born; Washington, where I worked; Cambridge, where I studied; about baseball (he too was a Yankee fan), basketball, and classical music as well as jazz; about Averell Harriman and Dwight Eisenhower; and, finally, about poetry and poets. He loved Carl Sandburg and Robert Frost. He thought Conrad Aiken was brilliant, and he worshipped T. S. Eliot. "My greatest delight is to read American poets," he declared. "Many evenings when I come home from work, I pick up an old 1927 anthology I have, with an introduction by Aiken, and read the poems over and over again." He smiled softly. "They pick me up and transport me to a dream world."

I had stumbled upon an English-language teacher who taught in a small technical school in Leningrad. In my diary I called him Sasha, although that was not his real name. He was forty-five years old, born in Ukraine, and raised in Moscow. In 1928 his father got a better job in Leningrad, and the family moved there. "This was the closest I could get to the West," he explained. "It is the most Western city in Russia, I would say."

We exchanged biographical information for more than an hour, and then I told Sasha about my interest in Russian history, especially the Soviet period. I told him about Uvarov, which produced a look of disapproval.

Busy Moscow street with the author, center. Russians across the street line up in front of food stores.

"You are not serious," he frowned. And I told him about the Voshchen-kov lecture, stressing that I had not heard anything as savagely anti-American in my time in the Soviet Union.

"What's going on?" I asked.

Sasha, looking uncomfortable, answered, "To be completely truthful with you, I pay very little attention to politics." He searched in my eyes for understanding. "Maybe that's why I love your American poetry so much. Much of it is so light, so tender, so individual, so loving, that it lifts me from this world and carries me to a sweet and fragrant paradise."

I asked, "Is 'this world' Russia and the 'fragrant paradise' America?"

Sasha apparently felt he could not be precise. But his English was so poetic that I often got lost in its beauty and missed a carefully nuanced political hint. He spoke often in flowing metaphors, quoting Sandburg and Frost by heart, and to strengthen his message, political or poetic, he would add a phrase from Aiken, always with a mysterious, faraway smile of satisfaction.

Hungary, though, was special. It brought Sasha back to politics, however reluctantly. "In recent time the only issue that made me raise my eyebrows," he admitted, "was Hungary. The effects have reverberated not only through Russia but also throughout the world. It has made many of us think, think really hard, for the first time in many years. I think it has had as great an effect on the Russian intelligentsia"—Sasha smiled as he used this phrase—"as the death of Stalin."

"Big words, Sasha, big words," I said. "As big as the death of Stalin?"

Sasha nodded, adding, "The information we have of course is limited, but I think the government probably did the right thing."

"The right thing?" His judgment left me momentarily speechless. How could a lover of American poetry condone his government's brutality in Hungary?

"Sasha, forgive me, but you are very, very wrong." I didn't want to elaborate but I couldn't stop. I wanted to "prove" to Sasha that he was wrong. "The facts about the Hungarian revolution are clear," I said. "A majority of the people rose up against communism and against Russia. They did not want either. This might be hard for you to accept, but the Hungarian people will never accept communism or the presence of Russian troops in their country. They hate both. Just remove the troops, and you will see how quickly the people will remove the last vestiges of communism." I reached for a summary thought: "In Eastern Europe communism rests on the bayonets of Red Army troops, and nothing more."

Sasha objected. He said I was exaggerating the crisis in Hungary, that in time the people would accept both communism and the Red Army, and be grateful for both. "But you know," he continued, "I think that even in the ugliness of the situation, there is still beauty. It is like Macaulay's essay on revolution when he writes that the ugliness of revolution can yield beauty in the long run, and we must not be blinded by temporary darkness to the possibility of a bright future."

"Sasha," I said, "you are a romantic. Your quotes sound nice, but the facts demand another conclusion. The Hungarians do not want the Russians there—it is as simple as that. You cannot export revolution on a Red Army tank. Surely that is not orthodox communism."

"No, it isn't. But it is orthodox Bolshevism."

His voice turned hard, almost confrontational, and I realized, as he did, that we had unintentionally allowed ourselves to slip into an argument. I apologized immediately—that was never my intent. But I could not understand Sasha's defense of the Russian crackdown in Hungary. "How can you condone such brutality?" I asked.

"What else am I to do?" Sasha said. For a few minutes, he bent over the table, his head down, his elbows on his knees.

On only one issue was Sasha unabashedly critical of his government. He wanted more artistic exchanges between the Soviet Union and the West, especially the United States. "My friends want books from the West. They want artistic exchanges. They do not believe that artistic freedom should be constrained by communist doctrine." His voice grew stronger as he continued. "We all feel that socialism is inevitable throughout the world. It is a law of history. It is inexorable. But at the same time we do not feel that art follows inexorable rules. We believe that socialist realism should be abolished as an artistic doctrine. It is harmful and restrictive."

Sasha reached across the table and held my hands. "You simply cannot imagine," he said, his eyes moist with emotion, "how happy we were this past summer, seeing so many foreigners in Russia, hearing and enjoying your great artists, like Isaac Stern, Jan Peerce, and the Boston Symphony Orchestra. We would like all of this to continue. We don't want a change to the old days." I reminded Sasha again of the tone of the lecture I had heard. "It looks to me like we are heading backwards, not forwards," I said.

Sasha disagreed. "I think you are too pessimistic," he said. "This won't happen. This cannot happen."

We had been talking for a long time. The waitresses were beginning to give us dirty looks. I suggested we go for a walk. Nevsky Prospekt was our destination. It was crowded and noisy. After a few blocks Sasha steered me toward a bus stop and we got on a bus. After a short ride he walked me to the front of the Astoria, but not into the lobby. He told me that he was grateful for the time we had spent together, and he promised to call me in a few days. I knew I had met a wonderful human being, a Russian I would like to call a friend, a Russian deserving of open borders and free exchanges. But I was left wondering whether he would call me in a few days, as he had promised.

Over the next few days, with my Russia clock quickly running out of time, I spent a great deal of my days at the Saltykov-Shchedrin Library and the Institute for Russian Literature, where I had been granted access to Uvarov's papers. My immediate problem was no longer bureaucratic but just time: I had too little of it to finish the job, no matter how much effort I put into the task. I took notes on the many documents I read, but there were simply too many documents and not enough time. I had an idea. During one break for tea and dark bread, I asked the *uchenyi sekretar* if I could microfilm the documents, letters, and papers I would not have the time to read during my stay in Leningrad. After finishing my research I would give the microfilm to Harvard's Widener Library as the opening of an exchange of scholarly data and documents between the Soviet Union and the United States.

His eyes lit up like a Christmas tree. He loved the idea, but neither of us had the authority to consummate any such deal. And we knew it. The *uchenyi sekretar* proposed instead that he would, on his own hook, microfilm the Uvarov papers I had before me, and I would then promise to deliver them to the Widener Library once I was finished with them. Not only was this an unorthodox proposal (Soviet officials, even *uchenyi sekretary*, did not negotiate on their own, and certainly not with foreign diplomats). It was also a very brave and generous act, considering the rigid, unyielding nature of the Soviet bureaucracy, especially when foreigners were involved.

"Thank you," I said, shaking his hand. "That was very kind of you." He laughed. "No one has ever shown an interest in Uvarov," he said, "so I wanted to help, if I could." We had a deal, sort of. Except for a little problem that we should have foreseen. We had both foolishly assumed that the library's microfilm apparatus would be working, but like so many other pieces of modern technology in Russia, that day it was "on remont"—being repaired. After a few telephone calls, the embarrassed *uchenyi sekretar* assured me that the microfilming of the Uvarov papers would be completed "tomorrow, late in the day." His use of the word "tomorrow" left me limp with anxiety.

"Do not worry," he assured me. "You have my word."

"What time tomorrow?" I asked.

"Five in the afternoon," he said. "No doubt about it."

His assurance left me more anxious than ever, but I had no alternative. He was doing me a favor. He knew it; I knew it. "See you tomorrow at five," I said, emphasizing the word "tomorrow." He again smiled. We agreed on the documents to be microfilmed and shook hands once more, and I returned to the Astoria, where, much to my surprise, I spotted Sasha pacing near the taxi line to the right of the main entrance.

"Come with me," Sasha said, putting his right hand under my left arm. "I want to show you what Leningrad is really like."

I had not expected to see Sasha until the following day—that is, if he called me at all, which I considered far from certain. "Were you waiting for me long, Sasha? I am so happy to see you."

"No, only a few minutes," he lied poorly.

"But where are we going?"

"I'll show you soon enough."

We walked briskly to a bus stop on the Nevsky Prospekt and boarded a waiting bus. After a few minutes, as I stared out the window, I had a feeling that we had just been transported in time and place, suddenly finding ourselves in another city. The streets were narrower, and dirtier, and the people were dressed in shabby clothes, looking nothing like the comparatively well-dressed members of the *nomenklatura* strolling along the Nevsky. I spotted a street sign—Prospekt Gaza, named for a Bolshevik worker at a nearby factory.

Sasha pointed out the window. "Further down this road are the Putilov Works. You remember, they played a very prominent role in the revolution." I did remember, of course, but Sasha continued anyway. "It's
very important, this factory, because in 1917, Stalin spoke there twice." It
was his sort of political humor.

We never did get to the Putilov Works. To my left, as we entered the
vast Narva Square, I saw the historic Narva Triumphal Arch, constructed
in 1814 to commemorate Russia's historic victory over Napoleon, and I
wanted to get off the bus and see it more closely. Sasha was delighted to
oblige. "In the old days, before the revolution, I'm told, the gate was in a
park filled with trees, and it was very beautiful. But now, as you can see,
it is surrounded by apartment houses, and it is not pretty at all." Maybe
not pretty, I agreed, but it was impressive and powerful, a reminder of a
great moment in Russian history. I had read somewhere that during the
Nazi siege the huge columns blocked German tanks from entering the
center of the city.

We walked through the vast square, stopping every now and then to
look more closely at an interesting frieze or cornice, and then we entered dark narrow streets, crowded with early-evening shoppers, the
women wearing heavy woolen scarves over their heads and shoulders
and the men wearing fur hats with ear flaps left defiantly open. Each
person seemed to be carrying a loaf of bread, essential for their dinner.
They moved past old, small houses with cracked walls and broken windows. Children played on the ice, sliding down small inclines on the seat
of their pants. They were having a good time.

"You were spending too much time on the Nevsky," said Sasha, breaking into my bleak urban reverie. "This is the real Leningrad, and these
are the people who made the revolution. They represent the true proletariat. The revolution was made in their name. Now look at them. Look
how they live, how they dress." Anger and disappointment swept over
his face, emotions so out of character with his generally mild, ascetic
appearance.

"How would you like to have a beer?" he asked. "It's not Ballantine,
but it'll have to do." He smiled when he said "Ballantine." "I know lots of

trade names, like Chevrolet, Chrysler—is Fritz Kreisler really the manager of the Chrysler automobile company?—and Coca-Cola—have you ever really drunk Coca-Cola?" A beer seemed like a good idea.

We entered a *pivnoy zal*, a beer hall. It was small and smoky, filled with round tables but no chairs. I attracted immediate attention, standing at least a head or more taller than most of the clientele, and I was wearing a tweed overcoat, Western in design. The men there all wore dark coats, and many were drunk. Their favorite drink, it seemed, was vodka with beer chasers. They cursed in loud voices and seemed to take an instant dislike to me.

Sasha ordered two beers and we brought them to a table. A few feet away, around another table, four very drunk Russians stared resentfully at me and Sasha. One snarled, raising his fist, as though ready to fight. "Why would a *stilyag* come here? Why, I ask? To show off, that's why. To show off." He took a menacing step toward me. Sasha held up his hand, urging everyone to stay calm, but his effort failed.

Now not one but two men staggered toward us. "I hate *stilyagi*," one of them hissed. He obviously thought we were rich Russians. "I hate you well-dressed *stilyagi*," he bellowed. "I hate you and your Western clothing." He turned toward his friend, and shouted, "I wouldn't give two kopecks for his coat, or his hat or his suit. I hate him. And, you know, he does not really look like a Russian. He looks like one of those Germans I used to see during the war, and I hate Germans, I hate Germans, and I hate *stilyagi*."

The atmosphere chilled. Everyone expected a fight to break out at any moment. The drunks formed a circle around us. I made a quick decision. I would speak in English and praise Leningrad. If I had spoken in Russian, they would have assumed I was a Soviet citizen, though perhaps not from Leningrad, maybe from the Baltic area or Moscow. "I love Leningrad," I said, with as much of a smile as I could manage, "and I admire the Russian people." A question clouded many faces. "Maybe he is a foreigner," I heard one Russian say.

"No," the loudest of the loud drunks exclaimed, before anyone else could speak. "He's a *stilyag*, a rich *stilyag*. They come here and boast about how rich they are. I know his type. They're all over here these days."

His friend, equally drunk but suddenly more cautious, asked me if I was a foreigner. I pretended I did not understand him. I repeated what I had said earlier—that I "loved" Leningrad and "admired" the Russian people. The loud drunk lunged toward me, but his more cautious friend intervened, grabbed him by the collar, and threw him to the floor.

"Stop it," he cried, shaking his head. "He may really be a foreigner."

The loud drunk got up from the floor and again staggered toward me, but this time he did not look as though he wanted to fight. He turned to his friends and roared, "I shall ask him." Sasha quickly stepped between us.

"Sasha," I shouted in English, "let him come. It'll be okay." Reluctantly Sasha pulled back but stayed close to me.

The drunk asked, "Are you a Russian?"

I looked at him, and in English answered, "I do not understand you."

The words in a foreign tongue seemed to strike him like a thunderbolt. He reeled back against his friend, who was standing directly behind him.

"Maybe he is a foreigner," he said, a question mark in his voice.

The drunk then retreated to his table, looking like a person who had just suffered a stunning humiliation. He belted back a vodka, and then another, and then he retraced his steps and apologized to me. "I did not know that you were a foreigner," he said. "I did not know." I shook my head, again explaining in English that I did not understand him. He again apologized and returned to his friends. There would be no fight between the worker and the "rich *stilyag*." Relieved, Sasha and I finished our beers and left.

"I feel terrible about what happened," Sasha started. "Please understand: I spend very little time in a *pivnoy zal*. I don't really know these people. I am as much a foreigner to them as you are."

"Sasha, please don't apologize. We both learned something today. I learned more about Russia in the last five minutes than I would have if I spent another week in the libraries. I should thank you. Today I met the Russian proletariat, and what's especially interesting is, I think today you met him too." Sasha nodded in agreement.

We decided to walk back to the Astoria. It was a long walk, but we had much to say to each other. Among other things: Sasha explained why he had not married the woman he loved (he was an intellectual, a teacher, of only modest means, and she was the daughter of a general, who insisted that she marry up, not down), and he also explained his feelings about communism pre-Hungary and post-Hungary. Pre-Hungary, communism was a "wonderful, idealistic idea, hardly perfect but certainly acceptable," he said. Post-Hungary, communism became "my private nightmare, a dream filled with hope, shattered by an ideology lacking hope."

Why, I wondered, had he not confided this change to me, when we discussed Hungary a few nights before? "I didn't trust you," he answered. "Just that simple."

We also discussed music and books, and as we approached the Astoria, I told him about my "negotiation" with the *uchenyi sekretar*. He was amazed. "You must be a good diplomat," he said, smiling. "Good luck. I hope tomorrow actually means tomorrow, and you get your microfilm."

"I hope so too," I said, a prayer hidden in my voice.

The following morning, at 11:00 a.m., I met with a young historian from Leningrad University whom I had first met a week earlier. He had assured me at that time that he knew a way to gain access to the Uvarov archives. "The Central Historical Archives," he whispered, as if he was conveying a big secret. "They're on Decembrist Square, near the statue of the Bronze Horseman."

I told him I appreciated his help, but the archives were under the control of the KGB, and any effort by a foreigner to gain access was an invitation to frustration and ultimately to failure. "I tried once in Moscow," I explained. "It didn't work then, and probably won't now."

The young historian exploded in anger. "This I cannot understand! What difference would it make to anyone if you saw Uvarov's personal papers? What difference at all? Certainly Uvarov's papers would reveal no state secrets." He lit a cigarette with shaky hands. "Sometimes I get so angry!"

After an awkward few moments, we swung the discussion to matters of Western historiography on Russia. I told him that in a number of American universities scholars were digging into the works of many pre-revolutionary Russian conservatives—the Slavophiles, Nikolai Karamzin, Count Sergey Witte, Pyotr Stolypin. My study of Uvarov was only one of many, and far from the most important.

"This is what we need to do too," the historian interjected. "We need real scholarship. We must be alert to all trends in history. Sticking only to Marxism cuts us off from the historical truth, which is made up of many different and even conflicting tendencies and trends."

My surprise at his blunt critique must have appeared on my face.

"What's the matter?" he asked. "Are you surprised to hear me say these things? Are you surprised to hear me say what I think and feel? If so, you should attend some of the student meetings I have been at recently. Many times, such a tumult is raised that the professors must end the meetings, because they simply cannot control them anymore."

I had heard the student tumult in Moscow, and it was gratifying to hear a young historian speak of similar eruptions in Leningrad.

███

Sasha called, and we agreed to meet at a small café on the Nevsky called the Seagull, named no doubt after Chekhov's play. Up to this point, with few exceptions, we had talked mostly about literary matters, but on this occasion Sasha also wanted to talk about politics.

"We may never see each other again," he began, startling me, "and I want to say I shall never forget you. You are the first American I ever met, the first one with whom I have spoken at length. You are so different from what I expected."

"What did you expect?" I asked. "I mean, did you believe what you read in your papers?"

"Well, not everything, but I do believe that certain circles rule your government and determine American policy."

"Who are these circles, Sasha. Describe them to me."

"Everyone knows that certain circles of capitalists are interested only in making enormous profits and finding these profits in the manufacture of military weapons and guns. These circles are on Wall Street, and they run Congress."

Sasha's entire frame of reference was Marxist. He saw everything through the prism of Marxism: large crowds of workers, growing larger but getting poorer, dominated by a small class of monopolists, growing smaller and getting richer. There was no difference between the Democratic and Republican parties—both reflected only capitalist interests. Corruption and misery—everywhere. Slums for the workers, Park Avenue for the capitalists, and no road between the two worlds.

He summarized his views. "Your country is technically very powerful, very productive economically. We know that your workers live better than ours. That is because you have a higher technology. We believed that if communism took over in America, there would be a real paradise on earth there, because you have such an advanced technology."

Average American workers, I explained, were not socialists, and certainly not communists. They were very bourgeois in their tastes and attitudes. In this respect, American workers resembled Hungarian workers. Neither wanted socialism. Sasha seemed incredulous. "Surely this is impossible," he insisted. "Workers love socialism. Socialism is a worker's doctrine. Socialism was created for workers. How can they not like socialism?"

"Sasha, let's face it: you are an intellectual, not a worker. You do not share their hopes and miseries. Hungary reveals one thing very clearly: the workers did not want socialism, at least Soviet-style socialism."

"But you must admit they did not want a return to fascism."

"In fact, I don't know what they wanted, but they did not want socialism. In the long term, maybe they had a plan, maybe they didn't. As in many revolutions, emotions carried the day." I paused for a moment. "They did not have a doctrine for tomorrow, only a hatred of yesterday."

Sasha weighed my argument carefully. When he did formulate a reply, it sounded prosaic, as if he was recalling *Pravda* editorials and regurgitating them. It was the safer way. "The Red Army had to move into Hungary," he began. "If it hadn't, the Western armies would have. We had to stem the rise of fascism. We hate fascism. The workers were misled by black reactionaries, and mistakes were committed. Honest communists were killed." He rambled on, his voice listless. He spoke as if he wanted to justify a doctrine on which his life had been based. To abandon it, in the absence of a sensible alternative, would translate quickly into ideological bankruptcy, a kind of emptiness, for which he was not ready.

He continued: "Capitalists distort news and information about the Soviet Union, about my country. The bourgeois press twists the truth almost beyond recognition. That's why you think this is a bad country. It is really a very good country. You write about a reign of terror, about fear, about misery, about a lack of culture."

"Sasha, it's true that we have written about a reign of terror, about fear, misery, and many other things. Some of these reports have been exaggerated, but basically they are true. Are they not?"

"No, they are false. They are all false." His voice reached a falsetto pitch.

"Sasha," I said in a whisper, "come back to the hotel with me."

My question seemed to stun him. "What did you say?"

"I asked you to come back to the hotel with me for a drink. Will you?" Sasha grew defensive. "No, I don't think I shall."

"But why? Why, Sasha? In America, this would be the normal thing."

"Someone might misinterpret my visit."

"But who, why?"

"Oh, someone might. Someone might." His voice trailed off, his shoulders slumped, and his face looked twenty years older. He looked up at me after a while. I saw tears in his eyes. His hands, trembling, reached out toward mine. "Oh, my friend, my dear friend," he said. "It is not easy. It is not so easy. Life is hard, very hard," and he held both of my hands in his for a long time before we both decided we needed a breath of fresh air.

Outside we were greeted with a burst of frigid air. It felt like a reprieve from political exile. We walked quickly through dark streets, past a large cathedral, past the spot where Alexander II was assassinated, heading back toward the Nevsky. "Sasha, have you ever seen the Russian moderns?" I asked, wanting to change the subject and lighten the mood. I had heard these priceless wonders were stored on the third floor of the Russian Museum, not open for public exhibition. "No, I have not, but would you like to see them?" Sasha had a friend, he said, who might be able to get me in. At the hotel, he said he would call me in the morning if he succeeded.

Sasha did call the following morning. He spoke in a quiet voice. "I saw my friend this morning," he said, "but I did not ask her for permission. And I did not ask her for permission for the same reason I did not come to your hotel for a drink last night." His voice started to crack. I assured him I would find a way to see the Russian moderns on my own, some other time perhaps, and I urged him not to be upset. "But I would have liked to help you, my friend, but I can't." He seemed to be taking a deep breath. "You're right, and I'm wrong, but what can I do?" Sasha then started to cry. He cried for a few second, and then I heard a click on the phone. He had hung up.

What more was there for me to do? I returned to the Saltykov-Shchedrin Library, where I found the *uchenyi sekretar* to be friendly and cooperative.

"You're early," he remarked.

"I was in the neighborhood," I fibbed, "and wondered if the microfilm was ready."

"No," he replied, "but I am expecting it back very soon." He confessed that he had sent the Uvarov file to a colleague at another library, where the microfilm machine was functioning, and he expected it to be returned by 5:00 p.m., the agreed-upon time for pickup. I said I'd be back, and then spent the next few hours walking through the city, soaking up last-minute impressions of Peter's "window on the West" and wondering, once again, whether Western values such as freedom and democracy would ever be enjoyed by Russians.

At 5:00 p.m. I walked back to the Saltykov-Shchedrin Library, hoping that the Uvarov file had indeed been microfilmed. The smile on the *uchenyi sekretar*'s face screamed out *yes*. I signed some papers, paid a very modest fee, and, microfilm in my coat pocket, walked back to the Astoria, had dinner by myself, and left for Moscow the following morning.

CHAPTER FIFTEEN

At the End of the Arc

The name of Stalin is inseparable from Marxism-Leninism.
—*Nikita Khrushchev*

On the long but pleasant train ride from Leningrad to Moscow, I put pen to paper in an effort to summarize my thinking about Russia before packing my toothbrush and heading back to Cambridge. I had arrived in late January 1956 and planned to leave in late January 1957, a span of time the Russians described as "the year of the thaw." What happened to Russia and the Russians during this time? What had I seen? What had I learned?

If the "thaw" could be imagined as a work of art, it would look like a brightly colored arc splashed across the backdrop of a decaying dictatorship. It started its upward trajectory with Khrushchev's stunning denunciation of Stalin at the 20th Party Congress in February 1956 and then, in early November, plunged downward with the Russian suppression of the Hungarian Revolution.

The Soviet Union was changing, no doubt about it. Along the way there were fits and starts, changes in leadership, and shifts in direction. But the change was continuing, driven by a mystical belief, held by many intellectuals, that one day their country would evolve into a kind of democracy drawn to the West but anchored in the political and cultural traditions of a Eurasian land mass stretching from Poland to the Pacific.

Stalin, the "great genius," as he was known for decades, was suddenly being portrayed as a brutal dictator who grossly distorted communist ideology. Throughout "the year of the thaw," the effect of this change was visible at every level of Soviet society. Senior officials fled from any association with Stalin, wrapping themselves whenever possible in the safer garb of Leninism. The Russian people were not officially informed of the Khrushchev speech until decades later, but thanks to their incredibly efficient grapevine they learned of its core message at roughly the same time as they began to experience an easing of the Communist Party's tight control over their lives.

It was as if a huge burden was being lifted from their shoulders. Intellectuals began to think more freely, discarding their ideological straitjackets. Teachers planned trips abroad. Foreign artists were invited to perform in Moscow. Students rebelled against dusty Marxist texts. Workers demanded better housing, clothing, and food. Some even dared to go on strike. Political dissidents, after spending years in Siberian camps, were released and allowed to return to Moscow and Leningrad. Unlike Stalin, Khrushchev showed up at foreign national day receptions, where he joshed with reporters and exchanged stories with diplomats. It seemed like the dawn of a new day.

By summertime the thaw was at its peak. Stalin's icy dictatorship was melting, and Russians and Eastern Europeans were beginning to assume that things would naturally continue to get better at home and abroad. The evidence was everywhere, they felt, even in the rigid ideology that still undergirded the system.

For example, Stalin had painted a gloomy picture of dangerous conflict with the capitalist world. War, even nuclear war, was not only possible but inevitable, he had proclaimed in speeches and pamphlets. Khrushchev, though, turned Stalin's bleak prognosis on its head, promoting a dramatically new vision of "peaceful coexistence" among nations with different economic and political systems. War, according to Khrushchev's rewrite of Stalin's orthodoxy, was no longer inevitable. For Khrushchev, coexistence replaced conflict.

But theory was one thing, practice another. Even though the theory of peaceful coexistence was appealing to many Russians, and also to many in Eastern Europe, its application, its conversion from theory into practice, ran into different interpretations. The obstreperous Poles could translate the theory in one way, the Kremlin in another, and the two could quickly find themselves on a collision course. By the time summer edged into fall, almost all of Eastern Europe was in some form of revolt against the Kremlin, the Russian thaw being the underlying reason for the unfolding upheaval. If Khrushchev could denounce Stalin, it was reasoned, then a Czech or a Bulgarian communist could likewise denounce the ultimate leader in his own country, and his policies as well.

It started in late June, when Poland's Communist leaders invited businessmen from communist and capitalist countries to the Poznan International Fair. It was a perfect example of Khrushchev's peaceful coexistence, except for one thing: the workers in nearby plants seized the moment and went out on strike, demonstrating for better salaries and improved labor conditions. They attacked Communist Party headquarters and torched the local prison. Before long, Polish tanks and troops, in an effort to restore order, opened fire on the demonstrating workers, killing many of them. The streets were suddenly awash with blood. The scene was hardly a good advertisement for communism.

Not too far away, in Czechoslovakia, students went on a rampage. Like their counterparts in Moscow, they questioned not only the presumed wisdom of communism as their governing philosophy but also the leadership of the Czech Communist Party. In one university town after another, students carrying anti-communist placards blocked traffic and brought life in the countryside to a virtual standstill. Only here, unlike in Poland, the police did not intervene, the troops stayed in their

Moscow's central marketplace, where the author often went to talk to Russian peasants, and sometimes to buy their fruits and vegetables.

barracks, and the country seemed to slow to a stop. These scenes were repeated in parts of East Germany, Romania, and Bulgaria.

The rush toward disaffection in Eastern Europe reached its climax in Hungary in late October. Angry workers and disillusioned intellectuals pushed the country into open revolt against communism and Russia. Khrushchev faced a crucial decision. If he ordered the Red Army into Hungary to crush the rebellion, many people would be killed, and the myth that Russia was Eastern Europe's best comrade-in-arms would be exposed as a lie. But if he did not order the Red Army into Hungary, he was certain he would lose all of Eastern Europe in a swirling anti-communist rebellion, and soon thereafter his post as first secretary of the Communist Party of the Soviet Union.

Khrushchev ordered his army into Hungary, feeling he had no other realistic option, and he suffered the consequences. His political position was severely weakened. In his Eastern European empire, now rent with bloody uncertainty, he was scorned and Russia was hated. And everywhere else, Russia was seen as a brutal dictatorship. All the glowing tributes he had earlier received from his anti-Stalinist shift in policy were reduced to rubble. Khrushchev knew it, and his political enemies knew it, too.

As the train rumbled slowly toward Moscow, I returned to my original question: What happened to Russia during the year of the thaw? One thing was clear: A dictatorship cannot be dismantled one speech at a time. Khrushchev had tried, and he clearly had failed in this effort. What else? After a year of conversations with Russians from Tashkent to Kiev, observing and talking with Soviet leaders (including Khrushchev), reading and translating the Soviet press every morning, and attending the Russian theater as often as my schedule would allow, and after cracking a small hole in the Soviet archives in my pursuit of the Uvarov file, four strong impressions of "Russia 1956" had formed in my mind.

1. Eleven years after the end of World War II, the Russian people were in a desperate need of peace. They had endured terrible hardships during the war. Tens of millions had been killed. No family had survived without tragic losses. More than anything, they wanted the chance to rebuild their lives. Khrushchev's attack on Stalin's rugged adherence to communist doctrine was designed in part to respond sympathetically to this popular yearning.

2. Russia was a huge, wealthy country, but it was locked into a woeful economic system that stifled creative growth, producing just enough to maintain the necessities of life but little more. The bottom line was that

the system, justifiably criticized at home and abroad, somehow worked. It worked badly, but it worked. Communist leaders promised annually that "next year" industrial production would soar, and things would get better. Workers had little choice but to buy the line, however reluctantly, or to become deep skeptics of the system itself, of communism as the driving dynamic of their lives. I met both kinds of workers. Only the peasants seemed chronically miserable. They wanted to own their own land and their own livestock, and they were tired of waiting.

3. Communism as a governing philosophy had lost its revolutionary magnetism. It was a dying ideology. Young people told me they would join a revolt against communism, if they thought it would do any good—but, shaking their heads, they expressed doubt that it would. I believed that communism would decay even faster if the Russian intellectual could find an emotional substitute of comparable appeal.

4. Russia was in a period of profound transition. One student told me that Russia was "between the old and the new." The "old" was communism under Stalin and now adjusted by Khrushchev. The "new" was an uncertain, distant dream.

When I returned to the American embassy that evening, I noted in my diary that the "Russian people are much too imaginative to live forever as the docile servants of a bloodless cause. They are no longer the illiterate and inert peasantry that Stalin ruled with an iron discipline. They now know how to read, and they are also beginning to think. In a dictatorship, thinking is dangerous."

The following day, a somewhat subdued Khrushchev attended a diplomatic reception and, in an astounding toast, raised a glass in tribute to Stalin, the Georgian he had attacked a year earlier as a criminal, a madman, a fiend. "God grant," he said with bombastic force, stressing the word "God," "that every communist be able to fight as Stalin fought!" His remark produced a startled hush. Diplomats turned to one another, puzzled looks on their faces. Reporters pulled notebooks from their pockets. They knew they had a story when they thought all they were getting was a drink. Khrushchev continued: "For all of us, Marxist-Leninists, who have devoted our lives to the revolutionary struggle for the interests of the working class and its militant vanguard, the Leninist party, the name of Stalin is inseparable from Marxism-Leninism."

Khrushchev, in rhetorical retreat, looked solemn, only occasionally cracking a smile, as he made his way out of the embassy. Had he just signaled an end to his controversial reform of Stalinist Russia? I did not think so. Too much had happened during this year of the thaw. Too many hopes had been lofted. Too much freedom had been tasted, and enjoyed, at home and throughout Eastern Europe. It could not all be put back in the bottle. The Molotovs of communism would try and, on occasion, succeed. But they, too, would be unable to hold up the train of Russian history. With the thaw, it had left the station on a journey yet to be charted.

Five Months Later . . .

One morning in June 1957, an assistant at Widener Library tapped me on the shoulder. "Marvin," she said softly, "you have a call, uh, from a man who says he is, uh, Edward R. Murrow."

"Oh, please," I brushed her off. "Edward R. Murrow is not calling me. Obviously a mistake—just, just hang up on him." I returned to my reading of an obscure nineteenth-century Russian manuscript, which at the time I found fascinating. I was a Ph.D. candidate in the History Department at Harvard. I had recently returned from a long trip through Southeast Asia after a year-long assignment at the American embassy in Moscow.

Later that afternoon the librarian was back. "Marvin," she said, this time with added resolve, "the same man is calling. You ought to talk to him." I still did not think it was Murrow, but . . . he might have read a few of my articles about the Soviet Union. Several had appeared in the *Saturday Review of Literature*, one in the *New York Times Magazine*. He certainly knew my brother, Bernard Kalb, a *New York Times* correspondent in Southeast Asia. They had both covered Chinese Premier Zhou Enlai's recent visit to Burma, as it was then called. It was not a totally nutty idea that Murrow might be the one on the phone. "Okay," I said, yielding to my curiosity. "Is it the phone in your office?" She nodded.

The moment I heard his voice, I realized I had made a huge mistake. "This is Ed Murrow," he said. I had been listening to his voice for years. "I hope I am not interrupting"—an oblique reference to his earlier call.

"No, no, no," I stumbled, apologetically, "not at all. I'm so happy to talk to you, sir."

Murrow quickly got to the point of his call. "I read your piece on Soviet youth, and I'd like to talk to you about it."

"Yes, sir," I replied. "I'd be honored, delighted. Uh, when?"

"How about tomorrow morning at nine?" he said. "Here in my office. In New York."

"Yes, sir!" I all but shouted.

I could not believe what had just happened. Murrow had called me. Unbelievable! He had just invited me to his office to talk about Soviet youth. Unbelievable! I had been listening to Murrow since World War II. "This . . . is London," the signature opening of his inspiring broadcasts from the British capital during the Nazi blitz. I admired him enormously. More than any other broadcaster, he had set a standard for broadcast news unparalleled in the history of the industry. And he had just called me. Unbelievable! Only in America!

I took a late-night train to New York and, with a fresh shirt and tie, arrived at 485 Madison Avenue, then headquarters of CBS News, a few minutes before nine. Kay Campbell, Murrow's secretary since his days reporting from London, greeted me with a smile. "No more than thirty minutes," she said. "He's got an exceptionally busy schedule today."

"Yes, absolutely," I replied. "I understand."

At exactly 9:00 a.m., Murrow opened his office door and, cigarette in hand, welcomed me. "Come in, Professor."

Murrow's office was tastefully furnished: a sofa and a few chairs on one side, his large, dark-brown desk on the other, and on the empty wall behind his desk a plaque that read, "If I had more time, I would write you a shorter letter." It was signed "Cicero."

"Coffee? Tea?" he asked, as he sat down behind his desk.

"No, thank you."

"Good," he said, "then let's get to it." We discussed Soviet youth. Murrow asked the questions; I tried to answer them. He wanted to know what young people thought about Khrushchev, their rambunctious leader; about his famous speech the year before denouncing Stalin; about communism as a governing ideology. He also wanted to know whether many truly believed in communism, or merely mouthed an allegiance to communism as a gateway to a secure job. He also wanted to know what they felt about family, marriage, religion.

We were well beyond the thirty minutes Kay Campbell had allotted for our meeting. Murrow seemed indifferent to the deadline. He was clearly enjoying the conversation, and I was thrilled to be part of it. Throughout he called me Professor, and I called him Sir, setting a pattern that was to last for years.

Murrow was especially interested in Khrushchev. "What sort of person is he? Does he have a sense of humor?" he asked. I decided to tell him the Peter the Great story. Murrow burst into laughter. "Did he really call you Peter the Great?" Apparently, he loved the story as much as I loved telling it. Then, rather abruptly, Murrow turned from Khrushchev to CBS News. "Ever think about working for CBS?" he asked, lighting another cigarette. I was flabbergasted. It had been one of my not-so-secret dreams for years, discussed with my brother and close friends. Maybe, with hard work and lots of luck, I could become the CBS equivalent of Harry Schwartz, the *Times*'s expert on Soviet affairs, or even the CBS correspondent in Moscow. I remembered Dan Schorr's offer months before. Had Schorr spoken to Murrow about my rejection?

"Yes, yes of course," I said, uncertain about what I should say or how I should say it. "It would be an honor, truly an honor."

"Delighted," Murrow smiled. He reached down to open a large drawer on the right side of his desk. Casually, he pulled out two large glasses and a bottle of Johnny Walker Black Label scotch. As he started to pour, I glanced at a wall clock, which noted unmistakably that it was only a few minutes after ten. My face must have reflected both surprise and shock.

"Oh, dear," Murrow made a face. "You don't drink."

"No," I replied. "Does that mean there's no job?"

"No, no, no," he answered with a wave of his hand. "But it does make things that much more difficult."

Murrow finished his drink and we quickly returned to the safer terrain of Russian history. Murrow was especially interested in the tumultuous eighteenth-century reigns of Peter the Great and Catherine the Great, which absorbed us for much of the next two hours. At noon, Campbell knocked at the door, opened it, and in a loud whisper reminded her boss that he had a lunch date. She shot me a look of distinct disapproval, as though I had violated a treaty we had both secretly negotiated. For an instant Murrow paused, as if he might cancel his lunch date, but then he quickly straightened his tie and put on his jacket. "Come with me," he said.

Outside the office he introduced me to Jesse Zousmer and Johnny Aaron, two of his producers. "This is Marvin Kalb. He's Bernie's brother. Knows a lot about Russia. Call Sig or John. Let's see what we can do about setting him up for a job here." Sig Mickelson was president of CBS News, and John F. Day was his vice president. I met both the following day. Upshot: I was offered, and accepted, a job at CBS, starting as a writer on the overnight shift for the local WCBS radio station. Pay was $137 per week. I was ecstatic.

By accepting Murrow's offer, I knew I would probably not be finishing my Uvarov dissertation and certainly I would be disappointing my mother. But it was an offer I felt I could not refuse. Seven months earlier I had turned down a similar offer from Dan Schorr. But in the interim, especially during my trip to Southeast Asia, where the guerrilla war in Vietnam was spreading, I found that my passion for daily journalism had deepened. Moreover, this offer had come from Murrow, who was my idol. How could I say no to Murrow? As I was soon to learn, his offer opened the door to a dream job. A world of opportunity beckoned.

In less than three months, I went from writing hourly newscasts for WCBS to writing commentaries on global communism for Murrow's nightly news program; working on a TV documentary, *The Red Sell*, with Walter Cronkite, who was then the rising star at CBS; soon thereafter promoting my first book about Russia, called *Eastern Exposure*; and appearing on a CBS television special on the Russian writer Boris Pasternak's Nobel Prize. I then applied for, and got, a CBS Foundation Fellowship, which I used to travel around the world and write a book at Columbia University about the splintering Sino-Soviet alliance. It was called *Dragon in the Kremlin*. In the spring of 1960 I was appointed CBS's Moscow bureau chief and correspondent. Larry LeSueur, a Murrow colleague from World War II, had been slated for the assignment, but for some reason the Russians refused to give him a visa.

During my time in Moscow as a correspondent I covered the U-2 incident in 1960, the Berlin crisis in 1961, and the Cuban Missile Crisis in 1962. I was also the first American network correspondent to visit Mongolia, in August 1962. Six months later I was transferred to Washington, D.C., where I was named chief diplomatic correspondent, the first such post at any network. Over the next thirty years I covered the many faces of the Cold War: the ups and downs of U.S.-Soviet relations, the costly, tragic Vietnam War, Henry Kissinger's shuttle diplomacy in the Middle East, and the attempted assassination of Pope John Paul II. Most of the time I loved my assignment. When my reporting passion ebbed in the late 1980s, however, I switched to teaching and writing more books.

Not too long ago a TV producer posed an innocent question: "What's your hobby?" I think he was expecting a short, inconsequential response, like "golf." His question, though, threw me into speechless embarrassment. I suddenly realized I had no real hobby. I didn't play golf or tennis, nor did I go on cruises. I could only think of one activity that could possibly be construed as a hobby.

"I write books," I replied. "I really like to write books."

Acknowledgments

memoir emerges from many interrelationships. Family members, friends, teachers, even strangers play a role. I thank them all.

This book focuses on my time in the Soviet Union in 1956, a very special year in modern Russian history, each day a seminar in the awkward dismantling of Joseph Stalin's dictatorship. I was a translator/interpreter/press officer at the U.S. embassy in Moscow. For a budding scholar it was, without doubt, an extraordinary experience.

While I was in Moscow, few colleagues were more helpful to me than Anna Holdcroft, a British expert on Soviet politics, and U.S. ambassador Charles Bohlen, the model diplomat at a challenging time in East-West relations. Unbeknownst to him, Soviet leader Nikita Khrushchev also helped me to understand how Kremlin politics worked, to the degree that it did.

Acknowledgments

Before reaching Moscow, I studied Russian history and language at City College of New York and Harvard University. Among my professors were Hans Kohn, Michael Karpovich, and Richard Pipes. Each was an inspiration, opening the door to a fresh appreciation of a very complicated country.

Many Russians shared their life stories with me, and I also learned much about the differences between Soviet theory and practice from the many diplomats and journalists I met in Moscow. CBS's Dan Schorr was at the top of my list, becoming my first mentor in broadcast news.

This is the first book in a projected three-part memoir. I have many to thank, but I start with Valentina Kalk, the former director of the Brookings Institution Press, who encouraged this ambitious project. I am grateful for her friendship and wise counsel. Others, also helpful, were William Finan, Janet Walker, Carrie Engel, Adam Juskewitch, Elliott Beard, and Yelba Quinn. They composed a friendly, cooperative team of professionals.

Jon Sawyer, executive director of the Pulitzer Center, where I hang my hat, was always encouraging, as was his wife, the incomparable Kem Sawyer, who read the manuscript and offered important editorial advice. I also extend my heartfelt gratitude to Nathalie Applewhite, Tom Hundley, Ann Peters, Akela Lacy, Jin Ding, and everyone else at the Center for their help and support, which came in many ways and was always appreciated.

I have benefited greatly from the wisdom and guidance of many at the Brookings Institution, where I am a nonresident senior fellow in foreign affairs. Among them are Strobe Talbott, Martin Indyk, Bruce Jones, Michael O'Hanlon, Fiona Hill, Stephen Hess, and my dear friend Vassilis Coutifaris, always prepared to extend a helping hand.

Mike Freedman, executive producer of *The Kalb Report*, helped enormously, more perhaps than he realized, often by simply listening to my ramblings about Russia and then offering a nugget of advice or opinion.

A number of friends read early drafts of the manuscript and offered incredibly valuable suggestions. Among them: Andrew Glass, Garrett Mitchell, James Masland, and Walter Reich.

My gratitude to my immediate family is without measure, each member contributing handsomely in his or her own way.

As always, with all my books, my brother, Bernard, read and edited the manuscript with his usual dedication to accuracy, clarity, and style.

My daughter Deborah, a writer, blogger, and editor herself, was always there, from beginning to end, with wise counsel and guidance.

My daughter Judith, a scholar of Russian language and literature, read and edited the manuscript and then carefully transliterated Russian words or expressions into understandable English.

Deborah's husband, David, a scientist, was a wonderful traveling companion during the tour for my previous book, *Imperial Gamble*, and a source of constant encouragement.

Judith's husband, Alex, also a scholar of Russian language and literature, provided invaluable editing and, as important, came up with the title for this book.

My wife, Madeleine, an author and specialist on Russian foreign policy, has been at my side for more than sixty years, and so knowledgeable about global history that in the family she is playfully referred to as Ms. Google. With her, everything is possible. She has my eternal gratitude.

To my grandson, Aaron, and my granddaughter, Eloise, both wise beyond their years (he's twelve, she's nine), both loving, helpful, and inspiring, I offer my hope that they will continue to live without fear in a land that cherishes individual freedom and democratic rule.

Marvin Kalb
Chevy Chase, Maryland

Index